EDGAR H. SCHEIN

WITH **PETER SCHEIN**

ORGANIZATIONAL CULTURE AND LEADERSHIP

5TH EDITION

WILEY

ISBN 978–1–119–21204–1 (paper)
ISBN 978–1–119–21213–3 (ePDF)
ISBN 978–1–119–21205–8 (ePub)

Printed in the United States of America

10 9 8 7 6 5 4 3 2 1

Contents

Part One: Defining the Structure of Culture

Part Two: What Leaders Need to Know about Macro Cultures

Part Three: Culture and Leadership through Stages of Growth

Part Four: Assessing Culture and Leading Planned Change

Acknowledgments

The six years since the last edition have been different in many respects. I am now living in Palo Alto, California, in a retirement complex close to my son, Peter, who has also become my colleague and coauthor. Living in Silicon Valley and seeing the world out here through the lenses of Peter's 25 years of experiences in a number of different start-ups and mature companies have given me a new perspective on organizational culture and leadership issues. I am therefore most grateful to Peter who is now also my partner in our Organizational Culture and Leadership Institute (OCLI .org), and to various friends and clients with whom I have worked out here. Peter's wife, Jamie Schein, has also provided great insights from her current leadership role in the administration of the Stanford Graduate School of Business.

I am especially grateful to Google, Human Synergistics, Genentech, Stanford Hospital, IDEO, The Institute of the Future, Intel, and the Silicon Valley Organization Development Network, which have provided a variety of opportunities for me to learn from and contribute to what goes on in this fascinating geographically contained pocket of innovation. My growing focus on the culture of medicine has led to many important insights about occupational cultures in particular, thus I want to thank Mary Jane Kornacki, Jack Silversin, Gary Kaplan, and the other members of the summer workshop that I attended for many years at Mary Jane's and Jacks' retreat on Cape Ann. Here in California I want to thank James Hereford and the members of the impromptu monthly lunch meetings that I have had with a group of doctors and administrators at the Stanford Hospital. Others who deserve thanks for educating me on the complexities of the medical world are Marjorie Godfrey, Kathy McDonald, Diane Rawlins, Dr. Lucian Leape, Dr. Tony Suchman, and my surgeon son-in-law Dr. Wally Krengel.

In my new life out here I have become less of a teacher and more of a writer and coach. In that regard I want to acknowledge the stimulation and help I have received from Steve Piersanti and his Berrett-Kohler publishing company that has facilitated my writing three new books in the applied areas of helping, coaching, and consulting, which supplement in important ways the scholarly work that underlies this book. I also want to thank iUniverse for working with me on my memoirs and thereby providing an opportunity to think much more broadly about the evolution of culture and leadership in my own career.

In the broad world of organization development, I have greatly benefited from many new local colleagues, particularly Tim Kuppler, Kimberly Wiefling, Jeff Richardson, John Cronkite, Stu and Mary Winby, and Joy Hereford. The network of trainers who run the training groups for the Stanford Business School's leadership program welcomed me and enabled me to stay in touch with my former world of "experiential learning" for which I thank them. Special thanks also to my overseas friends and colleagues—Philip Mix, Michael and Linda Brimm, David Coghlan, Tina Doerffer, Peter and Lily Chen, Charles and Elizabeth Handy, Leopold Vansina, Joanne Martin, and Michael Chen who is active in bringing my culture work into China. Many thanks also to my friend and colleague Joichi Ogawa who has been actively championing my work in Japan.

My three children, Louisa, Liz, and Peter, their spouses, Ernie, Wally, and Jamie, and my seven grandchildren, Alexander, Peter, Sophia, Oliver, Annie, Ernesto, and Stephanie, have always provided an important perspective on cultural matters. I especially appreciate their observations on how culture is changing, how the world changes with the generations, and how what they are growing into is a different world from what I experienced. The organizations they are entering are different from the ones I was familiar with, and the social values that are debated in the world today are different and in many ways more profound. I mention all of this because it has emboldened me in doing this fifth edition to get some new perspectives on what aspects of culture and leadership have to be considered for tomorrow and our future beyond.

Last but certainly not least, I have to acknowledge past and present colleagues and fellow scholars who have continued to stimulate me over the last six years—John Van Maanen, with whom I cowrote the new version of *Career Anchors*; Lotte Bailyn, whose wisdom continues to be awesome; Bill Isaacs and Gervaise Bushe, who brought me into the whole dialogic world; Otto Scharmer, who keeps opening up new worlds of thinking and learning; David Bradford, who provided much needed advice and stimulation out here; Noam Cook, whose philosophical insights provide important perspectives on cultural matters; and Steve Barley, Warner Burke, Amy Edmondson, Jody Gittell, Charles O'Reilly III, and Melissa Valentine, whose current research is pushing us into much needed new dimensions of cultural analysis.

As was the case with previous editions, the editorial staff from Wiley, Jeanenne Ray and Heather Brosius, were most helpful in first gathering feedback of how to improve this book and then facilitating the editorial process.

Preface

This fifth edition of my *Organizational Culture and Leadership* book is being written in Palo Alto, California, in the heart of Silicon Valley. I am acutely aware that I am writing in a different place and at a very different time. I have now partnered with my son who has experienced over his 25 years of change in various Silicon Valley technology companies all kinds of leadership and all kinds of organizational cultures. I cannot convey adequately how different things feel at this time and in this place from what I was experiencing in Cambridge in 2008 when I wrote the fourth edition.

I am happy to have Peter working with me on this next edition and to help me capture some of what we both feel, and that provides some of the flavor of what has happened to the concept of "organizational culture" during the past couple of decades. With his insights and our joint experience of the past several years, I can navigate a bit better through the various different culture "trees" without losing sight of the forest as a whole.

Much of what is new in this book is hinted at in Peter's Foreword. Before you get to that I want to say a few words about what I think is the same in this edition and what I think is different and to some extent "new." My three-level model of how to define and think about culture has held up well and remains the strong skeleton of this whole approach to cultural analysis. What is new is to begin to apply this thinking to the bigger picture of a multicultural world. To this end I have added as a case my study of the Economic Development Board of Singapore and followed that up with two chapters on the problems of analyzing and working with macro cultures such as nations or worldwide occupations. I have emphasized that every organizational culture is nested in other, often larger cultures that influence its character; and every subculture, task force, or work group is, in turn, nested in larger cultures, which influence them. I have enhanced the discussion of how one can begin to work across national culture divides.

Although it is not a new emphasis, I am much more concerned in this edition with focusing on how our own socialization experiences have embedded various layers of culture within us. The cultures within us need to be understood because they dominate our behavior and, at the same time, provide us choices of who to be in various social situations. These choices are only partially attributable to "personality" or "temperament"; rather, they depend on our situational understandings that have been taught to us by our socialization experiences. I have therefore introduced as an important element for leadership choices a description of the social "levels of relationship" that we all have learned as part of our upbringing. We can be formal, personal, or intimate and can vary that behavior according to our situation. In that way, recognizing and managing the cultures *inside* us becomes an important leadership skill.

I continue to be impressed that culture as a concept leads us to see the *patterns* in social behavior. I have, therefore, ignored much of the recent research that (1) picks out one or two dimensions of culture, (2) relates those to desired outcomes of various sorts, and then (3) claims that culture matters. I thought we always knew that. However, the growing interest in unraveling the patterns we see in nations and in organizations and the various typologies of culture that have sprung up deserve review and analysis in this edition. In that regard it is important to differentiate the quantitative diagnostic studies from the more qualitative dialogic inquiry processes, and, with help of my son, to reflect on some of the more recent "rapid" diagnostic methods.

My emphasis is on culture as what a group *learns*, the explanation of how leadership and culture formation are two sides of the same coin, and the fact that the role of leadership changes with the growth and aging of an organization. These remain the same and are the heart of the book. I have tried to shorten this edition by taking out material that was either redundant or irrelevant, and to make the suggestions to the reader more interesting.

I continue to believe that culture is serious business, but it will be a useful construct for us only if we really observe, study, and understand it.

Foreword

Ed and I have been partnering for the past year to expand his readership, grow his consulting business, and provide for more opportunities for helping and learning. It's a great honor to share some thoughts in this foreword to the book that provides us with the name for our venture, the Organizational Culture and Leadership Institute (OCLI.org).

When Ed first started this book in the early 1980s, organizational culture was a pretty new concept. Now, the concept is universally accepted, discussed, diagnosed, shaped, "changed," blamed, and so on. This has happened in a generation. When I was finishing my social anthropology undergraduate degree in 1983, Ed was finishing the first edition of *Organizational Culture and Leadership*. Earlier this year (2016), as Ed's granddaughter (my daughter) was finishing her undergraduate economics degree and was preparing to join an international management consulting firm, he asked her to describe the firm's culture. This was perhaps presumptuous on Ed's part as she had had only a summer internship's worth of experience in this culture with which to answer the question. Yet, with little hesitation she described key artifacts and espoused values of this firm's culture. We drew the inference that after just a couple of months she had been exposed to, even indoctrinated into, this culture deeply enough that she could articulate it and, ideally, thrive within it.

However, there is nothing surprising about this; mature corporations (in this case, firms that offer business advisory services) have studied their culture and have established imagery, metaphors, and a vocabulary with which to describe it and teach it. Is it surprising that such implicit cultural immersion or indoctrination would be part of the summer internship program? If there is one thing that a summer internship should test it is "fit" between the firm and the individual. So it does make perfect sense that both firm and individuals have figured out that as with industry, training, and job function, corporate culture is central to any assessment of mutual "fit" and is a critical priority at the beginning of an employment term.

Yet, should I be surprised that my daughter could easily answer this open-ended question about her prospective employer's culture? Like me, she grew up in a household and extended family that talks routinely about this stuff. It's in the DNA, so this question would never seem particularly out of context for her. Yet the facility with which she responded still stood out for me. I am pretty sure Ed asked me the same question about my first employer, and I'm pretty sure I fumbled around trying to articulate what I was experiencing. I had just as much corporate culture to observe, but none of it was made explicit, and I did not have the vocabulary with which to describe it.

Over the course of four editions of *Organizational Culture and Leadership*, we've moved from culture being something that everyone at work had a vague sense was guiding behavior and shaping decisions, to culture being understood and described with a common language, to being a vital measure of "fit" for retention, to being touted as a firm's greatest virtue, to being leveraged for strategic change. Culture, in this explicitly leading role in our consciousness of our work lives, is now the subject of numerous deeply analytical survey-based diagnostic systems as well as simple "app"-based dashboarding tools (some of which have garnered many millions of dollars of start-up investment from top-tier venture capitalists). "There's money in them thar hills" is now something that we can project without hesitation about the diagnosis, analysis, and change of organizational culture. This has happened within a generation.

My views on organizational culture have been shaped mostly from my approximately 25 years in Silicon Valley. Whether drawn from Apple in the early 1990s, or internet start-ups in web "1.0," or Sun Microsystems in the 2000s, I recognize that cultural norms in tech companies, while all different from each other, are also categorically different from typical norms in other industries and locales. One of the first explicit descriptions of Silicon Valley tech-company culture that I experienced was captured in this simple question—"Is it a penguin culture or a bear culture"? I did not know what this meant, though I assumed it must be better to be a "bear culture."

Whether or not it is possible to create a descriptive culture model that is value-neutral, devoid of any normative tilt, is not the focus here except to propose that the simpler the taxonomy the more likely it is to have a normative leaning, one way or the other. In this case, the two culture types differ when describing how a company or group responds to the challenge of an incompetent or weak member of the group. Bears attempt to nurture the weak pack member back to health—that is, to improve the underperforming team member. This was not the reason for my leaning to the bear culture that I expected before hearing the explanation. I assumed it would have something to do with strength and dominance coupled with intelligence. Instead it was about nurturing the weak. Penguins, by contrast, respond to the weak member of their flock by pecking the weakling to death. Rather than the cute sophistication we associate with penguins, this cultural foundation was all about brutal decisiveness.

Reflecting on this continuum, from penguin to bear, my first thought is that this is one fairly accurate way to delineate tech companies, ranking them along this nurturing-to-brutal dimension. But as we think about culture models, this simple example reveals two other important themes that Ed explores at length in this edition. First, we are drawn to simple, compelling models or taxonomies. For example, Cameron and Quinn's OCAI (Organizational Culture Assessment Instrument) represents an interesting culture model based on a "competing values framework" (as one could say bear versus penguin represent competing values). What I find most compelling about OCAI is the language and metaphor: cultures are described as "clan," "adhocracy," "hierarchy," or "market." These descriptors resonate; they make sense and stick with us as we try to understand or describe what we experience.

Similarly, technology innovators in Silicon Valley have relied heavily on metaphors from the very beginning to illuminate and sell breakthrough technology to the uninitiated and uninformed. For example, the "window" and "navigator" helped us understand PC user interfaces and internet browsers. With the right metaphors we can refer to things in standardized ways, describing disparate artifacts as conforming to a model. The "operating system" term has come to mean far more than OS X or Linux these days; these OS abstractions and standardizations are what made it possible for business and personal users to find general utility in highly complex machines. We have now come full circle to where we borrow personal computing metaphors to characterize business structures and functions. The "business operating system" notion provides metaphor and language to standardize the descriptions of an organization's way of doing things. And a company's culture is one abstraction that we now accept as integral to its "operating system." Silicon Valley has made a point of describing dimensions, attributes, and facts as fitting into nice compelling models described in memorable metaphors that provide just enough detail to represent a consistent model of a complex human system in an unforgettable symbolic way. This too has happened within a generation.

My emphasis on this progress over the past generation raises the question: Can we or should we project what the next generation will bring to the understanding of organizational culture, leadership, and change? While I am not a futurist, anticipating the impacts of two things in particular seems important. First, as I mentioned previously, there are many ways and new schemes continue to be created for measuring culture and climate. In general, we can predict that more and more of what we experience in our work and personal lives will be measured, benchmarked, and scored, all in the interest of fine-tuning and improving. With ubiquitous networks, powerful low-power sensors capable of instrumenting practically anything, and unlimited cloud computing and storage, there is no reason why nearly every aspect of our work lives (and home lives) can't be measured from one second to the next. "Big data" is a many-faceted phenomenon affecting most dimensions of leadership, including culture and climate.

There is the self-reinforcing notion that we can instrument and study so much of our productivity, so why not study at finer-tuned intervals? This might allow us to see patterns and interactions in data that we did not know were in any way related (trying to understand "the unknown unknowns"). Shouldn't we expect a system that provides the instrumentation that would allow us to study individuals, teams, interactions, conflicts, and resolutions to have real-time predictive *culture* analytics? Yes, this is cringe-worthy, which is probably why I would expect that whoever is developing these systems will have many options for sponsorship and financing. We are living in a "measure everything" world in which benchmarks and scorecards, particularly when standardized, are magnetic in their attraction and quite possibly radioactive in their potential (harm).

"More better" is now *more better faster*. Should we not expect a surge in popularity of culture models and culture analytics that provide for *more better faster*, catalyzing faster positive change? Whether we can change culture *more better faster* will not be proved or disproved anytime soon, and those arguing that only climate can really be changed faster will remain on higher ground. Regardless, surveys using standard 5-point scales constitute instrumentation, just as recording and coding natural language (e.g., interview transcripts) or logging yes/no responses on apps on smartphones is all instrumentation. We will, with increasing frequency, capture, code, parse, analyze, store, and re-analyze culture and climate, using all of the latest big data techniques until we far exceed the point of diminishing returns. And I do not think we are anywhere near that point today.

Are we headed back to the future, updated Taylor-ist "scientific management," and time-and-motion analytics using big data for knowledge workers because *more better faster* is ultimately better for everybody? The purpose of doing any of this instrumentation and rapid analysis is to create positive change, which will typically be judged by ROI metrics; businesses study their culture to drive positive change that is ultimately related back to profitability. Is there some other more altruistic reason to study organizational culture that is not explicitly tied to improving key performance indicators: profitability from increased productivity, "engagement," and retention? Ed has been asked many times over many years to help companies "do a culture study." I do not believe he has ever offered to help with a culture study without knowing what the problem was. There is little point in spending hours on ethnography, diagnostics, and analytics without knowing what truly concerns senior management. Similarly, there is little point in doing culture studies that do not factor in the shifting motivations and evolving norms of non-leader stakeholders and employees.

In 2016 there is much concern and hand-wringing about how "millennials" (those born from 1980 to 1995) will change everything in the workplace. (I should note here that "generation Z" is broadly considered to be a different post-millennial cohort; for the purposes of this discussion, I will include generation Z in the broader term.) Regardless of the reality that baby-boomers and Gen-Xers seemed different as well, many have pointed to a difference that millennials appear to be "entitled" and motivated by things other than corporate or even personal profitability.

The notion that "purpose-driven" millennials may make capricious work and career choices strikes fear in leaders of companies large and small. Is it possible that organization design and organizational culture can no longer assume rational economic self-interested behavior from the current cohort filling the workforce? Shaping artifacts and conventions around core beliefs that motivate newly indoctrinated employees is vital to corporate self-preservation and growth. Economic self-interest among most if not all members of a corporation is generally assumed to be a given and therefore leverageable. Yet if economic self-interest is less important among millennials than environmental, spiritual, or collective shared interest, the artifacts, conventions, and assumptions—the cultural DNA of the company— may be out of sync with the interests of the company's younger employees.

Engagement has become a central concern for senior management of all organizations, particularly those that employ younger workers. Many software-as-a-service companies offer survey solutions for benchmarking and tracking engagement. The promise is insight into and knowledge of employees' motivations that will provide levers for retention and hiring, not to mention improved productivity and optimized organizational designs (for example, "holacracy"). Engagement surveys can be very efficient (quick and smartphone-based), prime examples of *more better faster* ways to make work-life improvements adapted to perceived shifting motivations of millennials. The engagement survey typically measures an individual's response to a series of statements reflecting the climate and attitudes of the subject organization. Putting aside methodological concerns with quick online surveys, these are still individual surveys of individual attitudes. Central to the study of organizational culture, as Ed expands on in this edition, is the argument that point-in-time surveys of individual attitudes run the risk of missing the two most critical underpinnings of organizational culture and climate: (1) *group* attitudes and responses to challenges and (2) the precedent events that have led to the present—said another way, the history that is always present.

Perhaps rather than just surveying for engagement of individual millennials, it will be important to consider what is distinct about them as a group (a subculture) with reference to the history of their early work lives. What makes the subculture is more than the current attitudes of frequently surveyed individuals. Deal, Levenson (and Gratton) summarize in their excellent *What Millennials Want From Work* (2016) that for the culture of those born between 1980 and 1995, their coming-of-age milieu is critical to understanding any present-day motivations. Those entering the workforce this millennium have had the internet in their hands for many years (smartphones providing instant connectedness to facts, people, and opinions from everywhere). And this same cohort has seen more cataclysmic terrorism and recession than any group since the period from 1930 to 1950. Is it "entitlement" or is it self-determination drawn from the power of instant information and global personal networks, compounded by justifiable doubts about the permanence of jobs, companies, countries, and ways of life? If the engagement surveys echo "a sense of entitlement" among this cohort of the workforce, part of the understanding of this must be the history this group shares and how the group responds to the cultural DNA of the company in which it exists.

Another aspect of millennials holding access to the (digital) world in their hands is clock and time-zone flattening. The "always-on" device suggests a much different work day (>16 waking hours versus 9-to-5) for a millennial, particularly if there is no distinction made between work and home phone numbers or email addresses. Likely this engenders a very different attitude about blending work and personal life for this cohort. Yet, if these blurred lines are taken advantage of by employers, there are bound to be disconnects if not dis-satisfiers. Millennials are also inextricably bound to the "gig economy." Whether by choice or by accident, a thirty-something in 2016 or 2026 may have, or plan to have, a period in his or her career that is characterized by uncommitted gigs of low-engagement project work.

Companies have learned over the past generation how attractive it can be to build productivity through contract hiring. It offers effective risk mitigation and cost containment. Among the potential downsides, perhaps the biggest, is that the knowledge and training gained by the contract employee leaves the company when the gig is over. Regardless of the costs and benefits of the emerging gig economy, it is critical to recognize that millennials have not adapted to this change, they were born into the gig economy. And for many it is preferable for its freedom, flexibility, and exposure to many new people, new companies, and new networks. A millennial may be deeply engaged with many things, and the current work gig may just not be one of them, despite all of the emphasis placed on creating a culture of engagement at work.

Time-zone flattening matters because the personal networks woven together by savvy smart-device users have become global and inclusive of time and place. Social networks spawn affinity groups that thrive on diversity of country and culture of origin. Such global affinity groups are powerful overlays that shape or shift subcultural attitudes of the like-minded, wherever they may happen to live and work. Millennials may well arrive at work with a global cross-cultural awareness that demands the attention of managers and leaders seeking to retain them in light of their diffuse focus on their world and their lives that encircle their work.

Cultural stereotypes (norms) can be like bright lights to moths, attractive in their clarity, powerful in their simplicity, and incendiary in their effect. We know it is too easy to reduce millennials to a rigid collection of known attributes and expected behaviors. But if "entitlement" and "low engagement" are commonly associated with this cohort, managers and leaders will be justifiably compelled to study the behaviors and search for patterns that can be understood and generalized. Stereotyping is just another way of scaling information in the interests of operational efficiency. If all the *more better faster* survey approaches yield is echoes of stereotypes, the management responses that survey results suggest may be incendiary. Subcultural sediment, from age (or youth), history, geography, and technology, is subtle and requires more ethnographic and deliberative study than can be drawn from mechanical data-gathering approaches focused on individual employees.

In dealing with the deepest layers of culture, such as the tacit assumptions that may motivate millennials, Ed's fifth edition of *Organizational Culture and Leadership* expands on this central argument: organizational culture should be studied, with qualitative insights captured, shared, and steeped in the group, ever mindful of the founder's and the organization's history in which, and out of which, the culture evolves.

PETER A. SCHEIN

About the Authors

Ed Schein is Professor Emeritus of the Massachusetts Institute of Technology (MIT) Sloan School of Management. He was educated at the University of Chicago, Stanford University, and Harvard University, where he received his Ph.D. in Social Psychology. He worked at the Walter Reed Army Institute of Research for four years and then joined MIT, where he taught until 2005.

He has published extensively, including *Organizational Psychology, 3rd ed.*, (1980), *Process Consultation Revisited* (1999), a book on career dynamics (*Career Anchors, 4th ed.* with John Van Maanen, 2013), *Organizational Culture and Leadership, 4th ed.* (2010), *The Corporate Culture Survival Guide, 2nd ed.* (2009), a cultural analysis of Singapore's economic miracle (*Strategic Pragmatism*, 1996), and Digital Equipment Corp.'s rise and fall (*DEC is Dead; Long Live DEC*, 2003).

In 2009 he published *Helping*, a book on the general theory and practice of giving and receiving help. This was followed in 2013 by *Humble Inquiry*, which explores why helping is so difficult in Western culture, and which won the 2013 business book of the year award from the Dept. of Leadership of the University of San Diego. He has just published *Humble Consulting* (2016), which revises the whole model of how to consult and coach, and is currently working with his son, Peter, on *Humble Leadership* (2017), which challenges our current theories of leadership and management.

He continues to consult with various local and international organizations on a variety of organizational culture and career development issues, with special emphasis on safety and quality in health care, the nuclear energy industry, and the US Forest Service. An important focus of this new consulting is to focus on the interaction of occupational and organizational subcultures and how they interact with career anchors to determine the effectiveness and safety of organizations.

He is the 2009 recipient of the Distinguished Scholar-Practitioner Award of the Academy of Management, the 2012 recipient of the Life Time Achievement Award from the International Leadership Association, the 2015 Lifetime Achievement Award in Organization Development from the International OD Network, and has an Honorary Doctorate from the IEDC Bled School of Management in Slovenia.

Peter Schein is a strategy and OD consultant in Silicon Valley. He provides help to start-ups and expansion-phase technology companies.

Peter's expertise draws on over twenty years of industry experience in marketing and corporate development at technology pioneers. In his early career he developed new products and services at Pacific Bell and Apple Computer, Inc. (including *eWorld* and *Newton*). He led product marketing efforts at Silicon Graphics Inc., Concentric Network Corporation (XO Communications), and Packeteer (BlueCoat). He developed a deep experience base and passion for internet infrastructure as the web era dawned in the mid-1990s.

Thereafter, Peter spent eleven years in corporate development and product strategy at Sun Microsystems. At Sun, Peter led numerous minority equity investments in mission-critical technology ecosystems. He drove acquisitions of technology innovators that developed into multi-million dollar product lines at Sun. Through these experiences developing new strategies organically and merging smaller entities into a large company, Peter developed a keen focus on the underlying organizational culture challenges that growth engenders in innovation-driven enterprises.

Peter was educated at Stanford University (BA Social Anthropology, *Honors and Distinction*) and Northwestern University (Kellogg MBA, Marketing and Information Management, *Top Student in Information Management*).

Part One

DEFINING THE STRUCTURE OF CULTURE

To understand how culture works we need to differentiate two perspectives. The most obvious and immediate impulse is to look for culture *content*. What is the culture about, what are the key values that we need to understand, what are the rules of behavior? Different people have different biases and assumptions about what is important. In the current national context we see a great emphasis on the cultural content pertaining to the role of government, leadership, and management in deciding what is good for everyone and focusing on the values of individual freedom and autonomy. Another culture analysis might, however, say that this is totally irrelevant to what the values are around saving the planet and becoming environmentally responsible. A third person chimes in with the importance of family values and the threat to "our culture" of allowing civil marriage. Parents lament or praise the new values that their children are bringing into the culture, or are just plain puzzled about what this new "millennial" generation is all about. We have to watch our language lest we say something "politically incorrect" about racial or gender issues.

The point is that culture *content*, the values we care about are all over the map. To make some sense of this variety, we have to look first at the *structure* of culture and develop a perspective on how to analyze the complex cultural landscape we encounter. In the next four chapters I will develop a "model" of the structure of culture. We will analyze several organizational cultures, illustrate how nested they are in larger cultural units. Chapter 1 gives a dynamic definition of culture. Chapter 2 describes the basic three-level model of the "structure" of culture that will be used throughout the rest of the book. In Chapter 3 this model is illustrated with Digital Equipment Corporation, a U.S. computer company that I encountered in its early growth period and in which I could, therefore, observe the growth and evolution of a culture. In Chapter 4 I describe Ciba-Geigy, an old Swiss-German chemical company, that illustrates some of the problems of a mature industry in a very different technology and the impact of national culture. In Chapter 5 I describe the Singapore Economic Development Board, which illustrates both a fusion of Western and Asian national cultures and an organization in the public sector. The cases are intended to highlight that cultures are learned *patterns of beliefs, values, assumptions,* and *behavioral norms that manifest themselves at different levels of observability.*

1

HOW TO DEFINE CULTURE IN GENERAL

The Problem of Defining Culture Clearly

Culture has been studied for a long time by anthropologists and sociologists, resulting in many models and definitions of culture. Some of the ways that they have conceptualized the essence of culture illustrate the breadth as well as the depth of the concept. Most of the categories that follow refer primarily to *macro* cultures such as nations, occupations, or large organizations but some are also relevant to *micro* or subcultures. As you will see from the pattern of references, many researchers use several of these definitional categories, and they overlap to a considerable degree. Culture as we will see exists at many levels of "observabilty." The categories are arranged roughly according to the degree to which you, as an observer, will be able to see and feel those cultural elements when you observe an organization or group.

- **Observed behavioral regularities when people interact:** The language they use along with the regularities in the interaction such as "Thank you" followed by "Don't mention it," or "How is your day going so far," "Just fine." Observed interaction patterns, customs, and traditions become evident in all groups in a variety of situations (e.g., Goffman, 1959, 1967; Jones, Moore, & Snyder, 1988; Trice & Beyer, 1993; Van Maanen, 1979).

- **Climate:** The feeling that is conveyed in a group by the physical layout and the way in which members of the organization interact with each other, with customers, or with other outsiders. Climate is sometimes included as an artifact of culture and is sometimes kept as a separate phenomenon to be analyzed (e.g., Ashkanasy, Wilderom, & Peterson, 2000; Schneider, 1990; Tagiuri & Litwin, 1968; Ehrhart, Schneider, & Macey, 2014).

- **Formal rituals and celebrations:** The ways in which a group celebrates key events that reflect important values or important "passages" by members such as promotion, completion of important projects, and milestones (Trice & Beyer, 1993; Deal & Kennedy, 1982, 1999).

- **Espoused values:** The articulated, publicly announced principles and values that the group claims to be trying to achieve, such as "product quality," "price leadership," or "safety" (e.g., Deal & Kennedy, 1982, 1999). Many companies in Silicon Valley such as Google and Netflix announce their culture in terms of such values in all of their recruiting materials and in books about themselves (Schmidt & Rosenberg, 2014).

- **Formal philosophy:** The broad policies and ideological principles that guide a group's actions toward stockholders, employees, customers, and other stakeholders such as the highly publicized "HP way" of Hewlett-Packard or, more recently, the explicit statements about culture in Netflix and Google (e.g., Ouchi, 1981; Pascale & Athos, 1981; Packard, 1995; Schmidt & Rosenberg, 2014).

- **Group norms:** The implicit standards and values that evolve in working groups, such as the particular norm of "a fair day's work for a fair day's pay" that evolved among workers in the Bank Wiring Room in the classic Hawthorne studies (e.g., Homans, 1950; Kilmann & Saxton, 1983).

- **Rules of the game:** These are the implicit, unwritten rules for getting along in the organization, "the ropes" that a newcomer must learn to become an accepted member, "the way we do things around here" (e.g., Schein, 1968, 1978; Van Maanen, 1976, 1979b; Ritti & Funkhouser, 1987; Deal & Kennedy, 1999).

- **Identity and images of self:** How the organization views itself in terms of "who we are," "what is our purpose," and "how we do things" (e.g., Schultz, 1995; Hatch, 1990; Hatch & Schultz, 2004).

- **Embedded skills:** The special competencies displayed by group members in accomplishing certain tasks, the ability to make certain things that get passed on from generation to generation without necessarily being articulated in writing (e.g., Argyris & Schon, 1978; Cook & Yanow, 1993; Peters & Waterman, 1982; Ang & Van Dyne, 2008).

- **Habits of thinking, mental models, or linguistic paradigms:** The shared cognitive frames that guide the perceptions, thoughts, and language used by the members of a group and are taught to new members in the socialization or "onboarding" process as it is now often called (e.g., Douglas, 1986; Hofstede, 1991, 2001, Hofstede, Hofstede, & Minkov, 2010; Van Maanen, 1979).

- **Shared meanings:** The emergent understandings that are created by group members as they interact with each other where the same words used in different cultures can have very different meanings (e.g., Geertz, 1973; Smircich, 1983; Van Maanen & Barley, 1984; Weick, 1995; Weick & Sutcliffe, 2001; Hatch & Schultz, 2004).

- **"Root metaphors" or integrating symbols:** The ways that groups evolve to characterize themselves, which may or may not be appreciated consciously but become embodied in buildings, office lay-outs, and other material artifacts of the group. This level of the culture reflects the emotional and aesthetic response of members as contrasted with the cognitive or evaluative response (e.g., Gagliardi, 1990; Hatch, 1990; Pondy, Frost, Morgan, & Dandridge, 1983; Schultz, 1995).

I have provided these many ways of defining culture to give you a sense that culture covers pretty much everything that a group has learned as it has evolved. When we look at macro cultures (e.g., nations or occupations) and want do describe their cultures, we need all of these specific concepts to capture their culture. However, in moving toward a usable definition of culture that you can apply to the organizations and groups that you will encounter and that you will want to decipher, we need a more integrative dynamic definition that highlights how culture forms and evolves in organizations, subcultures, and micro systems. The foregoing categories will help to define the content of a given culture, but defining them has to be a more dynamic holistic process.

The reason for such a formal definition at this point is to forewarn you that you will find many groups of various sizes with different shared patterns that must be understood on their own terms. You will see articles about how to change or even create cultures that don't agree with each

---

A Dynamic Definition of Culture

The culture of a group can be defined as the accumulated shared learning of that group as it solves its problems of external adaptation and internal integration; which has worked well enough to be considered valid and, therefore, to be taught to new members as the correct way to perceive, think, feel, and behave in relation to those problems.

This accumulated learning is a pattern or system of beliefs, values, and behavioral norms that come to be taken for granted as basic assumptions and eventually drop out of awareness.

---

other or that don't make sense. This definition is deliberately focused on the general process of how *any culture* is learned and will evolve, but in practice you will have to focus on different elements of that formal definition to make sense of the particular organizational situation you encounter. So let's expand on and explain the importance of each component of that definition in preparation for the more detailed analysis of these elements that occur later on in this book.

Accumulated Shared Learning

The most important element of the definition is to note that culture is a *shared* product of *shared* learning (Edmondson, 2012). If you understand that culture is a shared product of shared learning, you will realize several important corollaries that make culture complex. To fully understand a given group's culture, we will need to know what kind of learning has taken place, over what span of time, and under what kinds of leadership. Deciphering such history is impossible with preliterate culture, nations, and some occupations; however, with contemporary organizations and work groups, it is possible and fruitful to begin culture analysis with historical analysis. I will keep referring to "the group," but I mean this to include organizations of all kinds as well.

If learning is shared, all the group forces of identity formation and cohesion come into play in stabilizing that learning because it comes to define for the group who we are and what is our purpose or "reason to be." The various components of what is learned then become a pattern of beliefs and values that give meaning to the daily activities and work of the group. If the group is successful in achieving its purpose and is internally well organized, it will come to take these beliefs and values along with the accompanying behavioral norms for granted and will teach them to newcomers as the way to think, feel, and behave. In many ways this can be thought of as the group's sense of identity, which has both an external component of how the organization presents itself to the outside and an internal component of what its inner sense of itself is.

Basic Taken-for-Granted Assumptions—The Cultural DNA

The earliest shared learning provides meaning and stability and becomes, in a sense, *the cultural DNA*: the beliefs, values, and desired behaviors that launched the group and made it successful. This early level of beliefs, values, and desired behavior becomes nonnegotiable and turns into taken-for-granted basic assumptions that subsequently drop out of awareness. Such assumptions come to be very stable, serving as the source of later ways of doing things and elaborating the culture. What needs to be mentioned here is that these elements, learned early and composing the cultural DNA, are the source of the group's stability and cannot be changed without changing the group altogether. This point has to be understood at the outset because culture-change programs can work only if they are consistent with the group's cultural DNA.

Solving Problems of External Adaptation and Internal Integration

One of the most consistent findings of the study of groups and organizations is that leaders and members differentiate the "task" of the group from the question of "how we will organize and maintain ourselves as a group?" This arbitrary distinction has taken many forms, such as the "managerial grid," which separately measures the degree of concern for task and of concern for people, leading to an "ideal" of maximizing both (Blake & Mouton, 1964, 1969; Blake, Mouton, & McCanse, 1989). In extensive studies of problem-solving groups, it was discovered that two kinds of leadership evolved and were necessary for long-range group performance: a task leader and a social-emotional leader who were usually different people within the group (Bales, 1958).

Studies of effective organizations have always shown that successful performance and effective learning hinge on not separating these two dimensions, thinking instead in terms of "socio-technical systems," in which the external and internal are at least aligned if not integrated. In business organizations, this issue has shown up in concern for a "scorecard" or a "double bottom line" that emphasizes the need for paying attention to both the economic health of the organization and the internal organizational health that allows it to function and maintain itself (Kaplan & Norton, 1992).

One of the great dangers inherent in culture-change programs is to assume that strategy and the external adaptation issues are somehow separate from culture and to focus the desired culture changes just on the *internal* mechanisms by which a group makes life pleasant for itself. All the emphasis recently on analyzing which company to work for creates the risk that you will go to the best company but will be out of a job in a few years because that same company did not understand that its strategy was also part of its culture and failed to evolve that strategy according to the changing needs of the situation (Friedman, 2014).

Solutions That Have Worked Well Enough to Be Considered Valid

Groups are created for a purpose. We huddle together for safety or security or to get something done, and the group's survival depends on the degree to which it accomplishes its purpose. Groups do not exist in isolation. To get something done requires some kind of action in the various environments in which the group is embedded. As the group acts, it gets feedback on whether or not it is accomplishing its purpose. If it succeeds and continues to succeed, the beliefs, values, and behavior patterns that launched the group will become taken for granted as the way to continue. With age and continued success, those beliefs and values will become part of the identity of the group and will automatically be taught to newcomers as "this is who we are, this is what we do, and these are our beliefs." Whereas those values and beliefs might have been debated at the launching of the group, they become nonnegotiable and are treated as "assumptions" that new members are expected to adopt as the price of admission to the group.

Perception, Thought, Feeling, and Behavior

As a group grows, has success, and develops an identity, the shared learning process broadens from just the minimum behavior we need to agree on to get the job done to a language, a way to think, and a way to feel. When a company is founded, there will be a common interest focused on the technology, the product or service, and the occupational competencies required to perform. This means that some common ways of thinking and perceiving are present at the outset by the common decision to be a group and do something together.

With success and further shared experience the group develops its own "jargon," often expressed as shorthand and acronyms, forms of humor, and expressions that symbolize some of the essence of the shared experience. In Digital Equipment Corporation (DEC), a company that we will be referring to frequently, the phrase "Do the right thing" symbolized the value of technical honesty, openness, and really solving the customer's problems. In Apple the phrase was "Do your own thing," which meant feel free to contribute in the best way you can but express yourself personally, which, at the time, meant "decorate your office any way you want, bring your pet to work, but do the job well."

We tend to think of culture as mostly behavioral (i.e., "This is how we do things around here") and forget that with time and shared learning we come to share how we talk, what we perceive in our relevant environment, how we think about it, and what makes us feel good or bad. The longer the organization has existed, the more the thoughts and emotions of the members come to be alike. This process is most visible at the national level, where we find that subsidiaries of companies that move to new countries have great difficulty in functioning efficiently because of differences in language, thought, and emotional processes. In some companies the corporate culture is so strong and well embedded that the local offices in different countries look like and function exactly the same way as the headquarters organization.

I was once asked to describe the culture of the Swiss-German company Ciba-Geigy to the U.S. subsidiary in New Jersey. I had studied this culture in Basel and gave my Basel speech in New Jersey, which elicited the shocked response: "My God, you have just described us perfectly!"

What You Imply When You Use the Word *Culture*

The concept of culture implies structural stability, depth, breadth, and patterning or integration that results from the fact that culture is for the group a learned phenomenon just as personality and character are for individuals learned phenomena.

Structural Stability. Culture implies some level of structural stability in the group. When we say that something is "cultural," we imply that it is not only shared but is also stable because it defines the group. I have referred to this as "basic assumptions" and cultural DNA. After we achieve a sense of group identity, which is a key component of culture, it is our major stabilizing force and will not be given up easily. Culture is something that survives even when some members of the organization depart. Cultural DNA is hard to change because group members value stability because it provides meaning and predictability.

At the same time, the more surface elements of culture are defined by the interaction among the group members. The more ritualized of those interactions support the DNA and provide additional stability, but as new conditions arise and as new members with different beliefs, values, and norms enter the group, there will inevitably be both reinforcement and change as new solutions are invented for the problems of internal and external survival. Culture is both stable and dynamic, just as our body is stable if we think of the skeleton and skin and organs but constantly changing if we think of cells and the various bodily processes. The stable parts like our bones can change but not easily or rapidly unless extreme circumstances cause "breaks." When companies go bankrupt or are taken over by a turnaround manager, the cultural DNA can be destroyed and a new organization can be launched.

Depth. The basic assumptions of a culture are the deepest, often unconscious part of a group and are, therefore, less tangible and less visible. From this point of view, many of the definitions of culture that I reviewed focus too much on the visible manifestations of culture, but they are not the "essence" of what we mean by culture. This essence, best thought of as the cultural DNA, consists of the taken-for-granted, nonnegotiable beliefs, values, and behavioral assumptions. When something is more deeply embedded, that also lends stability.

Breadth. A third characteristic of culture is that after it has developed, it covers all of a group's functioning. Culture is pervasive and influences all aspects of how an organization deals with its primary purpose, its various environments, and its internal operations. As we have pointed out previously, the most common mistake is to limit the concept to the internal workings of the group while forgetting that culture also covers mission, strategy, structure, and basic operational processes. All of these have been the product of shared learning and will limit the kinds of changes the organization can make.

Patterning or Integration. The fourth characteristic that is implied by the concept of culture and that further lends stability is patterning or integration of the elements into a larger paradigm or "gestalt" that ties together the various elements at a deeper level. Culture implies that rituals, values, and behaviors are tied together into a coherent whole, and this pattern or integration is the essence of what we mean by "culture." Such patterning or integration ultimately derives from the human need to make our environment as sensible and orderly as we can (Weick, 1995). Because disorder or senselessness makes us anxious, we will work hard to reduce that anxiety by developing a more consistent and predictable view of how things are and how they should be. "Organizational cultures, like other cultures, develop as groups of people struggle to make sense of and cope with their worlds" (Trice & Beyer, 1993, p. 4).

However, we will also discover that within the cultural DNA one finds conflicting themes based on different things learned at different times and in different ways. Furthermore, as organizations evolve and develop subgroups, those subgroups develop their own subcultures, which may conflict with each other or with the larger "corporate culture." As we will see, cultural dynamics can become very complicated.

Taught to New Members: The Process of Socialization or Acculturation

After a group has developed a culture, it will pass elements of this culture on to new generations of group members (Louis, 1980; Schein, 1968; Van Maanen, 1976; Van Maanen & Schein, 1979). Studying what new members of groups are taught is, in fact, a good way to discover some of the elements of a culture, but we learn about surface aspects of the culture only by this means. This is especially so because much of what is at the heart of a culture will not be revealed in the rules of behavior taught to newcomers. It will be revealed to members only as they gain permanent status and are allowed into the inner circles of the group, where group secrets then are shared.

However, the way people learn and the socialization processes to which they are subjected may indeed reveal deeper assumptions. To reach those deeper levels, we must try to understand the perceptions and feelings that arise in critical situations, and we must observe and interview regular members or "old timers" to get an accurate sense of the deeper-level assumptions that are shared.

Can culture be learned through anticipatory socialization or self-socialization? Can new members discover for themselves what the basic assumptions are? Yes and no. We certainly know that one of the major activities of any new member when she or he enters a new group is to try to decipher the operating norms and assumptions. But this deciphering will be successful only through experiencing the rewards and punishments that are meted out by long-standing members to new members as they experiment with different kinds of behavior. In this sense, there is always a teaching process going on, even though it may be quite implicit and unsystematic.

If the group has not evolved to the point of having shared assumptions, as will sometimes be the case, the new members' interaction with old members will be a more creative process of building a culture. But once shared assumptions exist, the culture survives through teaching those assumptions to newcomers. In this regard, culture is a mechanism of social control and can be the basis of explicitly manipulating members into perceiving, thinking, and feeling in certain ways (Van Maanen & Kunda, 1989; Kunda, 1992, 2006). Whether or not we approve of this as a mechanism of social control is a separate question that will be addressed later.

Can Culture Be Inferred from Behavior Alone?

Note that the definition of culture that I have given does not include overt behavior patterns, though some such behavior, especially formal rituals, would reflect cultural assumptions. Instead, this definition emphasizes that the shared assumptions deal with how we perceive, think about, and feel about things. We cannot rely on overt behavior alone, because it is always determined both by the cultural predisposition (i.e., the shared perceptions, thoughts, and feelings that are patterned) and by the situational contingencies that arise from the immediate external environment.

Behavioral regularities can occur for reasons other than culture. For example, if we observe that all members of a group cower in the presence of a large and loud leader, this could be based on biological-reflex reactions to sound and size, individual learning, or shared learning. Such a behavioral regularity should not, therefore, be the basis for defining culture, though we might later discover that, in a given group's experience, cowering is indeed a result of shared learning and therefore a manifestation of deeper shared assumptions. Or, to put it another way, when we observe behavioral regularities, we do not know whether or not we are dealing with a cultural manifestation. Only after we have discovered the deeper layers that I am defining as the essence or DNA of culture can we specify what is and what is not an "artifact" that reflects the culture.

Do Occupations Have Cultures?

The definition provided previously does not specify the size or location of the social unit to which it can legitimately be applied. We know that nations, ethnic groups, religions, and other kinds of social units have cultures. I call these *macro* cultures. Our experience with large organizations also tells us that even globally dispersed corporations such as IBM or Unilever have corporate cultures in spite of the obvious presence of many diverse subcultures within the larger organization.

But it is not clear whether it makes sense to say that medicine or law or accounting or engineering has cultures. If culture is a product of joint learning leading to shared assumptions about how to perform and relate internally, we can see clearly that many occupations do evolve cultures. If there is strong socialization during the education and training period and if the beliefs and values learned during this time remain stable as taken-for-granted assumptions even though the person may not be in a group of occupational peers, then clearly those occupations have cultures. For most of the occupations that will concern us, these cultures are global to the extent that members are trained in the same way to the same skill set and values. However, we will find that the macro cultures, the nations and religions in which members of those occupations practice, also influence how the occupations are defined—that is, how engineering or medicine is practiced in a particular country. These variations make it that much more difficult to decipher in a hospital, for example, what is national, ethnic, occupational, or organizational.

Where Does Leadership Come In?

Leadership is the key to learning. Learning occurs when something expected is not happening and the individual or the group feels hungry, hurt, disappointed, or in some other way "disconfirmed." If we are talking about culture formation, learning occurs through the leadership of a founder or entrepreneur who uses his or her personal power to demand some new behavior directed toward achieving some purpose. If the group gets into difficulty, it will again be leadership that will propose something new to try to get out of the difficulty. If the group is successful, the culture will define what is expected of its formal leaders. If the group then gets into difficulty again, formal leaders or other members of the group will demonstrate or demand some new behavior to solve the problem, which may evolve the culture.

The learning mechanism will vary with the nature of the difficulty. If the group is not doing something that it should be doing, the leader provides it; and if the group succeeds, that behavior is reinforced and is eventually justified with the appropriate beliefs and values. If the group is doing something wrong that produces undesirable results, that behavior is punished by the other cultures in the environment and the group learns never to do that again. But again, the learning of something new or stopping something inappropriate will be mediated by leadership behavior. This will be explored further in the subsequent chapters.

Summary and Conclusions

To summarize, the most useful way to arrive at a definition of something as abstract as culture is to think in dynamic evolutionary terms, to think of culture as what the group has learned in its efforts to survive, grow, deal with its external environment, and organize itself. If we can understand where culture comes from and how it evolves, we can grasp something that is abstract, that exists in a group's unconscious, yet that has a powerful influence on a group's behavior.

Any social unit that has some kind of shared history will have gone through such a learning process and will have evolved a culture. The strength of that culture depends on the length of time, the stability of membership of the group, and the emotional intensity of the actual historical learning experiences they have shared. As we will see in the case examples, leadership is involved in the creation of the culture and at every stage of the organization's growth and maturity.

Suggestions for Readers

- If you are a scholar or researcher, before you plunge into your research consider that you are about to study a complex, patterned, multifaceted human socio-technical system and decide what it is you are really trying to find out, what research method you will use, and how that research method might affect the system.

- If you are a student or potential employee, ask the recruiter about the history of the company and ask to meet some "old timers" to get their sense of how the company came to be.

- If you are a change leader, ask yourself the following question: If the group or organization I am trying to change has a learning history, what can I learn about that history before I begin to plan changes?

- If you are a consultant or helper who has been asked to build or change culture, be sure to ask the potential client what he or she has in mind and get as concrete a picture as possible of what problems the client is trying to solve before you agree to anything.

2

THE STRUCTURE OF CULTURE

Culture in general can be analyzed at several different levels, with the term "level" meaning the degree to which the cultural phenomenon is visible to you as participant or observer. These levels range from the very tangible, overt manifestations that you can see and feel to the deeply embedded, unconscious, basic assumptions that we are defining as the essence of culture or its DNA. In between these layers are various espoused beliefs, values, norms, and rules of behavior that members of the culture use as a way of depicting the culture to themselves and others. The three major levels of cultural analysis are shown in Figure 2.1.

Three Levels of Analysis

Artifacts—Visible and Feelable Phenomena

We think of artifacts as the phenomena that you would see, hear, and feel when you encounter a new group with an unfamiliar culture. Artifacts include the visible products of the group, such as the architecture of its physical environment; its language; its technology and products; its artistic creations; its style, as embodied in clothing, manners of address, and emotional displays; its myths and stories told about the organization; its published lists of values; and its observable rituals and ceremonies.

Among these artifacts is the "climate" of the group. Some culture analysts see climate as the equivalent to culture, but it is better thought of as the product of some of the underlying assumptions and is, therefore, a manifestation of the culture. Observed behavior routines and rituals are also artifacts, as are the organizational processes by which such behavior is made routine. Structural elements such as charters, formal descriptions of how the organization works, and organization charts also belong to the artifact level.

Figure 2.1   The Three Levels of Culture

---

1. **Artifacts**
   - Visible and feelable structures and processes
   - Observed behavior
     — Difficult to decipher

2. **Espoused Beliefs and Values**
   - Ideals, goals, values, aspirations
   - Ideologies
   - Rationalizations
     — May or may not be congruent with behavior and other artifacts

3. **Basic Underlying Assumptions**
   - Unconscious, taken-for-granted beliefs and values
     — Determine behavior, perception, thought, and feeling

The most important point to be made about this level of the culture is that it is both easy to observe and very difficult to decipher. The Egyptians and the Mayans both built highly visible pyramids, but the meaning of pyramids in each culture was very different—tombs in one, temples as well as tombs in the other. In other words, observers can describe what they see and feel but cannot reconstruct from that alone what those things mean to the given group. If you are entering a new culture, you will observe lots of things that may or may not make sense to you, and you will not have the insight to figure them out without asking insiders some questions.

It is especially dangerous to try to infer the deeper assumptions from artifacts alone, because your interpretations will inevitably be projections of your own cultural background. For example, when you see a very informal, loose organization, you may interpret that as "inefficient" if your own background is based on the assumption that informality means playing around and not working. Alternatively, if you see a very formal organization, you may interpret that to be a sign of "lack of innovative capacity," if your own experience is based on the assumption that formality means bureaucracy and standardization.

If you live in the group long enough, the meanings of artifacts gradually become clear and people explain to you "why we do it that way." If, however, you want to achieve this level of understanding more quickly, you must ask insiders why they do what they do? You will then get what we are calling the espoused beliefs and values.

Espoused Beliefs and Values

All group learning ultimately reflects someone's original beliefs and values— his or her sense of what ought to be, as distinct from what is. When a group is first created or when it faces a new task, issue, or problem, the first solution proposed to deal with it reflects some individual's own assumptions about what is right or wrong, what will work or will not work. Those individuals who prevail, who can influence the group to adopt a certain approach to the problem, will later be identified as leaders or founders, but the group does not yet have any shared knowledge as a group because it has not yet taken a common action in reference to whatever it is supposed to do. Whatever is proposed will be perceived only as what the leader wants. Until the group has taken some joint action and together observed the outcome of that action, there is not as yet a shared basis for determining whether what the leader wants will turn out to be valid.

For example, if sales begin to decline in a young business, a manager may say, "We must increase advertising" because of her belief that advertising always increases sales. The group, never having experienced this situation before, will hear that assertion as a statement of that manager's beliefs and values: "She believes that when one is in sales trouble it is a good thing to increase advertising." What the leader initially proposes, therefore, cannot have any status other than a value to be questioned, debated, challenged, and tested. If the manager convinces the group to act on her belief and the solution works, then the perceived value that "advertising is good" gradually becomes transformed, first into a shared value or belief and ultimately into a shared assumption (if actions based on it continue to be successful). If this transformation process occurs, group members will usually forget that originally they were not sure and that the proposed course of action was, at an earlier time, just a proposal to be debated and confronted.

Not all beliefs and values undergo such transformation. First of all, the solution based on a given value may not work reliably. Only those beliefs and values that can be empirically tested and that continue to work reliably in solving the group's problems will become transformed into assumptions.

Second, certain value domains—those dealing with the less controllable elements of the environment or with aesthetic or moral matters—may not be testable at all. In such cases, consensus through social validation is still possible, but it is not automatic. Third, the strategy and goals of the organization may fall into this category of espoused beliefs in that there may be no way of testing them except through consensus, because the link between performance and strategy may be hard to prove.

Social validation means that certain beliefs and values are confirmed only by the shared social experience of a group. For example, any given culture cannot prove that its religion and moral system are superior to another culture's religion and moral system, but if the members reinforce each others' beliefs and values, they come to be taken for granted. Those who fail to accept such beliefs and values run the risk of "excommunication," of being thrown out of the group. The test of whether they work or not is how comfortable and anxiety-free members are when they abide by them. In these realms, the group learns that certain beliefs and values, as initially promulgated by prophets, founders, and leaders, "work" in the sense of reducing uncertainty in critical areas of the group's functioning. Moreover, as they continue to provide meaning and comfort to group members, they also become transformed into non-discussible assumptions even though they may not be correlated with actual performance.

The espoused beliefs and moral or ethical rules remain conscious and are explicitly articulated because they serve the normative or moral function of guiding members of the group as to how to deal with certain key situations as well as in training new members how to behave. Such beliefs and values often become embodied in an ideology or organizational philosophy, which then serves as a guide to dealing with the uncertainty of intrinsically uncontrollable or difficult events.

If the beliefs and values that provide meaning and comfort to the group are not congruent with the beliefs and values that correlate with effective performance, we will observe in many organizations espoused values that reflect the *desired* behavior but are not reflected in *observed* behavior (Argyris & Schon, 1978, 1996). For example, a company's ideology may say that it values people and that it has high quality standards for its products, but its actual record in that regard may contradict what it says. In U.S. organizations, it is common to espouse teamwork while actually rewarding individual competitiveness. Hewlett-Packard's highly touted "The HP way" (Packard, 1995) espoused consensus management and teamwork, but in its computer division, engineers discovered that to get ahead they had to be competitive and political.

So in analyzing espoused beliefs and values, you must discriminate carefully among those that are congruent with the underlying assumptions that guide performance, those that are part of the ideology or philosophy of the organization, and those that are rationalizations or only aspirations for the future. Often espoused beliefs and values are so abstract that they can be mutually contradictory, as when a company claims to be equally concerned about stockholders, employees, and customers, or when it claims both highest quality and lowest cost. Espoused beliefs and values often leave large areas of behavior unexplained, leaving us with a feeling that we understand a piece of the culture but still do not have the entire culture in hand. To get at that deeper level of understanding, to decipher the pattern, and to predict future behavior correctly, we have to understand more fully the category of basic assumptions.

Taken-for-Granted Underlying Basic Assumptions

When a solution to a problem works repeatedly, it comes to be taken for granted. What was once a hypothesis, supported only by a hunch or a value, gradually comes to be treated as a reality. We come to believe that nature really works this way. Basic assumptions, in this sense, are different from what some anthropologists have called "dominant value orientations," in that such dominant orientations reflect the preferred solution among several basic alternatives, but all the alternatives are still visible in the culture, and any given member of the culture could, from time to time, behave according to variant as well as dominant orientations (Kluckhohn & Strodtbeck, 1961). In the United States, the preferred solution is clearly individualism, but teamwork as a means to an end is accepted.

Basic assumptions, in the sense defined here, have become so taken for granted that you find little variation within a social unit. This degree of consensus results from repeated success in implementing certain beliefs and values, as previously described. In fact, if a basic assumption comes to be strongly held in a group, members will find behavior based on any other premise inconceivable. For example, in a group whose basic assumption is that the individual's rights supersede those of the group, members find it inconceivable to commit suicide or in some other way to sacrifice themselves to the group even if they had dishonored the group. In a capitalist country, it is inconceivable that someone might design a business organization to operate consistently at a financial loss or that it does not matter whether or not a product works.

In an occupation such as engineering, it is inconceivable to deliberately design something that is unsafe; it is a taken-for-granted assumption that things should be safe. Basic assumptions, in this sense, are similar to what Argyris and Schon (1996) identified as "theories-in-use"—the implicit assumptions that actually guide behavior, that tell group members how to perceive, think about, and feel about things. Basic assumptions, like theories-in-use, are generally non-confrontable and non-debatable and hence are extremely difficult to change. To learn something new in this realm requires us to resurrect, reexamine, and possibly change some of the more stable portions of our cognitive structure, a process that Argyris and others have called "double-loop learning," or "frame breaking" (Argyris & Schon, 1974, 1996).

Such learning is intrinsically difficult because the reexamination of basic assumptions temporarily destabilizes our cognitive and interpersonal world, releasing large quantities of basic anxiety. Rather than tolerating such anxiety levels, we tend to want to perceive the events around us as congruent with our assumptions, even if that means distorting, denying, projecting, or in other ways falsifying to ourselves what may be going on around us. It is in this psychological process that culture has its ultimate power.

Culture as a set of basic assumptions defines for us what to pay attention to, what things mean, how to react emotionally to what is going on, and what actions to take in various kinds of situations. After we have developed and integrated a set of such assumptions, we will have created a "thought world" or "mental map." We will then be most comfortable with others who share the same set of assumptions and very uncomfortable and vulnerable in situations where different assumptions operate because either we will not understand what is going on, or, worse, we will misperceive and misinterpret the actions of others (Douglas, 1986; Bushe, 2009).

Culture at this level provides its members with a basic sense of identity and defines the values that provide self-esteem (Hatch & Schultz, 2004). Cultures tell their members who they are, how to behave toward each other, and how to feel good about themselves. Recognizing these critical functions makes us aware why "changing" culture is so anxiety provoking.

To illustrate how unconscious assumptions can distort data, consider the following example. If we assume, on the basis of past experience or education, that other people will take advantage of us whenever they have an opportunity, we expect to be taken advantage of, and we then interpret the behavior of others in a way that coincides with those expectations. If we assume that it is human nature to be basically lazy, and if we observe people sitting in a seemingly idle posture at their desk, we will interpret their behavior as "loafing" rather than "thinking out an important problem." We will perceive absence from work as "shirking" rather than "doing work at home."

If this is not only a personal assumption but also one that is shared and thus part of the culture of an organization, we will discuss with others what to do about our "lazy" workforce and institute tight controls to ensure that people are at their desks and busy. If employees suggest that they do some of their work at home, we will be uncomfortable and probably deny the request because we will figure that at home they would loaf (Bailyn, 1992; Perin, 1991).

In contrast, if we assume that everyone is highly motivated and competent, we will act in accordance with that assumption by encouraging people to work at their own pace and in their own way. If we see people sitting quietly at their desks, we will assume that they are thinking or planning. If someone is discovered to be unproductive in such an organization, we will make the assumption that there is a mismatch between the person and the job assignment, not that the person is lazy or incompetent. If employees want to work at home, we will perceive that as evidence of their wanting to be productive.

In both cases, there is the potential for distortion, in that the cynical manager will not perceive how highly motivated some of the subordinates really are, and the idealistic manager will not perceive that there are subordinates who are lazy and are taking advantage of the situation. As McGregor (1960) noted many decades ago, such assumptions about "human nature" become the basis of management and control systems that perpetuate themselves because if people are treated consistently in terms of certain basic assumptions, they come eventually to behave according to those assumptions to make their world stable and predictable.

Unconscious assumptions sometimes lead to ridiculously tragic situations, as illustrated by a common problem experienced by U.S. supervisors in some Asian countries. A manager who comes from a U.S. pragmatic tradition assumes and takes it for granted that solving a problem always has the highest priority. When that manager encounters a subordinate who comes from a cultural tradition in which good relationships and protecting the superior's "face" are assumed to have top priority, the following scenario has often resulted.

The manager proposes a solution to a given problem. The subordinate knows that the solution will not work, but his unconscious assumption requires that he remain silent because to tell the boss that the proposed solution is wrong is a threat to the boss's face. It would not even occur to the subordinate to do anything other than remain silent or, if the boss were to inquire what the subordinate thought, he might even reassure the boss to go ahead and take the action rather than challenge the boss.

The action is taken, the results are negative, and the boss, somewhat surprised and puzzled, asks the subordinate what he would have done or would he have done something different. This question puts the subordinate into an impossible double bind because the answer itself is a threat to the boss's face. He cannot possibly explain his behavior without committing the very sin he was trying to avoid in the first place—namely, embarrassing the boss. He may even lie at this point and argue that what the boss did was right and only "bad luck" or uncontrollable circumstances prevented it from succeeding.

From the point of view of the subordinate, the boss's behavior is incomprehensible because to ask the subordinate what he would have done shows lack of self-pride, possibly causing the subordinate to lose respect for that boss. To the boss, the subordinate's behavior is equally incomprehensible. He cannot develop any sensible explanation of his subordinate's behavior that is not cynically colored by the assumption that the subordinate at some level just does not care about effective performance and therefore must be gotten rid of. It never occurs to the boss that another assumption—such as "you never embarrass a superior"—is operating, and that, to the subordinate, that assumption is even more powerful than "you have to get the job done."

If assumptions such as these operate only in an individual and represent his or her idiosyncratic experience, they can be corrected more easily because the person will detect that he or she is alone in holding a given assumption. The power of culture comes about through the fact that the assumptions are shared and, therefore, mutually reinforced. In these instances, probably only a third party or some cross-cultural experiences could help to find common ground whereby both parties could bring their implicit assumptions to the surface. Even after they have surfaced, such assumptions would still operate, forcing the boss and the subordinate to invent a whole new communication mechanism that would permit each to remain congruent with his or her culture— for example, agreeing that, before any decision is made and before the boss has stuck his or her neck out, the subordinate will be asked for suggestions and for factual data that would not be face threatening. Note that the solution has to keep each cultural assumption intact. We cannot, in these instances, simply declare one or the other cultural assumption "wrong." We have to find a third assumption to allow them both to retain their integrity.

We have dwelled on this long example to illustrate the potency of implicit, unconscious assumptions and to show that such assumptions often deal with fundamental aspects of life—the nature of time and space; human nature and human activities; the nature of truth and how we discover it; the correct way for the individual and the group to relate to each other; the relative importance of work, family, and self-development; the proper role of men and women; and the nature of the family.

Broader assumptions about human nature often derive from the larger culture in which the organization is embedded or from occupational units that cut across organizations. In the United States, the assumption that meetings are a waste of time derives very much from our pragmatic rugged individualism,which works both against group and team work and immediately types meetings as something to be avoided, even as complex tasks become more interdependent and require more meetings.

The Metaphor of the Lily Pond

We can summarize this three-level model with a metaphoric lily pond. The blossoms and the leaves on the surface of the pond are the "artifacts" that we can see and evaluate. The farmer who has created the pond (the leadership) announces what he expected and hoped for in the way of leaves and blossoms and will provide publicly accepted beliefs and values to justify the outcome. The farmer may or may not be consciously aware that the outcome is really a result of how the seeds, the root system, the quality of the water in the pond, and the fertilizers he put in combined to create the blossoms and leaves. This lack of awareness of what actually produces the results may not matter if the announced beliefs and values are congruent with how the leaves and blossoms turned out.

Figure 2.2   The Lily Pond as a Metaphor for Levels of Culture

Source: Artwork by Jason Bowes - Human Synergistics

However, if the observer notes a discrepancy between what the farmer claims and what actually comes up as blossoms, they will both have to examine what is present in the water and in the root system. And if they want different color blossoms, painting them a different color will not work; they will have to examine how to change the seeds, the water quality, the fertilizer—that is, the invisible DNA of the pond. Leaders who want to change culture cannot do so by painting the blossoms or pruning the leaves. They have to locate the cultural DNA and change some of that.

Given this structural model one can analyze any culture, or, for that matter, any individual's cultural identity. Let's look briefly at how this would apply at the individual or group micro-system level and then in subsequent chapters apply it to organizations and larger cultural units.

The Individual from a Cultural Perspective

The individual as a cultural entity can be analyzed in terms of artifacts, espoused beliefs and values, and underlying basic assumption. We all carry within us assumptions about the state of the world and about the correct ways to engage in relationships. Some of those assumptions about relationship have come to be taken for granted and fall into the realm of the unconscious because we learned early some of the basic rules of how to get along in different kinds of situations. These assumptions and rules derive from the macro culture in that every society has learned from its own history what level of communication and openness is workable for people to get along.

All societies (i.e., macro cultures) evolve rules of etiquette, good manners, and tact that specify what is or is not appropriate to say in any given situation. Most of us are, therefore, walking repositories of rules that were taught to us when young and that represent early layers of cultural socialization. We learn as part of our acculturation into the family that in the interests of getting along with each other, it is important to withhold some of our perceptions and feelings because to say them out loud might hurt or offend others. And if we hurt others, that permits them to hurt us back, which makes social life generally too dangerous. We learn that some of these things can be said to friends and even more can be said to intimates.

However, the basic assumptions about *why* you cannot say certain things remain below consciousness, and the process by which you learned them is probably totally forgotten.

When we enter into a therapeutic or personal-development program, the leader and the setting usually create a "cultural island" in which some of the societal rules can be suspended and people are encouraged to be more open about what they normally would withhold. When the tasks we are asked to perform in a group require a high degree of collaboration, the team learning process or "teaming" (Edmondson, 2012) similarly creates conditions where some of our basic assumptions have to be surfaced. The best example would be to give team members feedback on how we react to their participation and to own up to our own doubts and fears in relation to task accomplishment. I have called this "here-and-now humility" to indicate that in such team situations formal status and rank become less important than patterns of who is dependent on whom at a given moment in accomplishing a task (Schein, 2016).

In summary, as individuals we can all be observed at the artifact level, we all have our espoused beliefs and values that may or may not be consistent with our behavior, and we all have deeper-level assumptions about why we do what we do. It is the degree of alignment or congruity between the three levels that determine how an individual's "sincerity," or "integrity" is judged by others.

The Group or Micro System from a Cultural Perspective

Groups also evolve "hidden agendas," "have elephants in the room," and, in various ways, espouse beliefs and principles to justify their overt behavior. If we apply the three-level model to group behavior by analyzing whether or not the observed behavior matches the espoused beliefs and values, we discover discrepancies that reveal the basic assumptions level (Bion, 1959; Marshak, 2006; Kantor, 2012).

A simple but telling example occurred in a company manufacturing team that was dedicated to good team work and espoused a climate of relevant participation by all members. Over several meetings I observed that one member was consistently ignored after he tried to say something, was never called on, and seemed to be very much on the margin. I pointed this out at one of the meetings and was met with a stony silence, a pause, and then a continuation of the discussion as if nothing had happened.

After the meeting, the chair pointed out to me that this member had been one of the important inventors of several of the company's products, was still too young to be early retired, and was still potentially useful to have around for consultation, but there was no place to "park" him except in this particular group. In early meetings they had welcomed him and jointly agreed that he was welcome to participate but that he would probably find that most of his ideas were now obsolete. He understood and accepted this.

My intervention in calling attention to this embarrassed everyone by surfacing the basic assumption "we accept you as a member but we all understand that you will not be a real contributing member of the group." Any discussion of this assumption would lead to further embarrassment for all concerned. It had become part of the group's culture to accept this person as a member without, however, feeling obligated to take his ideas seriously. The group had evolved the behavioral rule of "you must be polite and pay attention to him but you don't have to use his ideas."

Do all groups have cultures? It depends on the degree to which a given group has a shared history of learning together. A group that has constant change of membership and has not had to learn to do anything together will not have a culture. But any group that has a shared task, more or less constant membership, and some common history of learning together will have its own subculture as well as being nested in the culture of the organizational unit it is in and in the macro cultures of the occupations of its members, the organization, and the nation.

Summary and Conclusions

This chapter presents a three-level model of culture as the way to describe and analyze any cultural phenomenon, whether we are talking about an individual, a micro system, a subculture, an organization, or a macro culture. It is important to differentiate the observed and experienced "artifacts" from the "espoused values" and from the "basic underlying assumptions" that ultimately drive the observed behavior.

Suggestions for Readers

- If you are a scholar or researcher, try to classify all that you observe and know about the group that you are a member of into the basic categories of artifacts, espoused values, and basic assumptions. What additional questions do you need to ask of your colleagues to decipher the basic assumptions?

- If you are a student or potential employee, take a potential organization you are interested in, visit it to gather impressions and feelings, and then see whether what the organization claims fits what you have observed and felt. If you see discrepancies, ask questions to get at the basic assumptions.

- If you are a change leader, bring together a representative group of members of the organization you are trying to change and ask them to identify as many behavioral artifacts of the organization as they can. List these on flip charts. Then ask the group to identify the major espoused values of the organization and compare those values with the artifacts on the charts. Are they consistent? If you find discrepancies, ask the group to identify what the deeper assumption might be that would explain the artifacts, especially observed routine behavior.

- If you are a consultant or helper and are sure you know what specific changes the change leaders have in mind, invite them to bring together a group from their organization and take it through the preceding exercise to determine where identified beliefs, values, and assumptions might aid or hinder the proposed change program.

3

A YOUNG AND GROWING U.S. ENGINEERING ORGANIZATION

How culture works and how to analyze and assess cultural phenomena is best illustrated through cases that represent different stages of organizational evolution. In this chapter I review the case of an organization that I was fortunate enough to encounter in its youth and able to follow through its entire life cycle. At one level this is an "old" case from the 1960s, but the culture dynamics I encountered then continue to be visible in companies that I observed in recent years and seem to characterize technically based start-ups.

Case 1: Digital Equipment Corporation in Maynard, Massachusetts

Digital Equipment Corporation (DEC) was the first major company to introduce interactive computing in the mid-1950s, and it became a very successful manufacturer of what came to be called "mini computers." It was located primarily in the northeastern part of the United States, with headquarters in an old mill in Maynard, Massachusetts, but it had branches throughout the world. At its peak, it employed more than 100,000 people, with sales of $14 billion. In the mid-1980s it became the second largest computer manufacturer in the world after IBM. The company ran into major financial difficulties in the 1990s and was eventually sold to the Compaq Corp. in 1998. Compaq was in turn acquired by Hewlett-Packard in 2001.

There were innumerable stories written about why and how DEC "failed," but few of them provided a cultural perspective on either its rise or its failure. I was involved with DEC as a consultant from 1966 to 1992, and therefore was privy to much of the inside story of how this company grew, peaked, and declined (Schein, 2003). I was a consultant to the founder, Ken Olsen, and to the various executives over this entire period, which provided a unique opportunity to see cultural dynamics in action over most of the life of this company. DEC's history is a prime example of how the deeper cultural layers, the basic assumptions, explain both the rise and fall of the company and will be used throughout this book as a major case example that illustrates macro and micro culture interactions.

In this chapter we begin by analyzing the company's culture structurally, using the framework provided in Chapter 2. In later chapters I will refer to various cultural forces that illuminate DEC as a start-up, DEC as a mid-life company, and DEC in decline. Start-ups and old companies have received a lot of attention in the organizational literature, but there are not many studies of an entire life cycle of a single company under its founder. Such studies become especially important as organization theory puts increasing attention on agility and "ambidexterity" as a key property of organizations that have survived for a long time (O'Reilly & Tushman, 2016).

What these authors show with the use of this concept is that long-range survival seems to hinge on the ability to manage both the existing business, which has been the reason for success thus far, and at the same time to develop a new business that is more responsive to changing environmental conditions. If the organization cannot do that for itself, it will inevitably attract competitors who will "disrupt" the present business by creating new businesses that are more adaptive and will, therefore, eventually put the old business into decline (Christensen, 1997). So with this theoretical background, let's meet DEC.

Artifacts: Encountering the Company

To gain entry into any of DEC's many buildings, you had to sign in with a guard who sat behind a counter where there were usually several people chatting, moving in and out, checking the badges of employees who were coming into the building, accepting mail, and answering phone calls. After signing in, you waited in a small, casually furnished lobby until the person you were visiting came personally or sent a secretary to escort you into the work areas.

What I recall most vividly from my first encounters with this organization was the ubiquitous open-office architecture, the extreme informality of dress and manners, a very dynamic environment in the sense of rapid pace, and a high rate of interaction among employees, seemingly reflecting enthusiasm, intensity, energy, and impatience. As I would pass cubicles or conference rooms, I would get the impression of openness. There were very few doors, and I learned later that Ken Olsen, the founder, had forbidden doors on engineers' offices. The company cafeteria spread out into a big open area where people sat at large tables, hopped from one table to another, and obviously were intensely involved in their work even at lunch. I also observed that there were many cubicles with coffee machines and refrigerators in them and that food seemed to be part of most meetings. For morning meetings one or another member brought boxes of fresh donuts for all to enjoy.

The physical layout and patterns of interaction made it very difficult to decipher who had what rank, and I was told that there were no status perquisites such as private dining rooms, special parking places, or offices with special views and the like. The furniture in the lobbies and offices was very inexpensive and functional. The company was mostly headquartered in an old industrial building. The informal clothing worn by most managers and employees reinforced this sense of economy and egalitarianism.

I had been brought into DEC by Ken Olsen "to help the top management team improve communication and group effectiveness." As I began to attend the regular staff meetings of the senior management group, I was quite struck by the high level of interpersonal confrontation, argumentativeness, and conflict. Group members became highly emotional at the drop of a hat, interrupted each other constantly, and seemed to become angry at each other, though it was also noticeable that such anger did not carry over outside the meeting.

With the exception of the president and founder, Ken Olsen, there were very few people who had visible status in terms of how people deferred to them. Olsen himself, through his informal behavior, implied that he did not take his position of power all that seriously. Group members argued as much with him as with each other and even interrupted him from time to time. His status did show up, however, in the occasional lectures he delivered to the group when he felt that members did not understand something or were "wrong" about something. At such times, Olsen could become very emotionally excited in a way that other members of the group never did. I learned from further observation that this style of running meetings was typical and that meetings were very common, to the point where people would complain about all the time spent in committees. At the same time, they would argue that without these committees they could not get their work done properly.

My own reactions to the company and these meetings also must be considered as artifacts to be documented. It was exciting to be attending top management meetings and surprising to observe so much behavior that seemed to me dysfunctional. The level of confrontation I observed made me quite nervous, and I had a sense of not knowing what this was all about, but it also provided me an agenda as a consultant: how to fix this dysfunctional group in terms of what I knew from my training were the characteristics of effective groups.

The company was organized as a matrix, one of the earliest versions of this type of organization in terms of functional units and product lines, but there was a sense of perpetual reorganization and a search for a structure that would "work better." Structure was viewed as something to tinker with until you got it right. There were many levels in the technical and managerial hierarchy, but I sensed that the hierarchy was just a convenience, not something to be taken very seriously.

However, the communication structure was taken very seriously. There were many committees already in existence, and new ones were constantly being formed. The company had an extensive email network that functioned worldwide; engineers and managers traveled frequently and were in constant telephone communication with each other. Olsen would get upset if he observed any evidence of under-communication or miscommunication. To make communication and contact easier, DEC had its own "air force" of several planes and helicopters. Ken Olsen was a licensed pilot and flew his own plane to a retreat in Maine for recreation.

Analytical Comment. Many other artifacts from this organization are described subsequently; but for the present, this will suffice to give a flavor of what I encountered at DEC. The question now is, what does any of it mean? I knew that I reacted very positively to the informality but very negatively to the unruly group behavior, but I did not really understand why these things were happening and what significance they had for members of the company. To gain some understanding, I had to get to the next level: the level of espoused beliefs, values, and behavioral norms.

At this point I thought I was observing subcultures (the various work areas) and micro cultures (the various group meetings) that reflected primarily the technology driving the business—that is, inventing computers that would be interactive, could sit on a desk, and could create a new industry. I was also seeing the personal style of the founder, which seemed to be a reflection of the New England Yankee macro culture. What would I learn if I asked questions?

Espoused Beliefs, Values, and Behavioral Norms

As I talked to people at DEC about my observations, especially those things that puzzled and scared me, I began to elicit some of the espoused beliefs and values by which the company ran. Many of these were embodied in slogans or in parables that Olsen wrote from time to time and circulated throughout the company. For example, a high value was placed on *personal responsibility*. If someone made a proposal to do something and it was approved, that person had a clear obligation to do it or, if it was not possible to do, to come back and renegotiate. The phrase "*He who proposes, does*" was frequently heard around the organization.

Employees at all levels were responsible for thinking about what they were doing and were enjoined at all times to "*do the right thing*," which, in many instances, meant being insubordinate. If the boss asked you to do something that you considered wrong or stupid, you were supposed to "*push back*" and attempt to change the boss's mind. If the boss insisted and you still felt that it was not right, you were supposed to not do it and take your chances on your own judgment. If you were wrong, you would get your wrist slapped but would gain respect for having stood up for your own convictions. Because bosses knew these rules, they were, of course, less likely to issue arbitrary orders, more likely to listen to you if you pushed back, and more likely to renegotiate the decision. So actual insubordination was rarely necessary, but the principle of thinking for oneself and doing the right thing was very strongly reinforced.

It was also a rule that you should not do things without *getting "buy-in"* from others who had to implement the decision, who had to provide needed services, or who would be influenced by it. Employees had to be very individualistic and, at the same time, very willing to be team players; hence, the simultaneous feeling that committees were a big drain on time but were indispensable. To reach a decision and to get buy-in, the individual had to convince others of the validity of his or her idea and be able to defend it against every conceivable argument, which caused the high levels of confrontation and fighting that I observed in groups.

However, after an idea had stood up to this level of debate and survived, it could then be moved forward and implemented, because everyone was now convinced that it was the right thing to do. This took longer to achieve, but led to more consistent and rapid action. If somewhere down the hierarchy the decision "failed to stick" because someone was not convinced that it was "the right thing to do," that person had to push back, his or her arguments had to be heard, and either he or she had to be convinced or the decision had to be renegotiated up the hierarchy.

In asking people about their jobs, I discovered another strong value: each person should *figure out the essence of your job* and be very clear about it. Asking the boss what was expected was considered a sign of weakness. If your own job definition was out of line with what the group or department required, you would hear about it soon enough. The role of the boss was to set broad targets, but subordinates were expected to take the initiative to figure out how best to achieve them. This value required a lot of discussion and negotiation, which often led to complaints about time wasting; at the same time, everyone defended the value of doing things in this way and continued to defend it even though it created difficulties later in DEC's life.

I also found out that people could fight bitterly in group meetings, yet remain very good friends. There was a feeling of being a tight-knit group, a kind of extended family under a strong father figure, Ken Olsen, which led to the norm that *fighting does not mean that people dislike or disrespect each other.* This norm seemed to extend even to "bad-mouthing" each other; people would call each other "stupid" behind each others' backs or say that someone was a real "turkey" or "jerk," yet they would respect each other in work situations.

Olsen often criticized people in public, which made them feel embarrassed, but it was explained to me that this only meant that you should work on improving your area of operations, not that you were really in disfavor. In fact, people quipped that it was better to have Ken criticize you than not to notice you. Even if someone fell into disfavor, he or she was viewed merely as being in the "penalty box." Stories were told of managers or engineers who had been in this kind of disfavor for long periods of time and then rebounded to become heroes in some other context.

When managers talked about their products, they emphasized quality and elegance. The company was founded by engineers and was dominated by an engineering mentality in that the value of a proposed new product was generally judged by whether the engineers themselves liked it and used it, not by external market surveys or test markets. DEC engineers loved sophisticated customers like scientists and lab managers who could relate to the complex products, give good feedback, and thereby stimulate product improvements. Ordinary customers were talked about in a rather disparaging way, especially those who might not be technically sophisticated enough to appreciate the elegance of the product that had been designed.

Olsen emphasized *absolute integrity in designing, manufacturing, and selling.* He viewed the company as highly ethical, and he strongly emphasized the work values associated with the Protestant work ethic—honesty, hard work, high standards of personal morality, professionalism, personal responsibility, integrity, and honesty. Especially important was being honest and truthful in their relations with each other and with customers. As this company grew and matured, it put many of these values into formal statements and taught them to new employees. They viewed their culture as a great asset and felt that the culture itself had to be taught to all new employees (Kunda, 1992, 2006).

Analytical Comments. There is a great temptation at this point to conclude that we now understand the DEC culture. I now "knew" what the espoused values and principles were but did not really understand "why" some of these values were so strongly held. I was also struck by the fact that those values represented simultaneously the macro culture of academia, in which ideas always have to be attacked and tested; the macro occupational engineering culture, in which elegance is a high value; and the micro culture of a start-up, in which the founder's values and operational methods are the primary influence on how the organization evolves. Ken Olsen was a very puritanical New Englander, and he infused those personal values into the organization. For example, there was no alcohol allowed at off-site meetings. Olsen strongly emphasized frugality, drove a very inexpensive car, and disallowed perquisites like private assigned parking spaces and executive dining rooms.

In figuring out which of these nested values are dominant in determining the evolution of the organization, it is important to note that other technical start-ups such as Hewlett-Packard, Apple, Microsoft, and Google had very similar cultures at the early stages of their development.

Basic Assumptions: The Basic DEC Paradigm

To understand the implications of these values and to show how they relate to overt behavior, we must seek the underlying assumptions and premises on which this organization was based (see Figures 3.1 and 3.2).

Figure 3.1   DEC's Cultural Paradigm: Part One

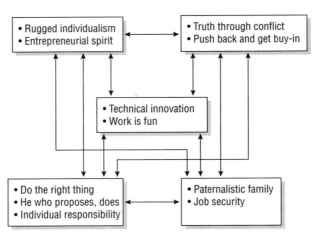

Figure 3.2   DEC's Cultural Paradigm: Part Two

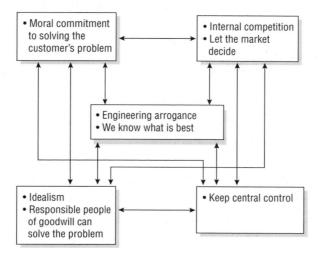

Analytical Comments. Only by grasping these first five assumptions can we understand, for example, why my initial interventions of trying to get the group to be "nicer" to each other in the communication process were politely ignored. I was seeing the group's "effectiveness" in terms of my values and assumptions of how a "good" group should act. The DEC senior management committee was trying to reach "truth" and make valid decisions in the only way they knew how and by a process that they believed in. The group was merely a means to an end; the real process going on in the group was a basic, deep search for solutions in which they could have confidence because they stood up even after intense debate.

After I shifted my focus to helping them in this search for valid solutions, I figured out what kinds of interventions would be more relevant, and I found that the group accepted them more readily. For example, I began to emphasize agenda setting, using the flip-chart to focus on ideas and to keep them visible in front of the group; time management; clarifying some of the debate; summarizing; consensus testing after the debate was running dry; and a more structured problem-solving process. The interrupting, the emotional conflicts, and the other behaviors I observed initially continued, but the group became more effective in its handling of information and in reaching consensus. It was in this context that I gradually developed the philosophy of being a "process consultant" instead of trying to be an expert on how groups should work (Schein, 1969, 1988, 1999a, 2003, 2016).

Additional Basic Assumptions

As I learned more about DEC, I also learned that the cultural DNA contained another five key assumptions, shown in Figure 3.2. These five additional assumptions reflected some of the group's beliefs and values pertaining to customers and marketing:

1. The only valid way to sell a product is to find out what the customer's problem is and to solve that problem, even if that means selling less or recommending another company's products.
2. People can and will take responsibility and continue to act responsibly no matter what.
3. The market is the best decision maker if there are several product contenders, which also implies that internal competition in product development is desirable.
4. Even as the company becomes very large and differentiated, it is desirable to keep some central control rather than divisionalizing. I think this was an imposition of Ken Olsen's personal needs as a founder instead of a strategic decision.
5. DEC engineers "know best" what a good product is, based on whether or not they personally like working with that product.

Analytical Comments. These 10 assumptions can be thought of as the DEC cultural paradigm. What is important in showing the interconnections is the fact that single elements of the paradigm could not explain how this organization was able to function. It was only by seeing the combination of assumptions—around individual creativity, group conflict as the source of truth, individual responsibility, commitment to each other as a family, commitment to innovation and to solving customer problems, and belief in internal competition and central control—that the observable day-to-day behavior could be explained. It is this level of basic assumptions and their interconnections that defines some of the *essence* of the culture—the key genes of the cultural DNA at this stage of DEC's development.

This paradigm is a mixed combination of U.S. macro-cultural values of individualism, competition, and pragmatism and family values such as loyalty, frugality, truth, and commitment to customers as represented by Ken Olsen and the engineers he hired. It illustrates the enormous power of the founder of an organization in how he infuses it with the values and assumptions he brings with him from his own cultural background.

How general was this paradigm in DEC? That is, if we were to study various micro systems such as the workers in the plants, salesmen in geographically remote units, engineers in technical enclaves, and so on, would we find the same assumptions operating? One of the interesting aspects of the DEC story is that at least for its first 20 or so years, this paradigm would have been observed in operation across most of its rank levels, functions, and geographies. Much of it was explicitly taught to all newcomers through periodic "boot camps," and much of it was written down as the DEC culture. Some of these assumptions were modified in functions such as sales and service where the pragmatic needs to relate well to customers created new and different subcultural elements—hierarchy, status rituals, more rapid decision making, and more discipline. As we will see subsequently, as DEC grew, aged, and evolved, some basic elements of the DEC culture began to change, whereas other elements that did not change, even as they became dysfunctional in the changing market environment, led ultimately to DEC's decline.

Because of my continuing contact with this company I was able to construct the detailed picture of the organization that is presented in the figures. This level of detail was needed to understand some of the puzzling behavior I had observed and to describe the organization to outside observers. But it must be noted that much of the current emphasis in culture research focuses on how one might *change* culture to improve performance. To change culture requires the insider change leaders to understand their culture at a detailed level and especially to identify various stable elements that were the source of the company's success, but it is not important for the researcher or outside observer to understand the culture in as much detail as I was able to gather. The consultant, the future employee, the investor, the supplier, or the customer needs to know some elements of an organization's culture, but he or she does not need to invest in the kind of clinical study that I was able to do in this case.

Summary and Conclusions

The crucial insight to take away from this case is that a young company's culture provides identity, meaning, and daily motivation. If the company is successful, that culture will become very strong and explicitly part of its identity. We see today articles and books by many organizations explicitly touting their culture and suggesting that it is the culture that is making those organizations successful. The DEC story should remind us that we cannot really make generalizations about culture without specifying the age, size, and underlying technology of the company, because each of those factors played a role in what the DEC culture became. We also have to consider in what way the given company culture is nested in various occupational and national macro cultures.

A second important lesson is that the presence of the founder or entrepreneur is a strong stabilizing force for the culture. The implication is that we cannot make generalizations about culture without specifying whether we are talking about a first- or a second-generation company still run by the founder or about a company run by general managers who have been appointed by boards and have worked their way up the managerial ladder. The stability of DEC's commitment to innovation even in the face of markets that wanted simpler turnkey products could be explained in part by the presence of the founder, whose deep assumptions and beliefs were difficult to challenge.

In the following chapter we will look at an entirely different kind of organization at a different stage of development and in a different industry.

Suggestions for Readers

For all readers, the main thing to do at this point is to *reflect* on the complexity of this organization's culture and how its micro and subcultures are nested in both the U.S. culture and the culture of engineering.

Can you think of other organizations that resemble DEC? What is similar and what is different, and why?

4

A MATURE SWISS-GERMAN CHEMICAL ORGANIZATION

A mature organization is culturally different in many ways. The main differences result from size, age, and that it is managed entirely by promoted general managers (not founders or their children). When we talk about culture, we have to remind ourselves to specify the kind of organization, the macro cultures it is nested in, and how big and old it is. This particular case is also one from the 1980s, but, as in the case of DEC, it shows in a very mature, large, diversified organization how different the cultural issues and cultural dynamics are, and still how representative they are of contemporary large mature organizations.

Case 2: Ciba-Geigy Company in Basel, Switzerland

The Ciba-Geigy Company in the late 1970s and early 1980s was a Swiss multinational, multidivisional, geographically decentralized chemical company dealing with pharmaceuticals, agricultural chemicals, industrial chemicals, dyestuffs, photographic chemicals, and some technically based consumer products. It eventually merged with a former competitor, Sandoz, to become what is today—Novartis. My consulting initially on career development evolved into numerous other consulting activities that lasted into the mid-1980s and focused on some major culture change.

Artifacts—Encountering Ciba-Geigy

My initial encounter with this company was through a telephone call from its head of management development, Dr. Jürg Leupold, inquiring whether I would be willing to give a talk to its annual meeting in Switzerland. Ciba-Geigy invited their top 40 to 50 worldwide executives along with one or two outsiders to a three-day meeting held at a Swiss resort. The purpose was to review strategy and operations and to stimulate the group by having outside lecturers present on topics of interest to the company. Dr. Leupold had asked me to give lectures and do some structured exercises around my research on career anchors at the 1979 annual meeting of its top executives (Schein, 1978, Schein & Van Maanen, 2013). The CEO, Dr. Samuel Koechlin, liked the fact that this research had shown that people are in their jobs for different reasons (the career anchors), but that in each kind of job one could be creative.

Koechlin was Swiss, but he had spent part of his career in the company's U.S. subsidiary and had become interested in all the emphasis he had observed in the U.S. culture on creativity and innovation. He requested that I visit him prior to the annual meeting to discuss how best to use the career-anchor exercise and to "test our chemistry with each other." I made a special flight to Basel to spend the night with him and his family. We decided that the career anchor booklet and job or role planning exercises were to be translated into German so that all the participants could do the exercise and discuss their career anchors at the annual meeting. I would lecture and draw out the implications for creativity and innovation following the exercises.

I was "briefed" by further phone conversations with Dr. Leupold whose first name was Jürg, but I never felt it was appropriate to use that. I learned that the company was run by a board of directors and an internal executive committee of nine people who were legally accountable as a group for company decisions. The chairman, Dr. Koechlin, functioned as the CEO, but the committee made most decisions by consensus. Each member of the committee had oversight responsibility for a division, a function, and a geographic area, and these responsibilities rotated every few years. Both Ciba and Geigy had long histories of growth and had merged in 1970. The merger was considered to be a success, but there were still strong identifications with the original companies, according to many managers. The CEO of Novartis when I asked him in 2006 how the Ciba-Geigy/Sandoz merger went said: "That merger is going fine, but I still have Ciba people and Geigy people!"

My first visit to Ciba-Geigy headquarters offered a sharp contrast to what I had encountered at DEC. I was immediately struck by the formality as symbolized by large gray stone buildings, heavy doors that were always closed, and stiff uniformed guards in the main lobby. This spacious, opulent lobby was the main passageway for employees to enter the inner compound of office buildings and plants. It had high ceilings, large heavy doors, and a few couches in one corner to serve as a waiting area.

Upon entering the Ciba-Geigy lobby, I was asked by the uniformed guard to check in with another guard who sat in a glassed-in office. I had to give my name and state where I was from and whom I was visiting. The guard then asked me to take a seat and to wait until an escort could take me to my appointed place. As I sat and waited, I noticed that the guard seemed to know most of the employees who streamed through the lobby or went to elevators and stairs leading from it. I had the distinct feeling that any stranger would have been spotted immediately and would have been asked to report as I had been.

Dr. Leupold's secretary arrived in due course and took me up the elevator and down a long corridor of closed offices. Each office had a tiny nameplate that could be covered over by a hinged metal plate if the occupant wanted to remain anonymous. Above each office was a light bulb, some of which showed red and some green. I asked on a subsequent visit what this meant; I was told that if the light was out, the person was not in; if it was green, it was okay to knock; and if it was red, the person did not want to be disturbed under any circumstances.

We went around a corner and down another corridor and did not see another soul during the entire time. When we reached Dr. Leupold's office, the secretary knocked discreetly. When he called to come in, she opened the door, ushered me in, then went to her own office and closed the door. I was offered some tea or coffee, which was brought by the secretary on a large formal tray with china accompanied by a small plate of excellent cookies. I mention that they were "excellent" because it turned out that good food was very much part of Ciba-Geigy's presented identity. Whenever I visited offices in later years in Paris and London, I was always taken to three-star restaurants.

Following our meeting, Dr. Leupold took me to the executive dining room in another building, where we again passed guards. This was the equivalent of a first-class restaurant, with a hostess who clearly knew everyone, reserved tables, and provided discreet guidance on the day's specials.

Aperitifs and wine were offered with lunch, and the whole meal took almost two hours. I was told that there was a less fancy dining room in still another building and an employee cafeteria as well, but that this dining room clearly had the best food and was the right place for senior management to conduct business and to bring visitors.

Ciba-Geigy managers came across as very serious, thoughtful, deliberate, well prepared, formal, and concerned about protocol. I learned later that whereas DEC allocated rank and salary fairly strictly to the actual job being performed by the individual employee, Ciba-Geigy had a system of managerial ranks based on length of service, overall performance, and the personal background of the individual rather than on the actual job being performed at a given time. Rank and status therefore had a much more permanent quality in Ciba-Geigy, whereas in DEC, fortunes could rise and fall precipitously and frequently with job assignment.

In Ciba-Geigy meetings, I observed much less direct confrontation and much more respect for individual opinion. Meetings were geared to information transmission rather than problem solving. Recommendations made by managers in their specific area of accountability were generally respected, accepted, and implemented. I never observed insubordination, and I had the impression that it would not be tolerated. Rank and status thus clearly had a higher value in Ciba-Geigy than in DEC, whereas personal negotiating skill and the ability to get things done in an ambiguous social environment had a higher value in DEC.

Analytical Comments. It was striking how different the initial encounters with this organization were from my first contacts with DEC and how hard it was from the beginning to determine whether this was a reflection of the Swiss-German macro culture, the effect of chemical technology (the basis of all their products), or the history of the company (which included the major merger of Ciba and Geigy), or the fact that the current leader had been "Americanized" through his years in the U.S. subsidiary.

I had the impression that things were very tightly organized and carefully planned; still, to meet Koechlin at his home with his family and spend the night contrasted sharply with my DEC experience. In my entire time as a consultant with DEC I never met any members of Ken Olsen's family nor the families of any other executives. It highlights the fact that even a concept like "informal" or "formal" can mean very different things in different macro cultures.

Whereas in DEC, kitchens and food were used as vehicles to get people to interact with each other, in Ciba-Geigy food, drink, and graciousness were handled very formally and carried additional symbolic meaning having to do with status and rank. Various senior officers of the company were pointed out to me, and I noticed that whenever anyone greeted another, it was always with their formal titles, usually Dr. This or Dr. That. Observable differences in deference and demeanor made it fairly easy to determine who was superior to whom within the organization. It was also obvious that the tables in the dining room were assigned to executives on the basis of status and that the hostess knew exactly the relative status of all her guests. I got to know a number of these executives over the years but another artifact was that I had to learn not to greet them in the dining room. If they acknowledged knowing me it would tell their peers that they needed consultation help, which apparently might be seen as a sign of weakness.

I reacted differently to the Ciba-Geigy and DEC environments. I liked the DEC environment more but could not decide whether it was the congruence with my U.S. identity, my experience in DEC that valued my more informal style, or the excitement of being in a start-up setting helping a company to grow versus trying to influence a very old culture to become more innovative. In performing a cultural analysis, a person's reactions are themselves artifacts of the culture that must be acknowledged and taken into account. It is undesirable to try to present any cultural analysis with total objectivity; not only would this be impossible, but a person's emotional reactions and biases are also primary data to be analyzed and understood.

I did not realize at the time that I was also confronting in these two companies an archetypal organizational issue: first, how to turn rampant creativity and innovation into a stable productive system and then, once a level of stability had been established, how to recapture some of the innovative capacity that is needed when a mature company faces changes in its technological, economic, and market environments. This issue has become a central focus of researchers on organizational structures and processes and has led to the concept of the "ambidextrous organization," which is to be able to both maintain its "old" business while simultaneously creating and protecting a new innovative business until it becomes mature and enables the company to survive in a new environment (O'Reilly & Tushman, 2016).

Espoused Beliefs and Values

Beliefs and values are usually elicited best when you ask about observed behavior or other artifacts that strike you as puzzling, anomalous, or inconsistent. If I asked managers in Ciba-Geigy why they always kept their doors closed, they would patiently and somewhat condescendingly explain to me that this was the only way they could get any work done and that they valued work very highly. Meetings were a necessary evil and were useful only for announcing decisions or gathering information. "Real work" was done by thinking things out, and that required quiet and concentration. In contrast, in DEC real work was accomplished by debating things out in meetings!

It was also pointed out to me that discussion among peers was not of great value and that important information would come from the boss or someone more technically expert. Formal and academic authority were highly respected, especially authority based on level of education and experience. The use of titles such as "Doctor" or "Professor" symbolized respect for the knowledge that education bestowed on people. Much of this had to do with a great respect for the science of chemistry and the contributions of laboratory research to product development. In Ciba-Geigy, as in DEC, a high value was placed on individual effort and contribution, but in Ciba-Geigy, no one ever went outside the chain of command and did things that would be out of line with what the boss had suggested.

In Ciba-Geigy, a high value was placed on product elegance and quality, and, as I discovered later, what might be called product significance. Ciba-Geigy managers felt very proud of the fact that their chemicals and drugs were useful for crop protection and creating the fertilizers that helped third-world countries deal with starvation, for curing diseases, and in other ways that helped to improve the world. The company had a clear worldwide identity that seemed to inform almost everything it did.

Assumptions—The Ciba-Geigy Company's Cultural Paradigm

Many of the values that were articulated gave a flavor to this company, but without digging deeper into assumptions, I could not fully understand how things worked. For example, the artifact that struck me most as I worked with this organization with the mandate to help it to become more innovative was the anomalous behavior connected with a memo I had written based on my learning how the company was successfully managing a difficult down-sizing process. I asked my contact client, Dr. Leupold, the director of management development, to distribute my memo to those managers he thought could most benefit from the information. Because he reported directly to Dr. Koechlin, he seemed like a natural conduit for communicating with those divisional, functional, and geographic managers who needed the information I was gathering. When I would return on a subsequent visit to the company and meet with one of the unit managers, without fail I would discover that he did not have the memo, but if he requested it from Dr. Leupold, it would be sent over almost immediately.

This pattern was puzzling and irritating, but its consistency clearly indicated that some strong underlying assumptions were at work here. When I asked one of my colleagues in the corporate staff unit that delivered training and other development programs to the organization why the information did not circulate freely, he revealed that he had similar problems in that he would develop a helpful intervention in one unit of the organization, but that other units would seek help *outside* the organization before they would "discover" that he had a solution that was better. The common denominator seemed to be that unsolicited ideas were generally not well received.

A third piece of information was that corporate marketing kept proposing integrated programs for all the divisions, only to be shot down with the comment: "How could there possibly be common training for Agri sales/marketing people who are slogging around in muddy fields talking to farmers, and well dressed MBAs visiting doctors in their hospital offices."

My colleague and I had a long exploratory conversation about this observed behavior and jointly figured out what the explanation was. At Ciba-Geigy, when a manager was given a job, that job became the private domain of that individual. Managers felt a strong sense of turf or ownership and made the assumption that each owner of a piece of the organization would be completely in charge and on top of his or her piece. Managers would be fully informed and make themselves experts in that area. Therefore, if someone provided some unsolicited information pertaining to the job, this was potentially an "invasion of privacy" and possibly an insult, as it implied that the manager did not already have this information or idea. The powerful metaphor that "giving someone unsolicited information was like walking into their home uninvited" came from a number of managers in subsequent interviews.

By not understanding this assumption, I had unwittingly put Dr. Leupold into the impossible position of risking insulting all his colleagues and peers if he had circulated my memos as I had asked. Interestingly enough, this kind of assumption means that even he could not articulate just why he had not followed my instructions. He was clearly uncomfortable and embarrassed about it but had no explanation until we uncovered the assumption about organizational turf and its symbolic meaning.

I realized that there was very little lateral communication occurring between units of the organization, so that new ideas developed in one unit never seemed to get outside that unit. If I inquired about cross-divisional meetings, for example, I would get blank stares and questions such as "Why would we do that?" Because the divisions were facing similar problems, it would obviously have been helpful to circulate some of the better ideas that came up in my interviews, supplemented with my own ideas based on my knowledge of what went on in other organizations. But here was a good example of a process that might work in the U.S. culture but might not even be considered in another macro culture. Of course, the irony in this example is that if I had understood this cultural characteristic I would have obtained a list of managers from Dr. Leupold and sent my memo directly to all of them. They would have accepted it as coming from the outside paid consultant and might even have viewed it as evidence that they were getting something useful from the outside expert.

Putting my interviews and direct observations together permitted me to construct a cultural paradigm for Ciba-Geigy, allowing, however, for the fact that I did not have nearly as much information in this instance as I had in the DEC case. Because these assumptions were not as tightly linked as the DEC ones, I present them only as a list.

1. Scientific research is the source of truth and good ideas.

2. The mission is to make a better world through science and "important" products.

3. Truth and wisdom reside in those who have more education and experience.

4. The strength of the organization is in the expertness of each role occupant. A job is one's own turf.

5. We are one family and take care of each other, but a family is a hierarchy and children have to obey.

6. There is enough time. Quality, accuracy, and truth are more important than speed.

7. Individual and organizational autonomy are the keys to success so long as one stays closely linked to one's "parents."

Analytical Comments. Ciba-Geigy had grown and achieved much of its success through fundamental discoveries made by a number of basic researchers in the company's central research laboratories. Much of its basic culture could be attributed to the macro culture of chemistry, which is a formal hierarchic discipline in which experimentation has to be done carefully to avoid explosions, fires, and bad odors. DEC was based on electrical engineering in which "fooling around" was not only possible but often desirable.

Whereas in DEC truth was discovered through conflict and debate, in Ciba-Geigy truth had come more from the individual wisdom of the scientist or researcher. Both companies believed in the individual, but the differing assumptions about the nature of truth led to completely different attitudes toward authority and the role of conflict. In Ciba-Geigy, authority was much more respected, and conflict was to be avoided. The individual was given areas of freedom by the boss and then was totally respected in those areas. If role occupants were not sufficiently educated or skilled enough to make decisions, they were expected to train themselves. If they performed poorly in the meantime, that would be tolerated for quite a while before a decision might be made to replace them.

In DEC if an individual was failing in a job the assumptions would be made that it was a mismatch rather than a personal failure and the individual would be allowed to negotiate a new assignment. In Ciba-Geigy, individuals would be expected to be good soldiers and do the job as best they could, and as long as they were perceived as doing their best they would be kept in the job. In DEC the individual was expected to negotiate his or her areas of freedom and then take full responsibility to report if things were not working out so that the job could be renegotiated, leading to a much more fluid job structure and much more vertical and lateral communication around work issues. Both companies had a "tenure" assumption that once people were accepted, they were likely to remain unless they failed in a major way or did something illegal or clearly immoral.

Both companies talked of being families, but the meaning of the word *family* was quite different in each company. In DEC, the essential assumption was that family members could fight, but they loved each other and could not lose membership. In Ciba-Geigy, the assumption was that parental authority should be respected and that children (employees and subordinate managers) should behave according to the rules and obey their parents. If they did so, they would be well treated, taken care of, and supported by the parents. They should not fight, and they should obey the rules and never be insubordinate.

Vertical and horizontal relationships in DEC were more personal whereas in Ciba-Geigy relationships were clearly more formal. This raises the interesting question of whether those differences reflected organizational culture and history or whether they reflected the macro cultures of the United States and Swiss Germany. If language is one of the major artifacts and characteristics of a national culture, one would note that English is a much less formal language than German, reflected even in the fact that in German the pronouns "du" and "sie" are used to differentiate how personal the relationship is meant to be.

In DEC, lifetime employment was implicit, whereas in Ciba-Geigy, it was taken for granted and informally affirmed. In each case, the family model reflected the wider macro-cultural assumptions of the countries in which these companies were located.

After I understood the Ciba-Geigy paradigm, I was able to figure out how to operate more effectively as a consultant. As I interviewed more managers and gathered information that would be relevant to what they were trying to do, instead of attempting to circulate memos to the various branches of the Ciba-Geigy organization through my contact client, Dr. Leupold, I found that if I gave information directly, even if it was unsolicited, it was accepted because I was an "expert." If I wanted information to circulate, I sent it out to the relevant parties on my own initiative, or, if I thought it needed to circulate down into the organization, I gave it to the boss and attempted to convince him that the information would be relevant lower down.

If I really wanted to intervene by having managers do something different, I could accomplish this best by being an expert and formally recommending it to the CEO, Dr. Koechlin. If he liked the idea, he would then "order the troops to do it." Inasmuch as he liked the career anchor idea, he ordered that everyone do the exercise for the summer program, but he mandated that in the following year all upper- and mid-level managers were to do the career anchor and job/role analysis, order their subordinates to do it, and then discuss it with them as part of the executive career development process. More will be said about Ciba-Geigy subsequently, but for now we need to explore the nesting concept again and ask a bigger question about macro cultures.

Can Organizational Cultures Be Stronger than National Cultures?

In terms of how cultures are nested within wider cultures, the question arises for both DEC and Ciba-Geigy as to what we would find in their various subsidiaries in other countries. They will, of course, vary for both type of organization and country of location, but some observations can be made about these two companies because they each had demonstrably strong organizational cultures.

I was able to visit subsidiaries of DEC in several European and Asian countries and found that at the artifactual level the DEC offices mirrored the headquarters in Maynard. The look of the place, the administrative procedures that were visible, and the informal climate looked and felt the same. Clearly the DEC culture attempted to replicate itself in other countries, but the administrative and managerial employees were mostly local and spoke the local language, which led to some modifications of the company culture.

Such modifications were most noticeable in the product-design area, where, for example, the German customers wanted certain modifications in the product that led first to difficult negotiations with U.S. product managers and eventually to permitting local engineering staff to make the modifications for the local customers. The country managers were mostly local so that they could speak the language but were rotated periodically to headquarters assignments so that they could absorb the "essence" of the DEC culture.

The most extreme version of this kind of company indoctrination was the story of an HP plant manager whom I met in Singapore. He had been hired in Australia but before taking over the Singapore plant he was flown to California and spent two entire weeks "shadowing" CEO and founder David Packard to "absorb" the "HP Way."

The strength of Ciba-Geigy's culture was best illustrated by the previously mentioned example that one year when the U.S. subsidiary manager in New Jersey invited me to give a talk to the top layers of management on what I had learned about the headquarters culture in Basel. After I gave the talk, I got the shocked reaction, "My God, you have just described us." Ciba-Geigy had evolved a systematic rotation of future executives into overseas assignments so that an effort to become more international would be reflected in all of its managers. The best example of the impact of that process was Samuel Koechlin himself, whose time in the United States subsidiary definitely influenced the Basel culture and made both the Basel and the U.S. cultures complex hybrids.

Summary and Conclusions

In the preceding two case analyses, I have tried to illustrate how organizational culture can be analyzed at several levels: (1) visible artifacts; (2) espoused beliefs, values, and behavioral norms; and (3) taken-for-granted basic underlying assumptions. Unless you dig down to the level of the assumptions, you cannot really decipher the artifacts, values, and norms. However, if you find some of those assumptions and explore their interrelationship, you are really getting at the essence of the culture and can then explain a great deal of what goes on. This essence can sometimes be analyzed as a paradigm in that some organizations function by virtue of an interlocking, coordinated set of assumptions. Whereas each one alone might not make sense, the pattern explains the behavior and the success of the organization in overcoming its external and internal challenges.

We should not assume that even these paradigms describe the whole culture, nor should we assume that we would find the same paradigm operating in every part of the organization. How general the assumptions are throughout the organization should be investigated empirically depending on your purpose. As a researcher trying to describe a whole culture, your needs for completeness would be quite different than if you were an employee or customer dealing with a local unit. If you are a manager trying to change the culture or are considering a merger or acquisition, it is the essence, the DNA of the culture, that you would be most concerned about. I discovered these assumptions as a helper and consultant primarily through observation and exploring with inside informants some of the anomalies that I observed. It is when we do not understand something that we need to pursue vigorously why we do not, and the best way to search is to use our own ignorance and naïveté.

What are some the lessons to be learned from these cases, and what implications do they have for leadership? The most important lesson for me is the realization that culture is deep, pervasive, complex, patterned, and morally neutral. In both cases, I had to overcome my own cultural prejudices about the right and wrong way to do things, and to learn that culture simply exists. Both companies were successful in their respective technological, political, economic, and broader cultural environments for a long time, but both companies also experienced environmental changes that led to their disappearance as independent economic entities.

In both cases, the powerful influence of early leaders and historical circumstance was evident. Cultural assumptions have their roots in early group experience and in the pattern of success and failure experienced by these companies. Their current leaders strongly valued their cultures, were proud of them, and felt it important for members of their organizations to accept the assumptions. In both organizations, stories were told of misfits who left because they did not like the way the company operated, or who were not hired in the first place because they either would have been disruptive or would not have liked it there anyway.

In both companies, leaders were struggling with changing environmental demands and were facing the issue of whether and how to evolve or change their ways of operating, but this was initially defined as reaffirmation of portions of the existing culture, not as changes in the culture. Though the companies were at different stages in their evolution, they both valued their cultures as important assets and were anxious to preserve and enhance them.

Finally, it is obvious that both companies reflected the national cultures in which they operated and the technologies that underlay their businesses. DEC was a U.S. company of creative electrical engineers evolving a brand new technology; Ciba-Geigy was a Swiss-German company of mostly highly educated chemical engineers working both with very old technologies (dye stuffs) and very new bio-chemical processes (pharmaceuticals). Electrical circuits and chemical processes require very different approaches and timetables for product development, which was pointed out to me many times. An important implication is that culture cannot really be understood without looking at core technologies, the occupations of organization members, and the macro-cultural context in which the organizations exist.

The major differences resulting from size, age, and leadership behavior were evident and will be spelled out more specifically in Chapter 11.

Questions for Readers

All readers should answer the following questions:

1. What struck you as most different in the two cases?
2. What do you think are the bases of those differences?
3. How much is attributable to their technologies?
4. How much is attributable to their national locations?
5. How much is attributable to their history, size, and age?
6. How well do you think you would fit into either company?

5

A DEVELOPMENTAL GOVERNMENT
ORGANIZATION IN SINGAPORE

Can this culture model be usefully applied to a different type of organization? To test this I decided to include a shortened version of one of the chapters from my book on the culture study I had done in the early 1990s as a paid researcher in Singapore (Schein, 1996b).

Case 3: Singapore's Economic Development Board

In thirty years Singapore has gone from being a third world country with a per capita GDP of $500 to having a per capita GDP of $15,000 and being on the edge of the rich industrial world. No country has ever developed faster.

(Lester Thurow from Foreword to Schein, 1996b)

The case of Singapore illustrates the structure of cultural analysis very well, because the visible artifacts of the dictatorial repressive political regime that evolved there cannot be understood without locating the taken-for-granted basic assumptions the leaders had when they founded an independent Singapore in the early 1960s. Singapore's story begins with a vision shared by its political leader, Lee Kuan Yew, and his fellow British-educated colleagues, who were combining their shared vision with a desire to make this ex-British colony into a "global city with total business capabilities."

This shared vision can be thought of as the "espoused beliefs and values" of the culture model. What makes the case interesting is that it is one of the rare cases I have encountered in which the artifacts, the espoused values, and the underlying assumptions were well aligned with each other, so that one could easily see how the three levels were consistent with each other and could explain each other.

To implement that vision, Lee Kuan Yew and his colleagues decided in 1961 to create the Economic Development Board (EDB), a quasi-governmental agency to implement a plan to attract foreign investment. In a predominantly Chinese culture that is averse to failure, the EDB had to create an organization that would "avoid punishing those who fail in the course of testing the limits of the system, but instead to punish those who are incompetent and those who do not learn from failure. Identify failure; change what does not work; create a learning environment. Easy advice—but hard to do unless one evolves a culture that supports such attitudes . . . create a long-range vision, build a team, draw out the best in team members. Demand total loyalty to the mission and a 120 percent commitment from everyone. Provide one-stop shopping for the clients from a totally professional organization devoted to teamwork, open communications, and a borderless organization. The rules are clear, there is no corruption, and integrity is total" (Thurow, Foreword to Schein, 1996b).

The EDB was very successful and decided in 1990 to have someone document its story. The EDB leaders originally hired a journalist to write this story but decided that it was their *culture* that was the key to their success, so they looked for someone who knew about culture. They consulted Lester Thurow, who was then Dean of the MIT Sloan School where I taught. He suggested that they approach me, which led to my agreeing to investigate their success story from three perspectives: (1) their view of themselves, (2) the view of the various CEOs who had decided to invest in Singapore by building plants and research organizations there, and (3) my analysis of the artifacts, espoused values, and basic assumptions that could be inferred from all of these data.

The EDB's view of itself was obtained through intensive interviews of all the leaders who had created and supported the EDB through the past three decades during several two-week visits to Singapore in 1994 and 1995. I then located and interviewed as many CEOs or other senior executives who had made the decision to invest in Singapore to determine why they had done so and how it had worked out. My analysis was supplemented by direct observation of how the EDB worked along with my attendance at various group meetings that had been set up to provide me with more information. The leaders of the EDB were clearly very proud of their accomplishments and wanted the study to document the positive elements of what they had done, but they also made it very clear that they wanted to learn from my analysis what their weak spots and future learning challenges might be. In other words, I was to be critical as well as positive.

The entire complex story of thirty years of development is told in my book *Strategic Pragmatism: The Culture of Singapore's Economic Development Board* (1996b) and is abstracted in this chapter.

The EDB Nested Cultural Paradigms

The structural model of artifacts, espoused values, and basic underlying assumptions proved to be necessary to make sense of all the interviews and observational information that I had gathered over the period of a year or so. The concept of cultures nested within other cultures was immediately evident in that the way the EDB setup reflected both the Chinese origins of the leaders and the impact of their British education and colonial experience. Furthermore, Singapore was originally embedded in the Malaysian Federation, which created cross-cultural tensions at the national level. Then, after Singapore broke away and became independent in 1965, that led to a period of economic *interdependence* because Singapore had no water supply of its own.

The basic assumptions that could be inferred and tested with the "insiders" thus fell into a "contextual" set that reflected the nesting and an "organizational" set that reflected the way in which the EDB as a separate organization managed its external and internal relationships. The contextual paradigm consisted primarily of a set of assumptions that Singapore's leaders held about economic development. These assumptions were shared by the EDB, but they also provided a broader context within which the EDB operated. The organizational paradigm consisted of a set of assumptions about how the EDB structured and managed itself.

1. The Contextual Paradigm: Assumptions about the Role of Government in Economic Development

The contextual paradigm consists of six interlocking and interrelated shared basic assumptions that reflect the mental models of the early leaders of Singapore and are largely taken for granted today. These assumptions are shared by Singapore's government in general and thus provide a cultural context within which the EDB operates. At the same time they are assumptions held by leaders and members of the EDB itself and thus influence more directly how the EDB operates. These assumptions led to the creation of the EDB and provided the espoused values that influenced how the EDB would define its mission and organize itself. We have here a case where the espoused beliefs and values are congruent with the observed artifacts—the work of the EDB.

1a. "State Capitalism." *Singapore's leaders and the EDB assumed and took for granted that government could and should play an active entrepreneurial role in economic development and should therefore exercise leadership through a quasi-governmental statutory board such as the EDB.*

1b. Absolute Long-Range Political Stability. A closely connected second core assumption that came to dominate Singaporean thinking and action is really a cluster of three interconnected assumptions that can be stated as follows. *Singapore's political leaders assumed (1) that economic development must precede political development, (2) that long-range successful economic development could occur only if there was political stability, and (3) that political stability could be achieved and maintained only by firm but benign government controls that steer all segments of the society.*

This was, of course, the most critical assumption to understand because it was the basis of the observed dictatorial regime that was set up around political and civil behavior. For example, severe punishment for littering or urinating in an elevator was justified on the grounds that Western businessmen would feel more confident working in a squeaky clean city. The rules and the heavy punishment were visible artifacts, but few observers really understood that there was a deep economic development assumption behind the rules and their implementation. The basic assumption that economic development justifies social control was never challenged as long as Singapore was succeeding in its development efforts.

1c. Collaboration among Sectors. *Singapore's political leaders assumed that economic development could succeed only if business, labor, and government actively collaborated with each other in fulfilling the common goal of building the nation ("Singapore, Inc.").*

Interorganizational collaboration was considered vital to provide the incentives and infrastructure needed to develop the manufacturing and service sectors—that is, roads, communication facilities, land, financial support for investment and training, a well-trained and motivated labor pool, housing, and so forth. One of the most notable aspects of this way of thinking was the decision to give the trade unions some responsibilities as owners and managers by having them own and operate one of the taxi companies and one of the insurance companies in Singapore. Some industrial-relations analysts might regard this as co-optation and undermining of the labor movement, but from Singapore's rulers' point of view, getting labor on their side was paramount, especially in view of the proximity of a communist China to the north.

1d. An Incorruptible, Competent Civil Service. *Singapore's political leaders assumed that favorable economic conditions for investors would be guaranteed only if the government and civil service were competent and incorruptible and operated with an open and consistent set of rules that were vigorously enforced.*

Here again we see nesting in that this assumption reflects the Chinese cultural legacy that rulers must be exemplars of virtue, the British traditions of a "clean civil service," and the early recognition on the part of Singapore's leaders that overseas investors would be attracted only to a developing nation in which there was not only political stability but also a competent government, a clear set of rules, and an absence of corruption.

1e. Primacy of People and Meritocracy. *Singapore's leaders assumed that the only resource they had were its people and their potential; it must, therefore, pick the best of them and develop them.*

Out of these assumptions grew the political decision to provide everyone with jobs and housing, to mandate English as the official language, and to create a lucrative government-sponsored scholarship program that would send the best students overseas to the best universities in exchange for a number of years of government service at salaries that were competitive with those offered by private industry.

1f. Strategic Pragmatism. Taken together these five assumptions describe what might best be labeled "strategic pragmatism" in that there was a clear long-range strategy reflecting Chinese cultural biases, but the implementation was thought through on a pragmatic daily basis and expressed in very detailed rules of how life was to be lived. This attention to pragmatic detail seemed more Western and was, in any case, aimed to attract Western business.

Singapore's leaders assumed that the survival of the city-state required a very long-range plan but that the implementation of that plan had to begin immediately on a very practical level with the creation of the EDB.

These long-range aspects included the decision to stabilize Singapore by attracting businesses that would make major capital investments and, therefore, would be committed to remaining. The leaders were very aware of how vulnerable city-states are that depend only on their port and shipping.

2. The Cultural Paradigm of the EDB as an Organization

The culture of the EDB as a separate organization nested within the contextual paradigm is a set of paradoxes and anomalies from a Western point of view, but its basic assumptions are consistent with each other and enabled the organization to function effectively. This paradigm is best described in terms of six basic assumptions that came to dominate daily activities and the way the EDB organized itself.

2a. Teamwork: Individualistic Groupism. The EDB assumed that the best kind of leadership is to build a team and that the ultimate responsibility of team members is to contribute to the maximum of their ability.

The EDB employees seemed equally comfortable working competitively with each other in producing results while being completely dedicated to the team, the EDB, and the nation-state. One sees here a cultural legacy from Confucian principles of concern for family combined with a Western concept of individual achievement. Underlying this assumption was the reality that the EDB always had to function as a team because it was a small organization in which members therefore had to help each other. However, this pragmatic reason for teamwork was also supported by a cultural tendency to be comfortable in a team setting, a kind of comfort that is noticeably absent in many Western teams. At the same time, all of the officers were educated in settings where individual achievement was highly valued, and they were constantly exposed to multinational company managers who lived by individualistic competitive rules and were encouraged to develop their individual careers within the EDB.

The organization attracted very strong individualists who did, in fact, compete with each other and noticed it when someone was promoted ahead of them. The competition was mitigated by the fact that they were all kept so busy that they had very little time to worry about each other's accomplishments. If you were too individualistic or political, you very quickly lost credibility with your colleagues and found yourself unable to do very much. So the two major distortions that could occur in the communications system—sitting on information or, at the other extreme, hyping up information and exaggerating what you know—were both mitigated by the need to maintain credibility and trustworthiness. To get anything done you had to build support, and to build support you had to maintain your credibility. Everything in the EDB had to be highly coordinated.

To be a successful performer in this kind of high-pressure family-team required a complex ability to collaborate with others and be a true team player while, at the same time, exposing individual talents and skills for purposes of promotion and career progress. This kind of balancing act was facilitated by the ability to think clearly, articulate clearly, write clearly, and be able to convince others to "join one's team" in support of a project. In other words, individual talent showed up most in the individual's quality of thinking and communicating, which was then tested in one's ability to create and work in a team. Individual achievement was recognized with awards and other forms of recognition.

The EDB's view of itself as a team and practically a family was partly based on everyone knowing everyone else. This level of acquaintance was maintained through many informal activities such as the weekly Friday afternoon teas; company functions such as picnics and sports outings that families were encouraged to attend; the monthly newsletter entitled "Network," in which a variety of personal news items, especially awards and individual accomplishments were given publicity; and the encouragement of romantic attachments among employees symbolized by the great pride in the number of married couples who h███████████ther as EDB employees and remained in their jobs.

Also supportive of this team spirit was a set of very flexible personnel policies that allowed part-time assignments or jobs in which one would not be required to travel if family responsibilities made travel difficult. The work of the EDB was so intrinsically motivating that there was never any question of loss of work motivation. Rather, the EDB tried to accommodate the needs of each employee because each was viewed as being valuable.

2b. Cosmopolitan Technocracy. If Singapore's fate rested on its ability to attract overseas investors, the EDB had to be able to deal with many other cultures and their officers had to be what sociologists have called "cosmopolitan" in their orientation. At the same time, to bring in the right investors and provide good services for them once they were in Singapore, the EDB had to staff itself with a cadre of people who would be both competent marketers or salesmen and entrepreneurs.

The EDB leaders and managers, therefore, had to be comfortable and knowledgeable in the global multicultural arena and at the same time very much in touch with the situation in Singapore and the potential of synergy between the multinationals and local industry. Their cartoon version of themselves depicted them as supermen and superwomen. To make all of this work required a particular personnel philosophy that could best be stated in terms of the following basic assumptions, many of which were explicitly espoused. *The EDB assumed that it could only succeed if it recruited*

1. *The "best and the brightest" based on scholastic performance.*

2. *Officers with a "cosmopolitan orientation" based on overseas education and interest in working with and in overseas business settings.*

3. *Officers who were technically oriented and trained because the kind of businesses that were to be promoted were usually technically based.*

4. *Officers who had high levels of personal initiative that enabled them to work in unpredictable and uncharted business and government arenas.*

5. *Officers and managers who were team oriented and had high levels of interpersonal skill_____ multiple cultures, with multiple hierarchical levels, and _____ boundaries of all kinds.*

Many of the qualities that were sought in the "officers" were already present in the leaders who created the EDB because they had grown up in a multicultural environment themselves—British, Malay, Tamil, and Chinese. Many of them had technical backgrounds and biased the education toward engineering and science from the outset, once again reminding us that the culture of the EDB was nested not only in the Singaporean culture but in the many other cultures that the early leaders brought into the picture.

2c. *Boundaryless Organization: Modulated Openness.* The EDB emphasized timely, accurate, and widely dispersed information as essential to decision making, often describing itself as a "boundaryless" organization. Two basic assumptions operated behind this principle, one referring to internal operations and one linking back to the contextual assumption about sector collaboration.

The EDB assumed that the only way it could fulfill its function effectively was for all managers, officers, and other relevant employees of the organization to be fully informed about all projects at all times. The EDB assumed that the only way it could fulfill its function was to develop and maintain open channels to the other sectors of the government as well as to private and labor sectors.

For the EDB to make quick and valid decisions about investments and investors, it believed that it was necessary for all relevant information for any given project to be available to all members of the organizations who might have an input to the decision, and certainly to the higher-level decision makers. This assumption resulted in the extensive global communication system that the EDB set up; its willingness to spend money on communications, travel, and meetings; and a standardized reporting system that allowed information to be efficiently centralized. Everything had to be written down, training was provided to employees in written communication, and, perhaps most important of all, the norm was articulated that "one must pass on all relevant information truthfully and not use information as a personal source of control or power."

The "modulated openness" referred to the potential problems of simultaneously working with many investor clients, many of whom were competing with each other. For example, Hewlett-Packard and Digital Equipment Corp. were both considering setting up manufacturing plants in Singapore.

If highly confidential plans were revealed, it was not always clear even within the EDB whose interests could be hurt by too much exposure of such plans. EDB officers therefore had to be very situationally careful while espousing maximum openness.

2d. Non-Hierarchic Hierarchy: The Boss as Patron, Coach, and Colleague.

The EDB culture implicitly assumed that managers could succeed only if they had a strong sense of autonomy in performing their task, a willingness to initiate decisions through formal proposals up the hierarchy, a willingness to be open and frank in revealing information up the hierarchy, a willingness to go around the hierarchy when tasks required it, and the ability to work with higher levels of management in the client organizations.

At the same time they assumed that managers had to show suitable deference to superiors when appropriate (particularly in public), to seek and accept guidance from above in revising proposals and in making decisions, to show good judgment in keeping their superiors fully informed when going around the hierarchy, and to show appropriate humility when being coached and guided by superiors and when dealing with higher-ranking managers in client companies.

The best way to characterize this set of relationships is to note that EDBers were expected to perform as one would in a boundaryless Western organization in which hierarchy is downplayed while performing as one would in an Asian (Chinese) organization in which deference and hierarchy are dominant. What the young senior officer had to learn in entering this organization was how to do that—how to develop the judgment and interpersonal skills to perform according to both sets of norms.

Interpersonal skills were especially relevant because, on the one hand, boundaries were nonexistent in the sense that one could always walk into a senior executive's office and talk very frankly to him. On the other hand, EDB officers knew that department heads might feel at a disadvantage when their subordinates went around them. Consequently, one of the important interpersonal skills was knowing how to keep the department heads feeling sufficiently secure so that they would not feel threatened if either a subordinate or a superior went around them. The implication is that one of the most important aspects of being socialized into the EDB was to learn the rules and develop the skills of being open and nonhierarchical without threatening the hierarchy.

2e. Extended Trust Relationships: Clients as Partners and Friends.

One of the important distinguishing features of the EDB was its conception that the overseas investor was to become a friend and partner and that the relationship was to be a long-term one that would be of mutual benefit to the company and to Singapore. Implicit in this concept was not only the long-range strategic goal but an extension of the Chinese philosophy of *guanxi*, or building trusted connections that can be used in the future. Whereas in the old Chinese system such connections were limited by personal acquaintance and patterns of mutual obligation that extended out from the family and clan, the EDB concept was a much more Western notion of forging strategic alliances and partnerships with investing companies to create the kind of industrial system that the strategy envisioned.

The EDB had set aside considerable investment funds to make such partnerships real by allowing itself to be an equity partner as well; the purpose was not to invest to make more money, but to ensure that the enterprise would succeed. Once a business was a going concern, the EDB always intended to sell off its share to make the money available for the next project. This general philosophy rested on two basic assumptions.

The EDB assumed that it could succeed only if it fully understood the needs of its clients (potential and present investors) and collaborated with them in solving their problems efficiently but without compromising its own basic goals, plans, or rules (strategic pragmatism). The EDB assumed that Singapore's long-range mission could be fulfilled only if initial investors continued to invest and became committed to transferring technology and training to Singapore's labor force. Such continued investment could be achieved only if the EDB became friends and partners with its initial investors.

It was never enough just to bring the investors in. Once they were in, they inevitably developed new needs and problems, and it was the EDB officer whom they would call when they needed help. Such help often laid the groundwork for further investment and an expanded relationship with Singapore. In that regard, possibly one of the most important dimensions of the EDB and Singapore culture was the attitude toward time. On the one hand, there was a lot of emphasis on long-range planning and figuring out how to create a set of incentives and activities that would encourage the investor, who was thinking about the long haul. On the other hand, there was tremendous pride in being a good host and doing whatever it took to help a foreign investor succeed in the short run. EDBers thought of themselves as instant problem solvers.

At the artifactual level, the long-range point of view was evident in the willingness to spend large amounts of money on training and education. The educational establishment was charged with offering the kinds of curricula that would fit the long-range needs of the country. Evidence for the short-run pragmatism comes from the frequent changes in social policy that the government was willing to undertake when a given policy did not accomplish what was intended. Singapore as a state and the EDB as an organization both displayed the ability to change course rapidly if their analysis indicated a need.

Singapore was neither a long-range planner like Japan nor a short-range pragmatist like Hong Kong or many Western countries that are driven by a monthly or quarterly business model. It is both, and it manages somehow to combine the two by having clear long-range goals and visions that are widely circulated throughout the nation-state and, at the same time, a sense that those goals and visions cannot be achieved if the daily problems of helping the industrial establishment are not solved immediately. The key to this combination is the building of relationships with investors so that their long-range interests will coincide with Singapore's. The day-to-day solving of problems ensures the solidity of the long-range partnership and friendship.

2f. Commitment to Learning and Innovation. Just as "strategic pragmatism" served as a kind of integrative assumption around the contextual paradigm, the commitment to learning and innovation serves to tie together the assumptions of the organizational paradigm. In a sense, commitment to innovation is also paradoxical because so much cultural analysis of Asian societies emphasizes a fatalistic view, acceptance of harmony with nature, and commitment to stability and harmony within the social structure. Clearly Singapore has blended whatever Asian legacy it has with a more Western proactive stance that anything is possible, symbolized in Singapore by the often-heard phrase "dare to dream." In assumption form this can be stated as follows:

The EDB (and the government of Singapore) assumed that the only way it could fulfill its vision of development was to learn from others and its own experience, and to continuously innovate in dealing with whatever problems were discovered to stand in the way of achieving the vision.

This attitude goes back to the early leaders' willingness to learn from other countries and from various non-Singaporean advisers; it was most clearly demonstrated in the continuous changing and refining of social policy. It is true that the policies are viewed by many as excessively controlling and a real restriction on the freedom of the individual, but in that perception one may miss the equally important point that the policies are constantly changing in response to new data. One of the important roles of the EDB is to stay in touch with what is going on in the rest of the world, which they did through a vast network of offices in all the major industrial centers. The knowledge acquired in this network became a major source of feedback to the government and provided the data needed to adjust government policy.

Various corporate seminars on marketing and strategic planning put on by the EDB became visible manifestations of the desire to stay open and learn. The EDB openly embraced the concept of the "learning organization," using Peter Senge's *The Fifth Discipline* and concepts of systems thinking (Senge, 1990).

Summary and Conclusions: The Multiple Implications of the Three Cases

The reader may well wonder why bother with such detailed cases. Should we not be looking for broad generalizations about organizational and national culture? There are several reasons for studying detailed cases.

First, the devil is in the details. Humans are complex at the personality level; groups, organizations, and nations are complex at the cultural level. We will later review some typologies that are intended to provide simpler models into which to sort cultures. For example, one popular model is to think of organizations as "markets," "hierarchies," or "clans" (Ouchi, 1981; Williamson, 1975). By that classification DEC, Ciba-Geigy, and Singapore's EDB would all have to be called clans, and we can see immediately that this would lose some of the important ways in which the clannish family feeling in each organization played out differently. The three organizations were at different stages of development, which strongly influenced the way the cultures evolved, and they were nested in entirely different national cultures.

Second, cultural details have to be understood to determine how these organizations evolved. The DNA of DEC's culture survived while the organization as an economic entity failed. Ciba-Geigy changed some of its externally focused DNA in abandoning some chemical businesses while enhancing the pharmaceutical business, but held on strongly to its way of dealing with people in making the changes; the EDB continued to be successful in helping Singapore to grow as a viable economic and politically stable city-state, thus reinforcing the complex mix of Asian and Western values that its cultural paradigm illustrates.

Third, how things work inside a culture and how employees and managers might feel on a daily basis can be inferred only by understanding the interrelationship of the cultural components, what I have labeled the cultural "paradigm" in each organization. As each case illustrates, to understand the paradigm one must identify both how the cultural components interact with each other and how they interact with the components of the cultures in which they are nested. DEC's sense of indifference to cost reduction was very much related to its individualistic values of not being willing to fire "good people." Ciba-Geigy's carefully orchestrated downsizing reflected to a considerable degree the Swiss-German and Basel community values. The EDB learned how to combine the traditional Chinese values with Western values to create its successes.

Fourth, when we examine the dynamics of *managed* culture evolution and change, we will see that the strategy and tactics of intervening successfully require a more detailed knowledge of the cultural elements and how they interact. We will not need analyses at the level of complexity of these cases, but we will need a process for quickly identifying which cultural elements will help us manage the desired changes and which ones will hinder us and become targets of change.

We have now reviewed the defining structure of culture and illustrated it with several detailed case studies. The cultural *dynamics* were covered to some degree in the cases, and the way organizational cultures are nested in macro cultures was illustrated. We now need to understand more about how to think about and assess those macro cultures.

Questions for Readers

Ask yourself the following questions:

1. In what way is this "government" agency different from a business?
2. How do the national cultures affect how the EDB functions?
3. What is the impact on the culture of what the organization's task is?

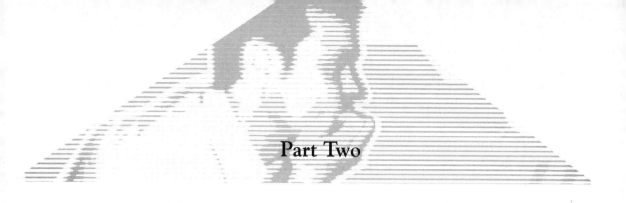

Part Two

WHAT LEADERS NEED TO KNOW ABOUT MACRO CULTURES

Macro cultures are nations, ethnic groups, and occupations that have been around for a long time and have, therefore, acquired some very stable elements, or "skeletons," in the form of basic languages, concepts, and values. At the same time they have evolved and will continue to evolve, primarily from contact with other cultures. To compare macro cultures we need general dimensions that cut across them and that have remained relatively stable in spite of historical experience. The problems of making multicultural groups work well is that those stable elements can clash in unanticipated ways and can cause both desired and undesired changes. To provide some historical context, let's begin with a couple of interesting stories from anthropology.

The murder of Captain Cook in Hawaii. The interaction of macro cultures can best be understood in historical examples such as those cited by Sahlins (1985) in his analysis of the interaction of the British with the Hawaiians and the Maori of New Zealand. The Hawaiian "mystery" was why Captain Cook was brutally murdered when he returned to Hawaii after a very successful first visit in 1778. When Captain Cook first landed in the Hawaiian islands he was viewed as the god that their mythology had predicted and was, therefore, highly revered. The Hawaiian women believed that sleeping with the sailors was culturally appropriate because the sailors were godly as well. Cook at first forbade this because it did not fit the British concept of appropriate naval behavior, but the women were so seductive that he relented, leading to a great deal of sexual behavior with the natives during his stay.

From the sailors' point of view this was great, but they felt that the women deserved something in return even though it seemed that sleeping with the godly sailors was enough for them. The sailors initially offered trinkets and beads, but as the women and their men found various metal objects on board they began to ask for those because they were very scarce in Hawaii. When they and their men brought back metal objects they gained status in their home community, so they asked for more and more, which eventually led the sailors to even pull up some of the metal nails on the ships. As the Hawaiian men and women gained status through this process, they also became more of a threat to the chiefs, who found many of their taboos violated by the women who were eating on board the ship together with men, something that was strictly forbidden in the local culture.

When Cook had finally been fully supplied and left he discovered after a week or so that the ships were not seaworthy because a number of metal nautical instruments had been stolen. He returned with the intention of confronting the chiefs and recovering his equipment. What he did not know was that the Hawaiian legend also said that a god who returns is a false god. As Sahlins summarizes it: "To the Hawaiian priests, Cook was always the ancient god Lono, even when he unexpectedly came back, whereas to the king, the god who appears out of season becomes a dangerous rival" (Sahlins, 1985, p. xvii). Cook's return so threatened and infuriated the Hawaiian chiefs that they fell upon him and murdered him as he was on his way to discuss with them the recovery of his equipment. This became a ritual sacrifice with thousands of stab wounds inflicted on him by the chiefs and the people. In the meantime the Hawaiian culture had been changed because of the increasing status of women who had been instrumental in the acquisition of metal in the Hawaiian society!

Cutting down flagpoles in New Zealand. The "mystery" in the New Zealand colonization was why the Maori kept chopping down British flagpoles even though they seemed to accept that they had been militarily and politically subjugated. On one occasion the Maori raided a British community and chopped down the flagpole at headquarters. This was interpreted as a sign of a bigger uprising, but nothing else like that occurred, suggesting that it was just a diversion to cut down the flag. This see-saw conflict lasted for many years and through many governors until one of them finally figured out what was going on.

The British interpreted the cutting down of flagpoles as an insult to their flag, an insult they would not tolerate, so they just put up another flagpole, which, in due course was cut down. What they had not understood was that in Maori culture, poles turned toward the sky had enormous symbolic importance in terms of legends of how the people were founded and the role of the poles in holding up the sky. The Maori did not care about the flag, and they accepted the British colonial rule, but they could not stand having the poles on British headquarters land. Once a new governor figured this out, it was easy to find an accommodation that preserved the British pride and their flag, while honoring the Maori need to be in charge of poles!

When organizational cultures from different nations meet we often see similar unexpected results that provide puzzles until we understand cultural variation around the basic categories that are provided in Chapter 6. Chapter 7 then proposes some ways in which a leader can set up the conditions for a multicultural group to explore the dimensions that may be critical to its own functioning.

6

DIMENSIONS OF THE MACRO-CULTURAL CONTEXT

Culture assessment can be either a vast bottomless pit or a focused exercise around specific issues based on the problem we are trying to solve. We sometimes need to assess the macro cultures of nations and occupations and to identify cultural DNA because we have specific problems to solve or changes to make. For this purpose we need selected dimensions that cut across macro cultures. This chapter will review the ways macro cultures can be assessed and show some of the dimensions that are useful in comparing macro cultures.

Travel and Literature

The three-level model for cultural analysis (see Chapter 2) can be helpful in looking at macro cultures like nations and occupations when we reflect on what we observe in our own national or ethnic culture and what we experience in other countries when we travel. The artifactual level is what we encounter when we travel as a tourist or, in the case of an occupation like medicine, what we experience when we visit our doctor or go to a hospital. The espoused-values level is found in the published ideology of nations or in the official mission statements of occupations. The basic assumptions, as with organizations, have to be inferred from talking to people, intensive personal observation over some period of time, or systematic observation and interviewing of "informants" as in ethnography.

If we want to learn about another culture without traveling to it, we read literary accounts of what others have observed and inferred or ethnographies, which provide a deeper analysis of the culture. This provides a partial analysis that can be supplemented by other sources such as the culture sections of guidebooks, films, novels, and other artistic media. Wikipedia carries a vast amount of cultural information, but it is not clear how much of all of this relates to the kinds of organizational issues we need to know about. If organizations are nested in macro cultures, what are the dimensions of those cultures that might be most relevant to understanding the beliefs, values, and norms of the organization? For that purpose we need the more focused work of ethnographers and researchers who have systematically surveyed national cultures.

Survey Research

Hofstede's IBM Study

Researchers have helped in providing us some dimensions into which nations can be categorized at their basic-assumption level. One of the earliest and most complete studies along these lines was Hofstede's analysis of questionnaire responses of a comparable group of IBM employees across all the nations in which IBM had offices (Hofstede, 2001; Hofstede et al., 2010). This work and subsequent follow-up studies have resulted in statistically derived dimensions in which nations can be compared. I think of these as basic-assumption dimensions because they reflect beliefs, values, and ways of thinking that are largely taken for granted and out of the conscious awareness of the members of those nations. All of the Hofstede dimensions are shown in Exhibit 6.1 but two of them are especially relevant to organizational culture analysis.

Individualism versus Collectivism. Based on Hofstede's original data and various kinds of follow-ups, the countries studied can be compared with each other, and clusters of countries that are similar in their overall profile can be identified. For example, Hofstede's comparative studies show countries such as the United States, Canada, Australia,

---

Exhibit 6.1   Hofstede's Basic Dimensions of Culture

Individualism—Collectivism: The degree to which the society is built around individual rights and duties versus the group being the basic unit of society to which individuals should subordinate themselves

Power Distance: The social and psychological status and authority distance between the highest and lowest powered people in the society

Masculinity—Femininity Distance: The degree to which gender roles are differentiated and linked to work versus home and family

Tolerance for Ambiguity and Uncertainty: The degree to which members of the society feel comfortable in uncertain and ambiguous circumstances; the need for clear structures, processes, and rules

Short-Run vs. Long-Run Time Orientation: The degree to which members of society plan for and fantasize about the distant future versus being concerned only about the near future

---

and the United Kingdom as more individualistic, whereas Pakistan, Indonesia, Colombia, Venezuela, Ecuador, and Japan come out as more collectivist.

In practice, every society and organization must honor both the group and the individual in the sense that neither makes sense without the other. Where cultures differ dramatically, however, is in the degree to which the espoused behavioral norms and values do or do not reflect the deeper assumption. On the surface, both the United States and Australia appear to be individualistic cultures, yet in Australia (and New Zealand), you hear many references to the "tall poppy syndrome"—that is, the tall poppy is the one that gets cut down. For example, an American teenager whose parents had relocated in Australia reported that after a brilliant ride on his surfboard, he had to say to his buddies, "Gee, that was a *lucky* one." A person does not take personal credit in an individualistic culture that has strong espoused collectivist values. In contrast, though the United States espouses teamwork, it is evident in sports that it is the superstar who is admired and that building teams is seen as pragmatically necessary, not intrinsically desirable.

Individualistic societies define roles in terms of personal accomplishment, license aggression through personal competition, put a high premium on ambition, and define intimacy and love in very personal terms. More collectivist societies define identity and role more in terms of group membership, license aggression primarily toward other groups, put less value on personal ambition, and funnel love primarily within the group.

Power Distance. All groups and cultures have the issue of how to manage aggression, so it is not surprising that broad surveys of cultures such as Hofstede's identified the dimension of "power distance"—countries vary in the degree to which people in a hierarchical situation perceive a greater or lesser ability to control each other's behavior. People in high power-distance countries, such as the Philippines, Mexico, and Venezuela, perceive more inequality between superiors and subordinates than do people in low power-distance countries, such as Denmark, Israel, and New Zealand. If we look at the same index by occupation, we find higher power distance among unskilled and semiskilled workers than among professional and managerial workers, as expected.

I will not comment on the other three dimensions because they are culturally so complex that one would have to study them one country at a time. The gender issue is also connected in a very complicated way with religion and ethnicity; in the United States, this results in a complex mix of norms and assumptions about the role of men and women. Tolerance for ambiguity and time orientation are discussed subsequently.

The Globe Study

A similar massive study was done by House and a team of researchers using survey data from 17,500 middle managers in several industries across 25 countries (House et al., 2004). They derived nine dimensions, as shown in Exhibit 6.2. The reader will note that many of the dimensions which House found are very similar to the Hofstede dimensions but the Globe study added several that are especially important for organizational analysis, especially Performance Orientation, Assertiveness, and Humane Orientation.

Exhibit 6.2   Globe Study Basic Dimensions of Culture

Power Distance: The degree to which members of a collective expect power to be distributed equally

Uncertainty Avoidance: The extent to which a society, organization, or group relies on social norms, rules, and procedures to alleviate unpredictability of future events

Gender Egalitarianism: The degree to which a collective minimizes gender inequality

Future Orientation: The extent to which individuals engage in future-oriented behaviors such as delaying gratification, planning, and investing in the future

Collectivism I (Institutional): The degree to which organizational and societal institutional practices encourage and reward collective distribution of resources and collective action

Collectivism II (In-Group): The degree to which individuals express pride, loyalty, and cohesiveness in their organizations or families

Performance Orientation: The degree to which a collective encourages and rewards group members for performance improvement and excellence

Assertiveness: The degree to which individuals are assertive, confrontational, and aggressive in their relationships with others

Humane Orientation: The degree to which a collective encourages and rewards individuals for being fair, altruistic, generous, caring, and kind to others

---

Can Surveys Identify Macro Culture Dimensions? From a research methodology point of view, the problem with surveys is that they reflect what the researcher put into the questions in the first place and thus are limited by the researcher's model of what should be asked for. It is also not clear whether reliance on individual responses to a survey can reveal collective beliefs, values, and norms, because individuals may be unaware of commonalities that an observer would pick up immediately or be able to elicit quickly in a group interview.

It is also not clear whether dimensions that are statistically derived by factor analysis can be viewed as fundamental constructs around which to build culture theory. The dimensions are statistically valid and permit useful comparison between countries, but they are incomplete and lack the depth that comes out of the combination of participant observation, ethnography, and group interviews in which *shared* beliefs, values, and norms become immediately visible. In the rest of this chapter, I review some important dimensions that come out of ethnographic research such as was done by Edward Hall (1959, 1966, 1977).

Ethnographic, Observational, and Interview-Based Research

Language and Context

The most obvious cultural dimension is, of course, the language that is spoken. The way we originally learn the culture of our own country is through the categories of what to look at, think about, and differentiate in our physical and human environment. We don't learn what something is by looking it up in the dictionary but by having our parents pointing it out and naming it at the same time. Language defines not only the categories of what we see, hear, and feel but how we think about things and define meaning, as is well illustrated by the cartoon in Figure 6.1.

To make matters worse, languages themselves differ in terms of what Hall described as "high context"—how hard a given word or phrase is

Figure 6.1

"Little Jack Horner sat in a corner, eating . . . What's a corner?"

Note: Reprinted with the permission of J. Whiting

to interpret because its meaning depends on context—or "low context" the words themselves are more precise and carry their meaning clearly. For example, one of my friends who worked in the Swiss subsidiary of the British parent bank NatWest asked me to help him figure out what the British bosses (high context) wanted from the Swiss subsidiary (low context) because they could never get a "clear" set of instructions. When I asked the Brits they assured me that they had been very clear and precise in what they had asked for! Ultimately I could not help much because I did not clearly understand what the Brits wanted either!

The Nature of Reality and Truth

A fundamental part of every culture is a set of assumptions about what is real and how to determine or discover what is real. Such assumptions tell members of a group how to determine what is relevant information, how to interpret information, and how to determine when they have enough of it to decide whether or not to act and what action to take. One useful distinction is whether we rely on "physical reality" or "social reality."

Physical reality refers to those things that can be determined empirically by objective or, in our Western tradition, "scientific" tests. For example, if two people are arguing about whether or not a piece of glass will break, they can hit it with a hammer and find out (Festinger, 1957). If two managers are arguing over which product to introduce, they can agree to define a test market and establish criteria by which to resolve the issue. However, if two managers are arguing over which of two political campaigns to support, both would have to agree that there are no physical criteria by which to resolve their conflict. They would have to then rely on whatever consensus they could achieve through more conversation or social tests that they might devise. High degrees of consensus then constitute "social reality," as sociologists have pointed out, if something is defined as *real, it is real in its consequences*.

Social reality comes into play when we deal with assumptions about the nature of human nature—the correct way for humans to relate to nature and to each other, the distribution of power and the entire political process, assumptions about the meaning of life, ideology, religion, group boundaries, and culture itself. These are obviously matters of consensus and are not empirically determinable. How a group defines itself and the values it chooses to live by obviously cannot be tested in terms of our traditional notions of empirical scientific testing, but they certainly can be strongly held and shared unanimously. If people believe in something and define it as real, it becomes real for that group. The dimensions identified in the surveys deal primarily with social reality. There is no way to physically test whether it is better to be more or less tolerant of ambiguity or more or less individualistic, or who is right about a territorial conflict or a belief system, as illustrated in the bad joke about the naïve diplomat who tells the Arabs and the Israelis to settle their differences in a good Christian manner.

Moralism versus Pragmatism.   A useful dimension for comparing national cultures is their approach to reality testing in terms of the moralism versus pragmatism dimension (England, 1975). In his study of managerial values, England found that managers in different countries tended to be either pragmatic, seeking validation in their own experience, or moralistic, seeking validation in a general philosophy, moral system, or tradition. For example, he found that Europeans were typically more moralistic, whereas Americans were more pragmatic. If we apply this dimension to the basic underlying assumptions that a group makes, we can specify different bases for defining what is true, as shown in Exhibit 6.3.

What Is "Information"?   How a group tests for reality and makes decisions also involves consensus on what constitutes data, what is information, and what is knowledge? As information technology has grown, the issue has become sharpened because of debates about the role of computers in providing "information," as captured well in the quip "garbage in, garbage out." We now have "big data" as a presumed source of truth, yet gatherers of such data find themselves having to hire analysts with PhDs who have been trained in the logic of science and, therefore, can teach the gatherers how to get from raw data to some approximation of truth on which decisions can be based. The question of how valid statistically derived relationships and concepts are remains very ambiguous because even the statistically announced degrees of "significance" is itself a social norm established by statisticians. Much of our presumed "knowledge" is

---

Exhibit 6.3   Possible Criteria for Determining Truth

Pure dogma, based on tradition or religion: It has always been done this way; it is God's will; it is written in the scriptures.

Revealed dogma, wisdom based on trust in the authority of wise men, formal leaders, prophets, or kings: Our leader wants to do it this way; our consultants have recommended that we do it this way; she has had the most experience, so we should do what she says.

Truth derived by a "rational-legal" process: As when we establish guilt or innocence via a legal process, we have agreed from the outset that there is no absolute truth, only socially determined truth; we have to take this decision to the marketing committee and do what they decide; the boss will have to decide this one, it is his area of responsibility; we will have to vote on it and go by majority rule; we agreed that this decision belongs to the production department head; we need consensus on this decision, we need unanimity.

Truth as that which survives conflict and debate: We thrashed it out in three different committees, tested it on the sales force, and the idea is still sound, so we will do it; let's discuss it and see where we come out; does anyone see any problems with doing it this way; if not, that's what we'll do.

Truth as that which works, the purely pragmatic criterion: Let's try it out this way and evaluate how we are doing.

Truth as established by the dogma of scientific method: Our research shows that this is the right way to do it; we've done three surveys, and they all show the same thing, so let's act on them."

For example, the U.S. culture and the occupational culture of electrical engineering are extremely pragmatic. Truth is discovered by trial and error, negotiation, conflict, and debate. Tradition and moral authority can be dismissed easily. Physical reality and scientific evidence are touted as the right basis for decision making. In some Asian societies the social or aesthetic traditions of how things are done may override pragmatism, as, for example, accepting nepotism as a good practice because family members can be trusted, while in the U.S. nepotism is rejected on the pragmatic ground that it leads to favoritism in decision making.

---

based on statistically significant correlations without sufficient replication or concern about whether a correlation between two things can be interpreted to mean that one causes the other.

Basic Time Orientation

Anthropologists have noted that every culture makes assumptions about the nature of time and has a basic orientation toward the past, present, or future (Kluckhohn & Strodtbeck, 1961; Redding & Martyn-Johns, 1979;

Hampden-Turner & Trompenaars, 1993). For example, in their study of the various cultures in the U.S. Southwest, Kluckhohn and Strodtbeck noted that some of the Indian tribes lived mostly in the past, the Spanish-Americans were oriented primarily toward the present, and the Anglo-Americans were oriented primarily toward the near future. Hampden-Turner & Trompenaars (1993, 2000), based on their own survey, found that among Asian countries, Japan is at the extreme of long-range planning, while Hong Kong is at the extreme of short-run planning.

How future oriented an organization should be is the subject of much debate, with many arguing that one of the problems of U.S. companies is that the financial context in which they operate (the stock market) forces a near-future orientation at the expense of longer-range planning. It is, of course, not clear which is cause and which is effect. Is the United States, culturally speaking, a near-future-oriented pragmatic society that has created certain economic institutions to reflect our need for quick and constant feedback, or have our economic institutions created the short-run pragmatic orientation?

In either case, the important point is that these cultural assumptions about time dominate daily thinking and activity to the point where a U.S. manager may have a hard time even imagining the alternative of a long-range planning process such as is typical in some Japanese industries. I have a Japanese colleague who is planning to translate and introduce some of my work to the Japanese market and already has planned either visits or video presentations for me in 2017 and 2018!

Monochronic and Polychronic Time. Hall (1959, 1966) points out that in the United States, most managers view time as monochronic, an infinitely divisible linear ribbon that can be divided into appointments and other compartments but within which only one thing can be done at a time. If more than one thing must be done within, say, an hour, we divide the hour into as many units as we need and then do one thing at a time. When we get disorganized or have a feeling of being overloaded, we are advised to do one thing at a time. Time is viewed as a valuable commodity that can be spent, wasted, killed, or made good use of; but once a unit of time is over, it is gone forever. Hassard (1999) points out that this concept of "linear time" was at the heart of the industrial revolution in the shift to measuring productivity in terms of the time it took to produce something, insertion of time clocks to measure the amount of work done, paying people by the amount of time they work, and emphasizing the metaphor that "time is money."

In contrast, some cultures in southern Europe, Africa, and the Middle East regard time as primarily polychronic, a kind of medium defined more by what is accomplished than by a clock and within which several things can be done simultaneously. Even more extreme is the cyclical concept of time as a recurring series of phases, rather circular in form. One season follows the next, one life leads into another as seen in some Asian societies (Sithi-Amnuai, 1968).

The manager who operates according to polychronic time "holds court" in the sense that he or she deals simultaneously with a number of subordinates, colleagues, and even bosses, keeping each matter in suspension until it is finished. Though there is an emphasis on monochronicity in the United States, polychronic time concepts do exist as when a doctor or dentist sees several patients in adjacent offices or a car salesman has several customers looking at cars and rotates among them. Modern information and social communication technologies have illustrated some of the potential problems of polychronicity by questioning whether texting or phoning can or should be done while driving.

Time concepts also define in a subtle way how status is displayed, as illustrated by the frustrating experiences that Americans and northern Europeans have in Latin cultures, where lining up and doing things one at a time are less common. I once stood in line at a small post office in southern France only to discover that some people barged to the head of the line and actually got service from the clerk. My friends pointed out to me that in this situation not only does the clerk have a more polychronic view of the world, leading the clerk to respond to those who shout loudest, but that a higher-status person considers it legitimate to break into the line and get service first as a display of status. If others live in the same status system, they do not get offended by being kept waiting. In fact, it was pointed out to me that by staying in line and fulminating, I was displaying a low sense of my own status; otherwise, I would have been up at the head of the line demanding service as well.

Planning Time and Development Time.   In a study of biotechnology companies, Dubinskas (1988) found an important difference between the occupational cultures of biologists and managers who worked together in the biotech industry. The managers viewed time in a linear, monochronic way, with targets and milestones that were tied to external objective realities such as market opportunities and the stock market. Dubinskas labeled this form of time *planning time*.

In contrast, the biologists seemed to operate from something Dubinskas called *development time*, best characterized as "things will take as long as they will take," referring to natural biological processes that have their own internal time cycles. To caricature the distinction, a manager might say we need the baby in five months to meet a business target, while the biologist would say, sorry, but it takes at least nine months to make a baby. Planning time seeks closure; open-ended development time can extend far into the future.

The Meaning of Space: Distance and Relative Placement

Our assumptions about the meaning and use of space are among the most subtle aspects of macro culture, because assumptions about space, like those about time, operate outside of awareness and are taken for granted. At the same time, when those assumptions are violated, very strong emotional reactions occur because space comes to have very powerful symbolic meanings, as expressed in the current phrase, "Don't get into my space." One of the most obvious ways that rank and status are symbolized in organizations is by the location and size of offices.

Hall (1966) points out that in some cultures, if someone is walking in a certain direction, the space ahead is perceived to belong to that person, so that if someone crosses in front of the individual, that person is "violating" the other's space. In other cultures, notably some Asian ones, space is initially defined as communal and shared, allowing for the complex flow of people, bicycles, cars, and animals you may see in a Chinese city street with everyone somehow moving forward and no one getting killed or trampled.

How we orient ourselves relative to others reflects our perception of what kind of relationship we are expressing. Formal relationships are generally conducted with a distance of several feet separating us, whereas intimate relationships allow for speaking to each other with just a few inches between us and physical contact. The greater the status gap, the greater the distance the subordinate will maintain, while the superior has the license to get close, especially if it is part of the job as in being a doctor or dentist.

Feelings about distance have biological roots. Animals have a clearly defined flight distance (the distance that will elicit fleeing if the animal is intruded upon) and critical distance (the distance that will elicit attacking behavior if the animal is intruded upon or "cornered"). Conditions of crowding not only elicit pathological behavior in nonhuman species but also elicit aggression in humans. Hence, most cultures have fairly clear rules about how to define personal and intimate space through the use of cues to permit what Hall (1959, 1966) calls "sensory screening," including partitions, walls, sound barriers, and other physical devices. We use eye contact, body position, and other personal devices to signal respect for the privacy of others (Goffman, 1959; Hatch, 1990; Steele, 1973, 1981).

We also learn how to manage what Hall (1959, 1966) calls *intrusion distance*—that is, how far away to remain from others who are in personal conversation without interrupting the conversation yet making it known that one wants attention when appropriate. In some cultures, including ours, intrusion occurs only when someone interrupts with speech (someone can stand close by without "interrupting"), whereas in other cultures, even entering the visual field of another person constitutes a bid for attention and hence is seen as an interruption. In these cultural settings, the use of physical barriers such as closed offices has an important symbolic meaning— it is the only way to maintain a feeling of privacy (Hall, 1966).

The Symbolism of Space. Every society develops ways of allocating space to symbolize important values. At the organizational level, clear norms emerge on how much space one should have and where it should be located. These norms reflect basic assumptions about the role of space use in getting work accomplished and space as a symbol of status. The best views and locations are usually reserved for the highest-status people. Senior executives are typically on the higher floors of buildings and often are allocated special spaces such as private conference rooms and private bathrooms.

Sociologists point out that one important function of private bathrooms is to enable leaders to present themselves properly to their subordinates and the public and to preserve the image of leaders as "super-human" beings who do not have the ordinary needs of those at lower levels (Goffman, 1967). In some countries or organizations, it would not be comfortable for the employee to find himself urinating next to the president of the corporation.

Some organizations use very precise space allocation as a direct status symbol. The headquarters building of General Foods was designed with movable walls so that, as product managers were promoted, the office size could be adjusted to reflect their new rank. The company had a department that allocated the kind of carpeting, furniture, and wall decorations that went with particular rank levels. Where buildings are located, how they are built, and the kind of architecture involved differ in different countries reflecting deeper values, as can be seen by the location and style of cathedrals and churches in different countries.

Because buildings and the environments around them are highly visible and relatively permanent, countries and organizations attempt to symbolize important values and assumptions through their design. The physical layout not only has this symbolic function but is often used to guide and channel the behavior of members of the organization, thereby becoming a powerful builder and reinforcer of norms (Berg & Kreiner, 1990; Gagliardi, 1990; Steele, 1973, 1981). The companies in Silicon Valley (e.g., Google, Apple, Facebook, Genentech, etc.) use their centralized spaces not as fortresses but as magnets, making the amenities so attractive that employees want to spend most of their time inside these areas, attractively called "campuses."

Body Language. One of the more subtle uses of space is how we use gestures, body position, and other physical cues to communicate our sense of what is going on in a given situation and how we relate to the other people in it. On the gross level, those we sit next to, physically avoid, touch, bow to, look at, and so on, convey our perceptions of relative status and intimacy. The foregoing discussion of "distance" that we maintain from others is a prime example. As sociologists have observed, however, there are many more subtle cues that convey our deeper sense of what is going on and our assumptions about the right and proper way to behave in any given situation (Goffman, 1967; Van Maanen, 1979).

Rituals of deference and demeanor that reinforce hierarchical relationships are played out in our physical and temporal positioning, as when a subordinate knows just where to stand at a meeting relative to the boss and how to time his or her questions or comments when disagreeing with the boss. The boss, for her part, knows that she must sit at the head of the table in the boardroom and time her remarks to the group appropriately. But only insiders know the full meaning of all these time or space cues, reminding us forcefully that what we observe around spatial arrangements and the behavioral use of time are cultural artifacts, difficult to decipher if we do not have additional data obtained from insiders through interview, observation, and joint inquiry.

It would be highly dangerous to use our own cultural lenses to interpret what we observe. In the South African coal mines, the white supervisors mistrusted the native employees because they were "shifty eyed and never looked you in the eye," not realizing that in the tribes from which they came it was a serious mark of disrespect to look directly into the eyes of a superior (Silberbauer, 1968). Special training programs had to be set up for the supervisors to teach them how to interpret employee behavior. However, in the United States where eye contact is considered a "good" indicator of attention, I have had difficulty convincing dialogue groups to "talk to the campfire" instead of directly to each other as is explained in the following chapter.

Time, Space, and Activity Interaction. Becoming oriented in both time and space is fundamental for an individual in any new situation. Thus far, we have analyzed time and space as separate dimensions, but, in reality, they always interact in complex ways around the activity that is supposed to occur. It is easiest to see this in relation to the basic forms of time. Monochronic time assumptions have specific implications for how space is organized. If someone must have individual appointments and privacy, he or she needs areas in which they can be held, thus requiring either desks that are far enough apart, cubicles, or offices with doors. Because monochronic time is linked with efficiency, the individual also requires a space layout that allows a minimum of wasted time. Thus it must be easy for people to contact each other, distances between important departments must be minimal, and amenities such as toilets and eating areas must be placed in such a way as to save time. In fact, in DEC, the liberal distribution of water coolers, coffee machines, and small kitchens around the organization clearly signaled the importance of continuing to work even as one satisfied bodily needs. The extensive facilities in Google suggest that the employee should not feel any need to leave the premises and should always be comfortable at work.

Polychronic time, in contrast, requires spatial arrangements that make it easy for simultaneous events to occur, where privacy is achieved by being near someone and whispering rather than by retreating behind closed doors. Thus, large rooms are built more like amphitheaters to permit a senior person to hold court, or sets of offices or cubicles are built around a central core that permits easy access to everyone. We might also expect more visually open environments such as the office bullpens that permit supervisors to survey an entire department so that they can easily see who might need help or who is not working.

When buildings and offices are designed in terms of certain intended work patterns, both distance and time are usually considered in the physical layout (Allen, 1977; Steele, 1973, 1981, 1986). These design issues become very complex, however, because information and communication technology is increasingly able to shrink time and space in ways that may not have been considered. For example, a group of people in private offices can communicate by telephone, email, fax, and videophone, and can even become a virtual team or meeting by using conference calls enhanced by various kinds of video software (Grenier & Metes, 1992; Johansen et al., 1991).

Human Essence and Basic Motivation

Every culture has shared assumptions about what it means to be human, what our basic instincts are, and what kinds of behavior are considered inhuman and therefore grounds for ejection from the group. Being human is both a physical property and a cultural construction, as we have seen throughout history. Slavery was often justified by defining slaves as "not human." In ethnic and religious conflicts the "other" is often defined as not human. Within the category of those defined as human, we have further variation. In their comparative study, Kluckhohn and Strodtbeck (1961) noted that in some societies humans are seen as basically evil, in others as basically good, and in still others as mixed or neutral, capable of being either good or bad.

Closely related are assumptions about how perfectible human nature is. Is our goodness or badness intrinsic so we must simply accept what we are, or can we, through hard work, generosity, or faith, overcome our badness and earn our salvation or nirvana? Where a given macro culture ends up in terms of these categories is often related to the religion that dominates that cultural unit, but, as we shall see, this issue is very much at the heart of leadership.

What assumptions do leaders make about the fundamental motivation of workers? In the United States we have seen a transition across several sets of such assumptions:

1. Workers as rational-economic actors
2. Workers as social animals with primarily social needs
3. Workers as problem solvers and self-actualizers, whose primary needs are to be challenged and to use their talents
4. Workers as complex and malleable (Schein, 1980)

Early theories of employee motivation in the United States were almost completely dominated by the assumption that the only incentives available to managers were monetary ones because it was assumed that the only essential motivation of employees was economic self-interest. The Hawthorne studies (Roethlisberger & Dickson, 1939; Homans, 1950) launched a new series of "social" assumptions, postulating that employees are motivated by the need to relate well to their peer and membership groups and that such motivation often overrides economic self-interest. The main evidence for these assumptions came from studies of restriction of output, which showed clearly that workers would reduce their take-home pay rather than break the norm of "a fair day's work for a fair day's pay." Furthermore, workers will put pressure on high producers ("rate busters") to work less hard and make less money to preserve the basic norm of a fair day's work.

Subsequent studies of work, particularly on the effects of the assembly line, introduced another set of assumptions: employees are self-actualizers who need challenge and interesting work to provide self-confirmation and valid outlets for the full use of their talents (Argyris, 1964). Motivation theorists, such as Maslow (1954), proposed that there is a hierarchy of human needs and an individual will not experience and work on the "higher" needs until lower ones are satisfied. If the individual is in a survival mode, economic motives will dominate; if survival needs are met, social needs come to the fore; if social needs are met, self-actualization needs become salient.

It is at this point not clear whether in any given organization it will be the deeper national assumptions or the managerial occupational assumptions that will dominate a particular reward system. In the Western capitalist system, money and the assumption that people are primarily motivated by it still appears to predominate in the managerial culture. But my recent conversations with Danica Purg, who runs a very forward-looking Management School in Bled, Slovenia, suggest that the countries that were dominated for decades by communism take full employment very seriously and make it very hard to "fire" someone; this makes life difficult for the young entrepreneurial type who has been bred on "no job security" and "no organizational loyalty expected."

Assumptions about Appropriate Human Activity

How do humans relate to their environment? Several basically different orientations have been identified in cross-cultural studies, and these have direct implications for variations we can see in organizations.

The "Doing" Orientation. At one extreme, we can identify a "doing" orientation, which correlates closely with (1) the assumption that nature can be controlled and manipulated, (2) a pragmatic orientation toward the nature of reality, and (3) a belief in human perfectibility (Kluckhohn & Strodtbeck, 1961). In other words, it is taken for granted that the proper thing for humans to do is to take charge and actively control their environment and their fate.

Doing is the predominant orientation in the United States and is certainly a key assumption of U.S. managers, reflected in the World War II slogan "We can do it," immortalized in the Rosie the Riveter posters and in the stock American phrases "getting things done" and "let's do something about it." The notion that "the impossible just takes a little longer" is central to U.S. business ideology. Organizations driven by this assumption seek to grow and to dominate the markets they are in.

The "Being" Orientation. At the other extreme is a "being "orientation, which correlates closely with the assumption that nature is powerful and humanity is subservient to it. This orientation implies a kind of fatalism: because we cannot influence nature, we must become accepting and enjoy what we have. We must focus more on the here and now, on individual enjoyment, and on acceptance of whatever comes. Many religions operate on this assumption. Organizations operating according to this orientation look for a niche in their environment that allows them to survive, and they try to adapt to external realities rather than create markets or dominate some portion of the environment.

The "Being-in-Becoming" Orientation. A third orientation, which lies between the two extremes of doing and being, is "being-in-becoming," referring to the idea that the individual must achieve harmony with nature by fully developing his or her own capacities, thereby achieving a perfect union with the environment. The focus is on development rather than a static condition. Through detachment, meditation, and control of those things that can be controlled (e.g., feelings and bodily functions), the individual achieves full self-development and self-actualization. The focus is on what the person is and can become rather than what specific thing the person can accomplish. In short, "the being-in-becoming orientation emphasizes that kind of activity which has as its goal the development of all aspects of the self as an integrated whole" (Kluckhohn and Strodtbeck, 1961, p. 17).

The definition of what constitutes growth and whether or not it should be encouraged varies widely. In Essochem Europe a talented country manager was refused a promotion to be European manager because he was "too emotional," which reflected the parent company's assumptions about management being of necessity unemotional. In contrast, DEC was extreme in the degree to which it allowed and encouraged all forms of self-development, which was later reflected in the degree to which "alumni" of DEC, now working on their own or in other organizations, used the phrase "I grew up in DEC."

In Ciba-Geigy, it was clear that each person had to fit in and become part of the organizational fabric and that socialization into the existing mode was therefore how development was defined. To succeed to senior executive levels, a manager had to have had a successful overseas assignment and had to develop cross-cultural skills mandated by the company.

Countries and the organizations within them differ in how much they consider the growth and development of their people to be an important management function, even as academics advocate that human development and successful organizational performance should both be possible (Chapman & Sisodia, 2015; Keegan & Lahey, 2016).

Assumptions about the Nature of Human Relationships

At the core of every culture are assumptions about the proper way for individuals to relate to each other to make the group safe, comfortable, and productive. When such assumptions are not widely shared, we speak of anarchy and anomie. This set of assumptions creates norms and behavioral rules that deal primarily with the two central issues of (1) what the relationship should be between higher and lower status people (and by implication between the individual and the group), and (2) what the relationship should be between peers and fellow team members.

These rules are taught early in life and come to be labeled as "proper behavior," etiquette, tact, good manners, and situationally appropriate behavior—that is, know your place in the structure and know what is appropriate. These rules change and reflect current social issues as is best exemplified by the importance of knowing what it is "politically correct" to say. What is proper and "situationally appropriate" varies with the degree of "intimacy" of the relationship, which in most cultures can be divided into four "levels" (Schein, 2016).

Levels of Relationship. The boundaries between these levels vary by country, religion, and ethnicity, but every macro culture has some version of these broad levels, as laid out in Exhibit 6.4. Understanding the rules of situational propriety becomes critical when macro cultures interact. For example, in a Brazilian subsidiary of a multinational chemical company a new CEO from the German branch opened his first meeting with a very formal agenda that included time allocations for each item and very precise instructions. He proudly presented the agenda to open the meeting and was greeted with laughter and joking, leading to his total humiliation and severely damaging his relationship with the local executives. Neither he nor the Brazilians who were used to very informal management understood that neither his nor their behavior was situationally appropriate.

Exhibit 6.4   Four Levels of Relationship in Society

Level -1. Exploitation, No Relationship or a Negative Relationship

Examples: Prisoners, POWs, slaves, sometimes members of extremely different cultures or those we consider underdeveloped, sometimes very old or very emotionally ill people, the victims or "marks" for criminals or con men

Comment: We recognize, of course, that inside these groups intense relationships form and that if we choose to build a relationship with someone in this category we are able to do so. But we don't owe them anything and don't have an expected level of trust or openness with them.

Level 1. Acknowledgement, Civility, Transactional Role Relations

Examples: Strangers on the street, seatmates on trains and planes, service people whose help we need, which includes professional helpers of all sorts whose behavior is governed by the defined role definitions in the culture

Comment: The parties do not "know" each other but treat each other as fellow humans whom we trust to a certain degree not to harm us and with whom we have polite levels of openness in conversation. Professional helpers fall into this category because their role definition requires them to maintain a "professional distance."

Level 2. Recognition as a Unique Person; Working Relationships

Examples: Casual friendships, people whom we know "as people," members of working teams, people whom we have come to know through common work or educational experiences, clients or subordinates who have developed personal but not intimate relationships with their helpers or bosses

Comment: This kind of relationship implies a deeper level of trust and openness in terms of (1) making and honoring commitments and promises to each other; (2) agreeing to not undermine each other or harm what we have agreed to do; and (3) agreeing not to lie to each other or withhold information relevant to our task.

Level 3. Strong Emotions—Close Friendships, Love and Intimacy

Examples: Relationships where stronger positive emotions are involved

Comment: This kind of relationship is usually viewed as undesirable in work or helping situations. Trust here goes one step beyond Level 2 in that the participants not only agree not to harm each other but assume that they will actively support each other when possible or when needed and be more open.

In terms of the levels of relationship, the German CEO treated the meeting as a Level 1 formal transaction and was not aware that the Brazilian group had evolved into a Level 2 personal set of relationships. When strangers meet and become confused about how personal to be, it can be awkward and uncomfortable, but when this happens across an important hierarchical boundary, it can be humiliating and destructive. Pragmatic, action-oriented U.S. executives in Asian and Latin countries often fail to understand that their Level 1 formal "professional" demeanor does not elicit the kind of trust and openness that the local executives want, and that makes them want to meet over dinner or informally before they talk business. They want some degree of Level 2 personalization to establish trust, while the U.S. executive will count on contracts and signatures.

A similar issue arises around peer relationships and teamwork. We always have a choice in any new relationship to define it as a Level 1 formal transaction or to make it a Level 2 more personalized relationship by opening ourselves up or asking personal questions (Schein, 2016). The big question is whether an appropriate level of trust and openness to allow effective work to be done can be established in a Level 1 relationship, or whether good working relationships always require some degree of Level 2 personalization. This issue has become more pressing as technological complexity has created more interdependence, not just among team members but even across the hierarchical boundaries. More and more managers and leaders are discovering that they are genuinely dependent on subordinates who know more and have more operational skills than they do, which highlights the degree to which leaders have to become humble and accept levels of vulnerability that they may not be used to (Schein, 2013, 2016).

Finding ways to establish common rules of situational propriety and defining together at what level of relationship we can work together will be the major challenges as we move into a more multicultural world.

Summary and Conclusions

This chapter has reviewed some of the major dimensions that have been proposed for understanding cultural differences at the macro culture national and ethnic level. My choice of what to include was premised on which dimensions would be most useful when we try to understand how organizational cultures are nested in broader macro cultures. We have now reviewed the major ways in which language, reality, time, space, truth, human activity, nature, and relationships can be categorized.

It is the patterning of assumptions around each of these issues that creates the totality we end up calling "the culture" of the country, recognizing that there are still other dimensions of what constitutes a culture that were not reviewed. Culture is deep, wide, complex, and multidimensional, so we should avoid the temptation to stereotype countries in terms of just a few salient dimensions as the survey-based models suggest.

The rules that govern relationships across hierarchical and functional boundaries are perhaps the most important area to explore when multicultural groups try to work together. A conceptual model of levels of relationship was proposed to organize that analysis and to suggest that the most important area of consensus to be sought is whether or not it is possible to build open and trusting relationships at the Level 1 transactional, professional level or whether the growing complexity of work requires always building some form of a personalized Level 2 relationship. We explore possible ways of doing this in the following chapter.

Questions for Readers

1. Which of the dimensions surprised you most, because you had never thought of culture in that way?

2. Which issues have bothered you most when you interact with someone from another culture?

3. What are your own attitudes about time? How late can a person be without offending you? How late do you allow yourself to be when you are running late?

4. Which excuses are legitimate for being late?

5. Have you observed the need to become "more personal" in your various relationships to build trust and open communication?

7

A FOCUSED WAY OF WORKING WITH MACRO CULTURES

Assessing macro cultures in terms of all of the dimensions mentioned in the preceding chapter is a huge task, but it is useful only for the researcher with a particular interest in a particular country or someone who wants to compare macro cultures. For the organizational leader or the person wanting to join an organization, a more applied and focused approach is needed. The best place to start is with the observation that multicultural task forces and projects will not only become more common in the future but have even acquired a new name—"collaborations." Such new kinds of work groups are well described in an article within the *Handbook of Cultural Intelligence* (Ang & Van Dyne, 2008):

> Participants in a collaboration may come together on a one-time basis, without anticipating continued interaction. A core set of members may remain involved for an extended period of time, but other participants may float on and off the effort, working only on an "as needed" sporadic basis. Further, collaborations may have periods of intensely interdependent interaction, but may otherwise consist of quite independent actors. Many are not embedded in a single organizational context, but represent either cross-organizational cooperation or participants may not have any organizational affiliation at all. Participants may feel as though they share a common purpose for the duration of a given project, yet may not view themselves as a "team." Collaborators may never meet face-to-face, may be geographically dispersed, and may be primarily connected by communication technology. Thus collaborations are more loosely structured, more temporary, more fluid, and often more electronically enabled than traditional teams.
>
> *(Gibson & Dibble, 2008, pp. 222–223)*

The two prototype situations to consider are (1) a team or task force in which every member comes from a different nationality, and (2) a team such as a surgical team in which every member comes from a different occupational culture with hierarchical differences within the team. The unique factor in these kinds of groups is that we are dealing with both national and status differences. From a culture management and change leadership perspective, how can such groups learn about the many layers of culture and how can such groups be made effective?

In each of these cases, the group must undergo some experiences that enable its members to discover some essential cultural characteristics of the other members that relate to the task at hand. To do this they must overcome the rituals of deference and demeanor that curtail open communication across status levels to develop some amount of understanding and empathy and to find some common ground. In particular, they must discover the norms and underlying assumptions that deal with *authority* and *intimacy*, because common ground in those areas is essential to developing feasible working relationships. This task is made especially difficult because each culture's social order has norms about "face" that make it difficult and dangerous to talk about these areas openly. Our own unconscious rules of politeness and fear of offending make it very likely that members will not easily reveal their deeper feelings about authority and intimacy to others nor will they think to ask about them.

We are not talking about how to manage a merger or joint venture when only two cultures are involved and where some formal mutual education might work. Instead we are now talking about how an Arab, an Israeli, a Japanese, a Nigerian, and an American, for example, can be shaped into a functioning work group even if they share some knowledge of English. Briefing the group on where each country stands on the Hofstede or Globe dimensions would do little to foster understanding or empathy. Or consider how a surgeon, an anesthesiologist, several nurses, and technicians who have to implement a new surgical technique can become a successful team, talk openly, and totally trust each other across the major hierarchical boundaries that exist in such a group (Edmondson, Bohmer, & Pisano, 2001; Edmondson, 2012). If you add the possibility that in this medical team, several of the members are from different countries and received their training in those countries, how would they find common ground? Lecturing to such a group about the culture of doctors and the different culture of nurses would only scratch the surface if the members need to collaborate constructively. What kind of education or experience would enable such groups to develop working relationships, trust, and task-relevant open communication?

To solve this puzzle it is necessary to draw on the concept of "levels of relationship," as was explained in the previous chapter. When multicultural groups come together, they will interact in the Level 1 transactional modes of their own country and will be especially cautious not to offend or "threaten face." I have seen multicultural classes go through an entire semester without anyone risking becoming more personal, and, as a consequence, not understanding each other's national cultures at all. If it is a working group, staying at Level 1 risks errors and low productivity, because members will not speak up lest they offend someone with higher status. It is necessary to remember that the social order in every society creates these Level 1 norms of politeness, tact, and face saving as an essential component of culture, designed to make society possible.

Every macro culture develops a social order, but the actual norms differ from culture to culture. For example, in the United States Level 1 face-to-face criticism is acceptable as part of performance appraisal; in Japan it is not. In some cultures, hiring relatives is the only way to have employees with whom it is possible to develop open trusting Level 2 relationships; in other cultures, it is called nepotism and is forbidden. In some cultures, trust is established with a handshake; in others, it can be established only with payoffs and bribes (even the word "bribe" is culturally loaded). Differences across occupational boundaries might not be as extreme, but they are just as important when teams that cut across hierarchical boundaries and occupations have to function together.

Cultural Intelligence

One approach to solving multicultural issues of this sort is to educate each member about the norms and assumptions of each of the cultures involved. I have already indicated that this approach would not only be cumbersome because of the number of different cultures involved, but it would also have to be so abstract that the learners would not know how to apply what they were told.

A second approach is to focus on cultural capacities and learning skills, which is increasingly being called *cultural intelligence* (Thomas & Inkson, 2003; Earley & Ang, 2003; Peterson, 2004; Plum, 2008; Ang & Van Dyne, 2008). Because there are very many macro cultures in the world, to learn their content appears to be a much less feasible approach than to develop the *learning skills* to quickly acquire whatever knowledge is needed of the cultures that are involved in a particular situation. The basic problem in multicultural situations is that the members of each macro culture may have opinions and biases about "the others" or may even have some level of understanding of "the others" but operate by the premise that their own culture is the one that is "right." Getting multicultural organizations, projects, and teams to work together, therefore, poses a much larger cultural challenge than evolving or managing cultural change within a single macro culture.

The concept of cultural intelligence introduces the proposition that to develop understanding, empathy, and the ability to work with others from other cultures requires four capacities: (1) actual knowledge of some of the essentials of the other cultures involved, (2) cultural sensitivity or mindfulness about culture, (3) motivation to learn about other cultures, and (4) behavioral skills and flexibility to learn new ways of doing things (Earley & Ang, 2003; Thomas & Inkson, 2003). For multicultural teams to work, therefore, implies that certain individual characteristics must be present to enable cross-cultural learning.

In their *Handbook of Cultural Intelligence* (2008), Ang and Van Dyne present a set of papers that describe the development of a cultural intelligence scale and show that teams with members that score higher on this measure perform better than lower-scoring groups. There are clearly individual differences in cultural sensitivity and learning capacity, and there is a vast psychological literature on what makes people more or less culturally competent, but selecting people for this capacity does not address two problems. First, in many work situations, we do not have choices as to whom to assign because of limited resources in the technical skills needed to do the work. Second, if a leader decides to increase the cultural competence of employees, what kind of experiences should they have? What should the leader do by way of designing learning processes that will stimulate such competence regardless of the initial state of cultural intelligence of the participants?

How to Foster Cross-Cultural Learning

Because culture is so deeply embedded in each of us, cross-cultural learning must confront the fundamental reality that each member of each culture begins with the assumption that what he or she does is the right and proper way to do things. We each come from a social order into which we have been socialized and therefore take its assumptions for granted. Intellectual understanding of other cultures may be a start in conceding that there are other ways to do things, but it does little to build empathy and does not enable us to find common ground for working together. More likely we begin by noting how the "other processes or positions won't work or are wrong."

To achieve a sufficient level of empathy and a context in which the group is motivated to engage in a mutual search for common ground requires a temporary suspension of some of the rules of the social order. We must be brought to the point of being able to reflect on our own assumptions and consider the possibility that some other assumptions may be just as valid as our own. This process starts with questioning ourselves, not with becoming convinced of the rightness of others. How is this to be done? What kind of social learning process has to be created to achieve such a state of reflection?

The Concept of a Temporary Cultural Island

A *cultural island* is a situation in which the rules of having to maintain face are temporarily suspended so that we can explore our self-concepts and thereby our values and tacit assumptions, especially around authority and intimacy. The first use of this term in the organizational domain was in Bethel, Maine, where human relations training groups met for several weeks to learn about leadership and group dynamics (Bradford, Gibb, & Benne, 1964; Schein & Bennis, 1965). The essence of this training process is based on the theory that this kind of learning has to be "experiential" in the sense that group members have to learn from their own efforts to become a group.

The groups are deliberately composed in such a way that all members would be strangers to each other so that no one had to maintain a particular identity vis-à-vis the others in the group. At the same time, the "trainers" or staff members of these T-groups (training groups) deliberately withheld any suggestions for the agenda, working method, or structure, thus forcing members to invent their own social order, their own norms, and their own ways of working together. The main impact of this kind of learning was that people confronted their own assumptions and observed how these differed from the assumptions of others.

The problems of authority, intimacy, and identity must be confronted immediately through personal experimentation and observation of an individual's impact on others. Members become acutely aware that there was no one best way to do things and that the best way has to be discovered, negotiated, and ratified, leading eventually to strong group norms that created a micro culture within each T-group. Such micro cultures often formed within a day or two in these groups and were viewed by each group as the best way to do things—"we are the best group." Members also discovered that they did not have to like each other to work together, but they had to have sufficient empathy to be able to accept others and work with them. A brief review of the theory underlying this learning progression is found in the introduction to the next part of this book.

What made T-group experiential learning possible was that the learning took place under conditions where members could relax the need to defend their own cultural assumptions because they were strangers to each other, were in a situation defined as "learning" rather than performing, and had the time and staff resources to develop their own learning skills. The total situation was designed by the staff to create a "container" in which the participants could feel psychologically safe.

For multicultural collaborations to work, the members must first learn about each other in a temporary cultural island. Making this work in a group that has to stay together and work together is more difficult than doing it with strangers in a T-group, but the same experiential assumptions apply. The group cannot be told how to work; it must learn from its own experience. The members must be enabled to get past Level 1 transactional norms, be encouraged to take some personal risks to personalize the situation, and begin to develop Level 2 relationships. The change leaders and managers who create such groups must therefore develop the skills to create temporary cultural-island experiences for the members to enable them to work effectively.

The basic logic is that to truly understand the deeper assumptions of the macro cultures involved in the group, we must create a micro culture that *personalizes* those assumptions and makes them available for reflection and understanding. I can read or be told that in the United States we have fairly "low power distance" and that my Mexican team member comes from a culture with "higher power distance," but this will mean nothing to me until we can concretize these generalizations in our own behavior and feelings. I need to discover within myself how I relate to people in authority, and I need to listen with empathy to how my Mexican teammate feels about his relationship to authority. If there are more than two of us, we must each develop some understanding and empathy for each other.

Cultural islands that attempt to facilitate this level of mutual understanding are sometimes created when we send teams to Outward Bound kinds of training and when we put teams in simulations, in role playing situations, in post-mortems or after action reviews, where a *review* of operations or experiences deliberately tries to minimize hierarchy and maximize open communication across the status levels of the participants (Conger, 1992; Darling & Parry, 2001; Mirvis, Ayas, & Roth, 2003). What these situations have in common is that they put participants into the cultural island, but then what they do within the cultural-island setting varies widely according to the purpose of the exercise. To focus the activity within the cultural island on obtaining multicultural insight and empathy, the participants need to create a conversation in a *dialogic* format (Isaacs, 1999; Bushe & Marshak, 2015).

Focused Dialogue in a Cultural-Island Setting

Dialogue is a form of conversation that allows the participants to relax sufficiently to begin to examine the assumptions that lie behind their thought processes (Isaacs, 1999; Schein, 1993a). Instead of trying to solve problems rapidly, the dialogue process attempts to slow down the conversation to allow participants to reflect on what comes out of their own mouths and what they hear from the mouths of others. The key to initiating this kind of dialogic conversation is to create a setting in which participants feel secure enough to *suspend* their need to win arguments, to clarify everything they say, and to challenge each other every time they disagree.

In "normal" Level 1 conversation in the United States, we are expected to respond to questions, to voice disagreements, and to "actively participate." In a dialogue the facilitator legitimizes the concept of *suspension*. If someone has just said something that I disagree with, I could hold back voicing my disagreement and, instead, silently ask myself why I disagree and what assumptions I am making that might explain the disagreement. Suspension thus facilitates learning about oneself, which is crucial in cross-cultural dialogues because we cannot understand someone else's culture if we cannot "see" our own cultural assumptions and discover the differences in an objective non-evaluative manner.

This form of dialogue derives from native cultures that made decisions through "talking to the campfire," allowing enough time for and encouraging reflective conversation rather than confrontational conversation, discussion, or debate. Talking to the campfire is an important element of this dialogue process, because the absence of eye contact makes it easier to suspend reactions, disagreements, objections, and other responses that might be triggered by face-to-face conversation. The purpose is not just to have a quiet, reflective conversation; rather, it is to allow participants to begin to see where their deeper levels of thought and tacit assumptions differ. Paradoxically such reflection leads to better listening in that if I identify my own assumptions and filters first, I am less likely to mishear or misunderstand the subtle meanings in the words of others. I cannot understand another culture if I have no insight into my own.

For this to work, all of the parties to the dialogue have to be willing to suspend their impulses to disagree, challenge, clarify, and elaborate. The conversational process imposes certain rules such as not interrupting, talking to the symbolic campfire instead of to each other, limiting eye contact, and, most important of all, starting with a "check-in." Checking in at the beginning of the meeting means that each member in turn will say something to the group as a whole (the campfire) about his or her present mental state, motivation, or feelings. Only when all of the members have checked in is the group ready for a more free-flowing conversation. The check-in ensures that everyone has made an initial contribution to the group and thereby has helped to *create* the group.

An example of discovering our own culture typically arises immediately around the instruction to talk to the campfire and avoid eye contact. For some people this is very easy, but for others—for example, U.S. human resource professionals—this is very difficult because in U.S. culture looking at each other is considered "good communication," and this is reinforced by the professional norms in the human resource field that "eye contact is necessary to make the other feel that you are really listening." It is often shocking for U.S. participants to learn how hard it is for them not to look at someone who is speaking because we consider that rude, not realizing that in many other cultures to look someone in the eye can be seen as disrespectful.

Talking to the symbolic campfire serves several important functions. First of all it encourages group members to become more reflective by not getting distracted by how others look and respond. Second, it preserves the sense of being one whole group by symbolically contributing each comment to the center, not to one or two other members, even though the comment may have been triggered by them. For example, if I have a specific question based on what member A has said, there is a consequential difference between my saying directly to A, "What did you mean by that?" versus saying to the campfire, "What A has just said makes me wonder what she meant." The second way of saying it raises the issue for the group as a whole. Third, the campfire avoids the common phenomenon of two members getting into a deep discussion while the rest of the group becomes a passive audience. The goal is to suspend many of the assumed rules of interaction coming from all the different cultural social orders and to create a new container within which members can talk more openly and can verbalize their reflections.

Using Dialogue for Multicultural Exploration

The norms created in a dialogue group lend themselves to the explorations of critical cultural differences, because the dialogue process allows for the articulation of macro-cultural differences at a personal level so that the participants not only learn how macro-cultures differ at a general level but can experience those differences immediately in the room. *This learning is achieved by using the check-in to focus on the critical issues of authority and intimacy.*

Case Example 7.1   The MBA Class

A group of 10 MIT MBA students from six different countries wanted to explore cultural differences within their group. They all spoke English but had a sense that they did not understand each other well enough to be able to work together on a joint task. We agreed to meet for a two-hour session to explore cultural differences.

Step 1. Setting Up the Dialogue Rules

As the faculty facilitator I explained the concept of dialogue and the basic rules that one spoke only to the "campfire," not to each other, that one did not have to respond to questions, that

(Continued)

one did not at any time interrupt, and that we would begin with a "check-in" by each answering two questions about themselves.

Step 2. First Check-In Question: Focus on Authority Issues

I asked each person to think for a moment about a past situation in which the boss or someone else in a position of authority was about to do something wrong in relation to the task they were engaged in. I then asked each person, in order and without being interrupted or questioned, to tell *the campfire* what they did or would do in that situation and give as much detail as possible. I emphasized that I did not want general comments about "their culture" but personal stories so that we would experience the culture through the personal experiences. Later we could follow up with general questions about each culture.

I then turned to the person on my right and asked him or her to begin. When that person was finished, I asked the next person to talk to the campfire and so on until they all had told their story. I enforced the rule of no questions or interruptions and kept the group members talking in order. If someone was not sure what I meant, I kept emphasizing that we wanted to hear from each member an actual incident or, if they had no actual experience, their account of what they think they would do if a boss was about to make a mistake or do something wrong. The goal was to push *down* the abstraction ladder, to get some concrete personal examples that we could all identity with.

Step 3. Reflection and Open Conversation

When all the participants had told their story, I asked for a few minutes of silent reflection on the variations we had heard and what common ground there seemed to be among the stories. I then asked for comments, observations, and questions but with the ground rule that we kept looking at and talking to the campfire. This was awkward at first, but the group learned within a few minutes that it was easier to say what was on one's mind if one did not look at a particular other group member even if the question was directed to him or her. If the group included members of obviously different rank or status, I asked for reflection on the implications for this group of what they had heard. This conversation went on for about 15 to 30 minutes. I then introduced the second question.

Step 4. Second Check-In Question: Focus on Intimacy and Trust

I said we would now again go in order to each talk about a situation in which the person had to decide whether or not he or she could trust a coworker and how he or she had made the decision. What kinds of behavior would they look for in the other person to determine whether or not that person could be trusted? What criteria did they use in deciding whether to trust the person and how did it work out? Again, each person, in order and without interruption, was to tell his or her story of how this worked out.

Step 5. Open Conversation to Reflect on Intimacy and Trust Stories

Here again I imposed the rule of talking only to the campfire as the group explored differences and similarities in what they heard from each other. I asked the group to reflect on the

(Continued)

(*Continued*)

implications of what they had heard for this group's ability to work together. At an appropriate point I shifted the conversation to the next step.

Step 6. Reflection and Exploration

I asked the group when everyone had spoked to reflect on what everyone had said and asked them to tell whether this helped them to understand each others' culture better. We then discussed how the dialogue format had influenced members' understanding of themselves and each other.

Analytic Comment. The learning goal was to show members that cross-cultural understanding can be achieved through a dialogue process and that they can set up such a process whenever they get stuck in the future. I emphasized the importance of getting personal experiences from everyone on how the specific problems of authority and intimacy were handled by them in their culture. Other dimensions of the macro cultures could come into the discussion, but the critical issues for the group to be able to work together were authority and intimacy.

This form of conversation is powerful because it *personalizes* the cultural issue. Instead of talking about how a particular country has evolved its approach to hierarchy and authority, it brings the issue into the room among the individuals who will have to work together. Personal accounts shift the conversation from Level 1 role-related transactions to stories with which every member of the group can identify. Imitation and identification are fundamental learning processes that become available when we shift to Level 2, where we treat each other as persons rather than as roles. In work with groups that have been historically in conflict with each other it has been found that the only way to begin any kind of conflict resolution work is to get each side to tell its story (Kahane, 2010).

Legitimizing Personalization in Cross-Cultural Conversation

I have pointed out that in a cross-cultural conversation people usually choose to stay in a Level 1 transactional, role-related mode because it is safe. I observed in my classes of Sloan Fellows, which often included as many as 20 non–U.S. members of the class of 50, that even after many months of attending classes and social events together, I had the sense that they had not broken through to any deeper level of understanding of each other's cultures. We assumed that if they were at MIT for a full year with their families that Level 2 and even Level 3 relationships would arise, and indeed some intimate friendships had been made, but overall I felt that a more systematic process for mutual cultural exploration had to be provided as part of their education. I tried an experiment along these lines.

Case Example 7.2

During the spring term some months before the end of the program I announced that I wanted to explore macro-cultural, national differences a bit more deeply and would run a three-hour class one evening if enough people volunteered. About 30 members wanted to try this, and some requested permission to bring their spouses along. A date was set, and a large flexible open-space classroom was booked.

Opening of the evening class: "Thank you all for coming to this experiment. What we will do tonight is quite different, so be prepared to think and feel differently as we go through the evening. My goal is to provide you with an opportunity to understand other cultures more deeply and personally. You have now met and gotten to know members of other countries, have done many things with them, and have a feeling you somewhat know how to deal with them.

"But my hunch is that you have also found yourself wondering about some aspects of how they feel or see things that you were afraid to ask about because it might be too personal. If you agree, for at least three hours tonight we will suspend some of the rules of etiquette and give each other permission to ask the questions we dared not ask. Will you join me in this experiment?" (Everyone nodded, no one asked any questions.)

"OK, for the next half hour I want you to find a partner from a different culture, find a corner of the room where you can talk quietly, and one of you begin the conversation with some version of 'You know, I have always wondered about. . . .' Or 'I have never understood why in your country. . . ?' Or, 'How do you handle your kids when they are disobedient?' I am presuming that you already know each other well enough to trust each other with these questions and to tell each other if a question is *too* personal. This is an experiment, so let's see what happens."

Half hour of spontaneous talk. I observed that people quickly formed themselves into two- or three-person groups, and within a few minutes they were in deep and intense conversation.

Review and reflection. At the end of the half hour, I brought the whole class together for debriefing and reaction. Without going into content detail, there was unanimous agreement that the conversations had been different and very meaningful in revealing aspects of national cultures that had previously not been understood even after being together for many months.

Round two of spontaneous talk. After about 15 minutes I asked the group whether they were ready for another set of pair conversations. At this point, a variety of alternative ideas emerged. Some pairs wanted to continue in their pair, some people wanted to try new pairs, some wanted to get into bigger groups with one person from another country—for example,

(Continued)

(Continued)

five U.S. Sloan Fellows wanted to meet with two members of an Asian country, and another group wanted to meet with one of the African-American Sloans because they needed to understand better how he had overcome his southern rural background but had always been afraid to ask. He indicated that he would be delighted to share. We broke into groups to talk.

Half hour of spontaneous talk. The various groupings then went to different parts of the room and immediately started what became very intense conversations that I finally broke up after 45 minutes.

Review and analysis. When the group came together again to review, it was obvious that this exercise had been very meaningful from the high energy that was apparent and the positive comments about how much they had learned. They agreed that something like this should be done with every class, but not right away. The six months of casual Level 1 relationship building, punctuated by some social Level 2 relations was thought to be necessary to allow the deeper Level 2 conversations to occur. It was also agreed that having a facilitator who creates the safe container was an important element that made the evening work.

The Paradox of Macro Culture Understanding

Both of the cases I reviewed reinforce the paradox that to understand another macro culture, you and your counterpart have to violate a deep rule of your own culture: "Be careful not to offend people in another culture," which translates into "stay at a safe Level 1 transactional level." The implication for multicultural working groups within organizations is that they need to experience cultural islands in which the rules of etiquette and face work can be suspended to enable mutual learning to occur. A cultural island can be deliberately created by leaders and facilitators or sometimes is created by circumstances such as work crises.

An excellent example was provided by Salk (1997) in her study of a German–U.S. joint venture. Each parent company had provided lectures on the main characteristics of the "other culture," which equipped everyone with clear stereotypes. Each group quickly discovered evidence in the other group that the stereotype was accurate and settled into adapting to it, even though it made collaboration awkward. This mutual adaptation at Level 1 went on for several *years* when a major problem arose with the union that threatened an immediate strike. Both parent companies said to the subsidiary: "Solve the problem and solve it *now*," which created crisis conditions and forced immediate emergency action. Suddenly the two groups had to get together under crisis conditions, which revealed them to each other as whole people rather than as employees in formal roles. They solved the problem, and from that point on they had a much easier time collaborating with each other. As they put it, "We finally got to know each other!"

Echelons as Macro Cultures

The discussion so far has focused on national cultures, but the problems of miscommunication and misunderstanding can be just as severe between rank levels in hierarchically structured organizations. White supervisors not understanding Bantu employees refusing to look directly at their superiors is an extreme example, but especially in the high-hazard industries that I have worked with I have seen equally dramatic cases of misunderstanding even when the same national language was spoken. The reason is that culture forms around shared experience, and in most organizations the shared experience of being an operator on the line is different from being a supervisor, which is different from being a middle manager, which is different from being an executive.

Going down the hierarchy, the main problem is misunderstood instructions and orders; going up the chain of command, the main problem is lost information, which causes productivity, quality, and safety problems not to be noticed or addressed effectively. The more technical and complex the industry, the greater the potential problem. I am addressing this issue in this chapter because I believe it is a problem of macro-cultural misunderstanding but has not been recognized as such.

For example, in the arena of *safety* in high-hazard industries such as nuclear power, airlines, and health care, the biggest obstacle to effective performance is the failure of *upward* communication. It is sad to see how many fatal accidents over the years have resulted from communication failures that have cultural roots. When it comes to multinational groups, the problems are, of course, worse, because there may not even be a common language with which to have a dialogue. In such a situation, the actual learning of a common language can itself be a facilitative cultural island.

As Gladwell (2008) points out in his reconstruction of the Colombian airlines disaster in 1990, at the root of it was (1) the failure of the Colombian co-pilot to understand that the JFK controllers did not translate "we are low on fuel" into "EMERGENCY," and (2) that the co-pilot did not know that being put at the head of the line for landing occurred only if you declared an *emergency*. The traffic controllers pointed out that there might at any time be four or five aircraft that reported "running out of fuel."

Gladwell further reports that the Korean airline had a series of disasters in the 1990s because of communication failures across rank levels within the cockpit and that this eventually was ameliorated only by shifting the cockpit language to English. The change in language provided the cultural island that permitted the introduction of new rules that led to better communication in the cockpit but, tragically, did not reveal the subtle occupational semantics of the difference between "running out of fuel" and "emergency."

Along these same lines, "procedures" and "checklists" are devices that can function as cultural islands in the sense that going through the list is a culturally neutral process. The subordinate is licensed to ask challenging questions of the more senior person if it is a checklist item without thereby threatening the senior person's face. Checklists and procedures have been very helpful in the medical context in that they neutralize the dangerous status gap between nurses and technicians on the one hand and doctors on the other hand, especially when they are also likely to be of different nationalities. The checklist or procedure can become a superordinate authority that puts the doctor, nurse, and technician on an equal status level as they go through the procedure. Insisting that dialogue conversations be "to the campfire" in a multinational group serves the same neutralizing function in implying that each culture is of equal rank and validity.

Analytical Comment. The analysis of safety issues in high-hazard industries and in the health care field has revealed several important facts that need to be highlighted because they operate both within and across cultures. Let me put these into a sequential logic:

1. Many failures in the safety arena could have been prevented if there had been better communication across cultural boundaries.

2. Some of these boundaries are technical; people did not understand the jargon and subtle meanings and hence either failed to understand or misunderstood.

3. Some of these boundaries are rank levels where communication breaks down because of cultural norms of deference and demeanor, leading to face protection rather than open sharing of task-relevant information.

4. Some of these boundaries are macro-cultural, reflecting national or occupational norms and values that lead either to not communicating things in the first place or dismissing communications from culture members who are viewed as "wrong" or "not knowing" or "having the wrong values."

5. These three kinds of cultural boundary problems are highly visible in multicultural groups that involve either nations or major occupational groups, but they operate just as much in organizations within a given national culture because of the subcultures that evolve around ranks and functions.

6. Theories of organizational effectiveness emphasize the importance of trust and open communication vertically and laterally, but they fail to acknowledge that such communication has to occur across cultural boundaries and requires some learning in cultural-island settings to ensure understanding and empathy. Exhorting the surgeon and the nurse to be open with each other is not enough; they have to have some kind of mutual cultural-island experience that builds common ground and mutual understanding.

7. A cultural perspective that acknowledges the existence of national and occupational macro cultures, functional subcultures, and subcultures based on rank and common experience is an essential component of organizational leadership.

8. The organizational leader must therefore become aware of when and how to create temporary cultural islands to enable various members of the organization to reach Level 2 relationships in which they can communicate with each other more openly.

9. When and how this is done is itself a function of the macro culture in which the organization and the leaders are operating. For example, a culture in which time is measured in very short units and is considered a key to productivity might have to speed up some version of the dialogue process. The important point is not how long it takes but the creation

of the climate of neutrality and temporary suspension of the rules of the social order.

Summary and Conclusions

As organizations and working groups become more multicultural, new ways of building workable relationships will have to be invented, because just training everyone to be more culturally intelligent and composing groups with the most intelligent will not be practical. Existing groups will have to find experiential ways of learning through creating cultural islands and learning new forms of conversation such as dialogue. The most essential characteristic of these new conversational forms is that they be personal stories, because only through such stories can people from different cultures identify with each other.

As organizations become more decentralized and electronically connected, some new versions of cultural islands will have to be invented to enable people who have not met face-to-face (and may not ever meet each other) to develop understanding and empathy. It is quite possible that the dialogic format can work well in a network if the participants tell their own stories of authority and intimacy to each other by email, Facebook, or whatever technology is extant at the time. The world is changing rapidly, but the issues of how we treat each other and how we handle status and authority remain remarkably stable. Perhaps more dialogues around these issues will stimulate some new ideas on how to get along better.

Suggestion for the Change Leader: Do Some Experiments with Dialogue

How to Set Up a Dialogue

1. Identify the group that needs to explore intercultural relationships.

2. Seat everyone in a circle or as near to it as possible.

3. Lay out the purpose of the dialogue: "To be able to listen more reflectively to ourselves and to each other, to get a sense of the similarities and differences in our cultures."

4. Start the conversation by having the members in turn check in by introducing who they are and answering the relevant question about authority relations as they see them—for example, "What do you do when you see your boss doing something wrong?" Ask each person to talk to the campfire, avoid eye contact, and prohibit any questions or comments until everyone has checked in.

5. After everyone has checked in, launch a very general question, such as, "What differences and commonalities did anyone notice?" Ask members to continue to talk to the campfire even if they are addressing a particular member. Encourage an open conversation on what everyone has just heard without the constraints of proceeding in order or having to withhold questions and comments.

6. When the topic runs dry or the group loses energy, introduce the second question—for example, "How do you know whether or not you can trust one of your coworkers?" Again, have everyone in turn give an answer before general conversation begins.

7. Let the differences and commonalities emerge naturally; don't try to make general statements because the purpose is mutual understanding and empathy, not necessarily clear description or conclusions.

8. After this topic runs dry, ask the group to poll itself by asking each person in turn to share one or two insights about his or her own culture and any other cultures that he or she has heard about during the dialogue.

9. Ask the group to identify common ground and what, if any, problems they see in working together, given what they have heard about authority or power and intimacy or trust.

10. Ask the group members what next steps they feel they need to work on together.

Suggestion for the Recruit

Get a group of friends together, sit in a circle, announce the rule about just talking to the campfire, put some symbolic object in the center, and begin with a check-in with "How are you feeling right now?"; go in order around the room; then just let the process go for a half hour and see how you feel at the end of it. What was different? What did you learn about conversation?

Suggestion for the Scholar or Researcher

Set up the conditions for a dialogue with a few friends, brief them on the concept and the rules, do a quick check-in, and then take an hour to practice just talking to the campfire. The topic does not matter; in fact, it can sometimes be most illuminating if you say, "Let's just begin with our check-in, turn to the right and say, "Why don't you begin."

Suggestion for the Consultant or Helper

When you are working with a group that consists of members of different cultures or status levels, ask them to talk about experiences involving authority and status in a dialogue format.

Part Three

CULTURE AND LEADERSHIP THROUGH STAGES OF GROWTH

How is culture created; how does it evolve; and how is it managed, manipulated, and influenced by human intervention? As I have indicated previously, an excellent way to define the unique function of leadership is to say that *leadership is the management of culture*. However, what we mean by *leadership* has to be understood in the context of the stage of growth of the organization or group.

Leaders as entrepreneurs, prophets, and politicians create new groups, organizations, and movements, thereby *creating new cultures*. But once organizations have succeeded in establishing themselves, their beliefs, values, norms, and basic assumptions (i.e., have created a culture), that culture will now define what kind of leadership will be valued and tolerated. The role of the leader now shifts to *maintaining and consolidating the existing culture*. Whereas leaders initially defined the basic values of the culture, the culture now defines what are the desired characteristics of leadership!

But cultures are nested within other cultures and create environments for each other that are dynamic and changing. Organizations then may find themselves with beliefs, values, norms, and basic assumptions that are to some degree dysfunctional and will require change that will typically

involve some "culture change." It now falls to leadership again to identify the problem, to assess how the existing culture will aid or hinder the
required changes, and to launch what can now be appropriately called a
"culture-change program." This is the third way in which leaders manage
culture—*leaders now manage the direction of the evolution of the culture*.

This third leadership role is often labeled by superficial commentators
as "culture creation," ignoring the reality that the organization already has
a culture that is both a source of strength (and therefore should mostly be
preserved) and a source of constraints (and therefore probably needs to be
partially changed).

These cultural issues and the required leadership roles will be explored
for all of the stages of growth in the chapters of this part. Chapter 8 describes
how culture begins in a group, provides an analytical model of this process,
and discusses the role that founders play in that process. Chapter 9 reviews
all the external and internal challenges that organizations face as they survive and grow; Chapter 10 then shows how successful leaders embed the
elements of the culture that they value. Chapter 11 analyzes what happens
with growth and age, especially the way this changes the leadership role.

8

HOW CULTURE BEGINS AND THE ROLE
OF THE FOUNDER OF ORGANIZATIONS

To fully understand cultural evolution and the role of leadership in that evolution, we have to begin with a bit of group theory. Culture is ultimately a characteristic of a group, just as personality and character are ultimately characteristics of an individual. Just as personality theory is relevant to understanding individuals, group dynamics theories and models are relevant to understanding culture. Founders of groups and organizations may not be aware of the dynamic issues they are grappling with, but those issues are there and need to be considered as determinants of the kind of culture that ends up being created.

A Model of How Culture Forms in New Groups

Groups have been studied intensively throughout history, but it is only in the post–World War II years that social psychologists led by Kurt Lewin in the United States and Wilfred Bion of the Tavistock Clinic in the United Kingdom began to formulate concepts that could be applied widely to all kinds of new and old groups (Lewin, 1947; Bion, 1959). In the United States this model of the stages of group evolution was well summarized by Bennis & Shepard (1956) and was then later described "poetically" by Tuchman (1965) as *forming, storming, norming, and performing*. The underlying psycho-dynamic logic is discussed in the following subsections.

Stage 1, Forming: Finding One's Identity and Role

The group is brought together for some purpose such as "learning" as in the groups referred to in the previous chapter or performing some task. There is a convener, leader, and founder unless environmental circumstances or some crisis like an accident throws a group of people together into a shared-fate situation.

The new members automatically face the questions of *identity and role* (Who am I to be in this group?); *authority and influence* (Who will control whom in this group, and will I have my own influence needs met?); and *intimacy* (How will I relate to the other members of this group and at what level?).

These issues will preoccupy a new member no matter how structured the group is and no matter how much the convener assigns roles and states norms. However, the convener's approach and style will determine the direction in which these issues are worked out by the members, as we will see in the case examples of founders creating companies. This stage can be as short as a pre-meeting lunch or as long as years if there is no informal time provided for building relationships. In any case, it will overlap with the inevitable next stage.

Stage 2, Storming: Resolving Who Will Have Authority and Influence

To sort out their identity, role, influence, and peer relationships, group members begin by explicitly or implicitly confronting and testing each other. That testing inevitably starts around the issue of authority and influence and will show up in confronting the convener and any emergent leader. The convener can "bury" the issue by being a strong chair or relying compulsively on Robert's Rules of Order, but the issue will then surface around disagreements and challenges on the task work itself. It is for this reason that it is not wise to give a brand-new group a task; the members will work out their own identity issues around the task without paying enough attention to the task itself.

The convener or founder can freeze the group at Level 1, leave the door open for spontaneous personalization to arise in the group, or stimulate Level 2 immediately by being more personal himself or herself. Entrepreneur founders will have an enormous influence at this stage according to how they present themselves to the people they recruit, hire, and train as well as the kinds of formal systems they create for how work will be done. This matter is covered in detail in the subsequent chapters.

Analytical Comment. If you are an observer of a new group, the process to focus on is what happens right after someone makes a confrontational remark, challenge, or proposal that requires some response from the group. If someone makes a move to influence the group, does the group ignore, waffle, fight, or accept? Who does what? What does the formal leader do? If the explicit or implicit fighting continues, how does the group move forward?

What the observer will see is that not everyone has the same needs to influence and some members' personalities are less concerned about whether or not they are the leader. The members who are less conflicted about authority will at some point identify the fighting process and name it, thereby forcing some resolution. This enables the group to deal with it explicitly and reach some consensus on how it wants to be led and how it wants to make decisions. With this consensus often comes a feeling of relief, success, and the illusion that the group can now get to work because it believes itself "to be a great group in which everybody now likes each other."

However, as the group tries to work, especially if it is competing with other groups, members discover not only that they don't all like each other but that under the pressure of time and competition some members become more active and others are ignored or shut down, revealing that some members are seen as contributing more than others, that there has grown up a status system within the group. Recognizing this reality moves the group into the next stage of dealing with how the members will treat each other and how personal and intimate the group will become.

Stage 3, Norming: Resolving at Which Level of Relationship We Want to Operate

How does such "recognition" come about? It is again a matter of making explicit what has been going on implicitly by naming it. Some member will say, "Why are we always ignoring what Mary is trying to say," or "Let's just get this done, Joe seems to have the right direction," or "Do we all have to participate equally?" If the group is relatively open, someone might even say, "For this task I think we should let Helen be the leader, because she knows the most about it, but when we need quick action, Pete always seems to get us there faster." "Do we all want to stay task focused and efficient [Level 1], or do we want to get to know each other a bit [Level 2]?"

It is again the persons who are least conflicted about the issue of closeness that will see and name the issue. The convener or leader is also in a critical position to do this by pointing out that the members are all different and have different talents and needs, and that the strength of the group is in the variety rather than the homogeneity. That insight makes it possible for members to replace the *illusion* of "we all like each other" with the *reality* that "we can all understand, accept, and appreciate each other." This insight creates Stage 4.

Stage 4, Performing: The Problem of Task Accomplishment

Only when this stage is reached can the group really use its resources to work effectively. Unfortunately, many groups get stuck either at stage 1, with members continuing to struggle for influence and power, or at stage 2, believing they are great and all like each other. In both cases the members are still thinking about themselves and their role in the group and are, therefore, unable to give full attention to the group's task.

The leader now has to ensure that consensus is reached on what the task is and how best to tackle it, especially with regard to the problem-solving methods, the decision processes, and the assessment method the group should use to track its progress. With this general model in mind, let's now examine how organizations are created and how this creates culture.

The Role of the Founder in the Creation of Cultures

The several cases presented in this chapter illustrate how organizations begin to create cultures through the actions of founders who operate as strong leaders. The cases of Amazon, Facebook, Netflix, and Google can be analyzed the same way, but I did not have enough first-hand information to tell their stories. Sometimes the company tells its own story, but these are generally just the espoused beliefs and values and cannot easily be checked against actual behavior to determine whether they reflect basic assumptions (Schmidt & Rosenberg, 2014).

I am not suggesting that leaders *consciously* set out to teach their new group certain ways of perceiving, thinking, and feeling (though some leaders probably do precisely that). Rather, it is in the nature of entrepreneurial thinking to have strong ideas about what to do and how to do it. Founders generally have well-articulated theories of their own about how groups should work, and they most often select as colleagues and subordinates people who they sense will think like them.

New organizations begin with someone wanting to do something different. If it works out for the group, a new culture is born. Ken Olsen created DEC because he wanted to build small interactive computers that did not exist in the early 1950s. Ciba-Geigy came about because several leaders in Basel saw the potential of joining a film company with an industrial chemical company. The EDB and the Singapore miracle came about because Lee Kuan Yew and his colleagues wanted to change a moribund British colony into a viable third-world city-state economy.

The histories of Apple, Microsoft, Facebook, Google, Hewlett–Packard, Intel, and Amazon all reveal single founding leaders or small groups of founders that wanted to do something different. Another way of saying this is that leadership creates changes; if those changes produce success for a group and the leader's vision and values are adopted, a culture evolves and survives. If someone wants to do something different and either does not get anyone else to go along, or if they go along but the group does not succeed, then we have "failed leadership" and usually never hear about it. We call it leadership only when it succeeds.

When leaders produce a whole new organization, a new political party, or a new religion, we hold them up as "models" of great leadership. However, those founding acts always are nested in macro cultures that already exist so we have to be careful not to overlook the existing cultural conditions that make certain changes possible or necessary. Leadership is necessary, but it succeeds only when the new way fits what was needed.

Founders usually have a major impact on how the group initially defines and solves its external adaptation and internal integration problems. Because they had the original idea, they will typically have their own notion, based on their own cultural history and personality, of how to fulfill the idea. Founders not only have a high level of self-confidence and determination, but they typically have strong assumptions about the nature of the world, the role that organizations play in that world, the nature of human nature and relationships, how truth is arrived at, and how to manage time and space (Schein, 1978, 1983, 2013). They will, therefore, be quite comfortable in imposing those views on their partners and employees as the fledgling organization fights for survival, and they will cling to them until such time as they become unworkable or the group fails and breaks up (Donaldson and Lorsch, 1983).

Example 1: Ken Olsen and DEC Revisited

The culture of DEC was described in detail in Chapter 3. How did DEC's founder, Ken Olsen, create a management system that led eventually to that culture. Olsen developed his beliefs, attitudes, and values in a strong Protestant family and at MIT, where he worked on Whirlwind, the first interactive computer. He and a colleague founded DEC in the mid-1950s because they believed they could build small interactive computers for which there would eventually be a very large market. They were able to convince General Doriot, then head of American Research and Development Corp., to make an initial investment because of their own credibility and the clarity of their basic vision of the company's core mission. After some years the two founders discovered that they did not share a vision of how to build an organization, so Olsen became the CEO (Schein, 2003).

Olsen's assumptions about the nature of the world and how one discovers truth and solves problems were very strong at this stage of DEC's growth and were reflected in his management style. He believed that good ideas could come from anyone regardless of rank or background, but that neither he nor any other individual was smart enough to determine whether a given idea was correct. Olsen felt that open discussion and debate in a group was the only way to test ideas and that one should not take action until the idea had survived the crucible of an active debate. One might have intuitions, but one should not act on them until they had been tested in the intellectual marketplace. Hence, Olsen set up a number of committees and internal boards to ensure that all ideas be discussed and debated before they were acted on.

Olsen bolstered his assumptions with a story that he told frequently to justify his thrusting issues onto groups. He said that he would often refuse to make a decision because, "I'm not that smart; if I really knew what to do I would say so. But when I get into a group of smart people and listen to them debate the idea, I get smart very fast." For Ken Olsen, groups were a kind of extension of his own intelligence, and he often used them to think out loud and get his own ideas straight in his head.

Olsen also believed that one cannot get good implementation of ideas if people do not fully support them and that the best way to get support is to let people debate the issues and convince themselves. He often told the story, "I remember making a decision once; I was walking down that road and turned around, only to discover that there was no one else there." Therefore, on any important decision, Olsen insisted on a wide debate, with many group meetings to test the idea and sell it down the organization and laterally. Only when it appeared that everyone wanted to do it and fully understood it would he "ratify" it. He even delayed important decisions if others were not on board, though he was personally already convinced of the course of action to take. He said that he did not want to be out there leading all by himself and run the risk that the troops were not committed and might disown the decision if it did not work out.

Olsen's theory was that one must give clear and simple individual responsibility and then measure the person strictly on that area of responsibility. Groups could help to make decisions and obtain commitment, but they could not under any circumstances be responsible or accountable. The intellectual testing of ideas, which he encouraged among individuals in group settings, was extended to organizational units if it was not clear which products or markets should be pursued. He was willing to create overlapping product and market units and to let them compete with each other, not realizing, however, that such internal competition eventually undermined openness of communication and made it more difficult for groups to negotiate decisions.

Recognizing that circumstances might change the outcome of even the best-laid plans, Olsen expected his managers to renegotiate those plans as soon as they observed a deviation. Thus, for example, if an annual budget had been set at a certain level and the responsible manager noticed after six months that he would overrun it, he was expected to get the situation under control according to the original assumptions or to come back to senior management to renegotiate. It was absolutely unacceptable either not to know what was happening or to let it happen without informing senior management and renegotiating.

Olsen believed completely in open communication and the ability of people to reach reasonable decisions and make appropriate compromises if they openly confronted the problems and issues, figured out what they wanted to do, and were willing to argue for their solution and honor any commitments they made. He assumed that people have "constructive intent," a rational loyalty to organizational goals and shared commitments. Withholding information, playing power games, competitively trying to win out over another member of the organization on a personal level, blaming others for one's failures, undermining or sabotaging decisions one has agreed to, and going off on one's own without getting others' agreement were all defined as sins and brought public censure.

This "model" of how to run an organization to maximize individual creativity and decision quality worked very successfully in that the company experienced dramatic growth for over 30 years and had exceptionally high morale. However, as the company grew larger, people found that they had less time to negotiate with each other and did not know each other as well personally, making these processes more frustrating. Some of the paradoxes and inconsistencies among the various assumptions came to the surface. For example, to encourage individuals to think for themselves and do what they believed to be the best course for DEC, even if it meant insubordination, clearly ran counter to the dictum that one must honor one's commitments and support decisions that have been made. In practice, the rule of honoring commitments was superseded by the rule of doing only what one believes is right, which meant that sometimes group decisions would not stick.

DEC had increasing difficulty in imposing any kind of discipline on its organizational processes. If a given manager decided that for organizational reasons a more disciplined autocratic approach was necessary, he ran the risk of Olsen's displeasure, because freedom was being taken away from subordinates and that would undermine their entrepreneurial spirit. Olsen felt he was giving his immediate subordinates great freedom, so why would they take it away from the levels below them? At the same time, Olsen recognized that at certain levels of the organization, discipline was essential to getting anything done; the difficulty was in deciding just which areas required discipline and which areas required freedom.

When the company was small and everyone knew everyone else, when "functional familiarity" was high, there was always time to renegotiate, and basic consensus and trust were high enough to ensure that if time pressure forced people to make their own decisions and to be insubordinate, others would, after the fact, mostly agree with the decisions that had been made locally. In other words, if initial decisions made at higher levels did not stick, this did not bother anyone—until the organization became larger and more complex. What was initially a highly adaptive system ideally suited for innovation began to be regarded by more and more members of the organization as disorganization—chaotic and ill adapted to a more mature market.

The company thrived on intelligent, assertive, individualistic people who were willing and able to argue for and sell their ideas. The hiring practices of the company reflected this bias in that each new applicant had to be approved by a large number of interviewers. Over the course of its first decade, the organization tended to hire and keep only people who fitted the assumptions and were willing to live in the system even though it might at times be frustrating. The people who were comfortable in this environment and enjoyed the excitement of building a successful organization found themselves increasingly feeling like members of a family, and they were emotionally treated as such. Strong bonds of mutual support grew up at an interpersonal level, and Ken Olsen functioned symbolically as a brilliant, demanding, but supportive and charismatic father figure.

Analytical Comments. Ken Olsen is an example of an entrepreneur with a clear set of assumptions about how things should be, both at the level of how to relate externally to the environment and the level of how to arrange things internally within the organization. His willingness to be open about his theory and his rewarding and punishing behavior in support of it led to the selection of others who shared the theory and to strong socialization practices that reinforced and perpetuated it. Consequently, the founder's assumptions were reflected in how the organization operated well into the 1990s. DEC's economic collapse and eventual sale to Compaq in the late 1990s also illustrates how a set of assumptions that worked under one set of circumstances may become dysfunctional under other sets of circumstances.

This story raises the whole question of how organizations transition out of the influence of their founders, because the presence of the founder stabilizes the culture and makes it "sacred" in the sense that symbolically changing the culture would be destroying the father figure. That, in turn, raises the issue of who "owns" the company and has the power to replace the founder with a different leader who may have different beliefs and values that are more in line with the new economic and technological realities in the environment. Olsen pretty much chose his own board of directors and listened seriously only to General Doriot, the original investor. Unfortunately Doriot died in 1987 so that when things began to go badly in the late 1980s and early 1990s neither he nor Gordon Bell who had been Olsen's highly respected chief technical adviser were around to influence what had become a dysfunctional economic entity. Bell had a heart attack in 1983 and retired from DEC shortly thereafter. We will return to why and how DEC became dysfunctional in the next chapters when we discuss cultural evolution in organizational midlife.

Example 2: Sam Steinberg and Steinberg's of Canada

Sam Steinberg was an immigrant whose parents had started a corner grocery store in Montreal that became Steinberg's in 1917. His parents, particularly his mother, taught him some basic attitudes toward customers and helped him form the vision that he could succeed in building a successful enterprise. He assumed from the beginning that if he did things right he would succeed and could build a major organization that would bring him and his family a fortune. Ultimately, he built a large chain of supermarkets, department stores, and related businesses that became for many decades a dominant force in Quebec and Ontario.

Sam Steinberg was the major ideological force in his company throughout its history, and he continued to impose his assumptions on the company until his death in his late seventies. He assumed that his primary mission was to supply a high-quality, reliable product to customers in clean, attractive surroundings and that his customers' needs were the primary consideration in all major decisions. There are many stories about how Sam Steinberg, as a young man operating the corner grocery store with his wife, gave customers credit and thus displayed trust in them. He always took products back if there was the slightest complaint, and he kept his store absolutely spotless to inspire customer confidence in his products. Each of these attitudes later became a major policy in his chain of stores and was taught and reinforced by close personal supervision.

Sam Steinberg believed that only personal examples and close supervision would ensure adequate performance by subordinates. He would show up at his stores unexpectedly, inspect even minor details, and then—by personal example, by stories of how other stores were solving the problems identified, by articulating rules, and by exhortation—would "teach" the staff what they should be doing. He often lost his temper and berated subordinates who did not follow the rules or principles he had laid down. Sam Steinberg expected his store managers to be highly visible, to be very much on top of their own jobs, to supervise closely in the same way he did, to set a good example, and to teach subordinates the "right way" to do things.

Most of the founding group in this company consisted of Sam Steinberg's three brothers, and one "lieutenant," who was not a family member, was recruited early and became, in addition to the founder—the main leader and culture carrier. He shared the founder's basic assumptions about "visible management" and set up formal systems to ensure that those principles became the basis for operating realities. After Sam Steinberg's death this man became the CEO and continued to perpetuate those same management practices.

Sam Steinberg assumed that one could win in the marketplace only by being highly innovative and technically in the forefront. He always encouraged his managers to try new approaches, brought in a variety of consultants who advocated new approaches to human resource management, started selection and development programs through assessment centers long before other companies tried this approach, and traveled to conventions and other businesses where new technological innovations were being displayed. This passion for innovation resulted in Steinberg's being one of the first companies in the supermarket industry to introduce bar-code technology and one of the first to use assessment centers in selecting store managers.

Steinberg was always willing to experiment to improve the business. His view of truth and reality was that one had to find them wherever one could; therefore, one must be open to one's environment and never take it for granted that one has all the answers. If things worked, Sam Steinberg encouraged their adoption; if they did not, he ordered them to be dropped. He trusted only those managers who operated by assumptions similar to his own and he clearly had favorites to whom he delegated more authority.

Power and authority in this organization remained very centralized, in that everyone knew that Sam Steinberg or his chief lieutenant, Jack Levine, could and would override decisions made by division or other unit managers without consultation and often in a very peremptory fashion. The ultimate source of power, the voting shares of stock, were owned entirely by Sam Steinberg and his wife, so that after his death his wife and his three daughters were in total control of the company. Though he was interested in developing good managers throughout the organization, he never shared ownership through granting stock options. He paid his key managers very well, but his assumption was that ownership was strictly a family matter, to the point that he was not even willing to share stock with Jack Levine, his close friend, and practically co-builder of the company. Because he was nested in a macro culture in which family was sacred, he wanted only his children to inherit ownership.

Sam Steinberg introduced several members of his own family into the firm and gave them key managerial positions. As the firm diversified, family members were made heads of divisions, often with relatively little management experience. If a family member performed poorly, he or she would be bolstered by having a good manager introduced under him or her. If the operation then improved, the family member would likely be given the credit. If things continued badly, the family member would be moved out, but with various face-saving excuses.

Though he wanted open communication and a high level of trust among all members of the organization, he never realized that his own assumptions about the role of the family and the correct way to manage were, to a large degree, in conflict with each other. He did not perceive his own conflicts and inconsistencies and hence could not understand why some of his best young managers failed to respond to his competitive incentives and even left the company. He thought he was adequately motivating them and could not see that for some of them the political climate, the absence of stock options, and the arbitrary rewarding of family members made their own career progress too uncertain. Sam Steinberg was perplexed and angry about much of this, blaming the young managers while holding onto his own assumptions and conflicts.

Several points should be noted about the description given thus far. By definition, something can become part of the culture only if it works in the sense of making the organization successful and reducing the anxiety of the members. Steinberg's assumptions about how things should be done were congruent with the kind of environment in which he operated, so he and the founding group received strong reinforcement for those assumptions.

Following Sam Steinberg's death, the company experienced a long period of cultural turmoil because of the vacuum created by both his absence and the retirement of several other key culture carriers, but the basic philosophy of how to run stores was thoroughly embedded and was carried on by Steinberg's chief lieutenant. After he retired, a period of instability set in, marked by the discovery that some of the managers who had been developed under Sam Steinberg were not as strong and capable as had been assumed. Because none of Sam Steinberg's daughters or their spouses were able to take over the business decisively, various other family members continued to run the company. None of them had Sam Steinberg's business skills, so an outside person was brought in to run the company. This person failed because he could not adapt to the culture and to the family.

After two more failures with CEOs drawn from other companies, the family turned to a manager who had originally been with the company and had subsequently made a fortune outside the company in various real estate enterprises. This manager stabilized the business for a time because he had more credibility by virtue of his prior history and his knowledge of how to handle family members. Under his leadership some of the original assumptions began to evolve in new directions, but disagreement among the three daughters caused new turmoil, lawsuits, and the eventual sale of the company in 1989, as was documented in a published family history (Gibbon & Hadekel, 1990).

Analytical Comments. One clear lesson from this example is that a strong culture does not survive if the main culture carriers depart and if the bulk of the members of the organization are experiencing some degree of conflict because of a mixed message that emanates from the leaders during the growth period. Steinberg's had a strong culture, but Sam Steinberg's own conflicts became embedded in that culture, creating conflict and ultimately a lack of stability. Those conflicts could be attributed to his "personality," but it is equally plausible to say that he was nested in his Jewish macro culture at a time when launching an enterprise from humble beginnings hinged on very tight family connections and efforts by all members of the family to make the enterprise work.

The unfortunate reality that none of his three daughters had either the inclination or the talent to take over the business also clearly influenced the outcome. I was involved for several years in an effort to "coach" one of the husbands who was being tried as CEO, but he also had neither the talent nor the motivation to function in this role. It is of incidental historical interest that at the same time Steinberg's was founded (1914), the Stop and Shop supermarket chain was being launched in New England by Irving Rabb, who also had only daughters. One of them, however, married a man who was a highly motivated and competent manager, leading to longer-range success for this organization.

Example 3: Fred Smithfield: a "Serial Entrepreneur"

After graduating from MIT's Sloan School, Fred Smithfield built a financial service organization, using sophisticated financial analysis techniques in an area of the country where insurance companies, mutual funds, and banks were only beginning to use such techniques. He was the conceptualizer and salesman, but once he had the idea for a new kind of service organization, he found others to invest in, build, and manage it. He believed that he should put only a very small amount of his own money into each enterprise because if he could not convince others to put up money, maybe there was something wrong with the idea.

Smithfield always started with the initial assumption that he did not know enough about the market to gamble with his own money, and he reinforced this assumption publicly by telling a story about the one enterprise in which he had failed. He had opened a retail store in a Midwestern city to sell ocean fish because he loved it. He assumed that others felt as he did, trusted his own judgment about what the market would want, and failed. He realized that if he had tried to get others to invest in the enterprise, he would have learned that his own tastes were not necessarily a good predictor of what others would want.

Because Smithfield saw himself as a creative conceptualizer but not as a manager, he not only kept his financial investment minimal but did not get very personally involved with his enterprises. Once he put together the package, he found people whom he could trust to manage the new organization. These were usually people like himself who were fairly open in their approach to business and not too concerned with imposing their own assumptions about how things should be done.

His creative needs were such that after a decade or so of founding financial service organizations, he turned his attention to real estate ventures; he became a lobbyist on behalf of an environmental organization, tried his hand at politics for a while, and then went back into business, first with an oil company and later with a diamond mining company. Eventually, he became interested in teaching, and ended up at a Midwestern business school developing a curriculum on entrepreneurship.

One can infer that Smithfield's assumptions about concrete goals, the best means to achieve them, how to measure results, and how to repair things when they were going wrong were essentially pragmatic. Whereas Sam Steinberg had a strong need to be involved in everything, Smithfield seemed to lose interest once the new organization was on its feet and functioning. His theory seemed to be to have a clear concept of the basic mission, test it by selling it to the investors, bring in good people who understood what the mission was, and then leave them alone to implement and run the organization, using only financial criteria as ultimate performance measures.

If Smithfield had assumptions about how an organization should be run internally, he kept them to himself. The cultures that each of his enterprises developed therefore had more to do with the assumptions of the people he brought in to manage them. As it turned out, those assumptions varied a good deal. Moreover, if one analyzed Smithfield Enterprises as a total organization, one would find little evidence of a "corporate" culture, because there was no group that had a shared history and shared learning experiences. But each of the separate enterprises would have a culture that derived from the beliefs, values, and assumptions of their Smithfield-appointed managers.

Analytical Comments. This brief case makes the point that founders do not automatically impose themselves on their organizations. It depends on their personal needs to externalize their various assumptions. For Smithfield, the ultimate personal validation lay in having each of his enterprises become financially successful and in his ability to continue to form creative new ones.

If we examine entrepreneurship in today's innovation areas such as Silicon Valley, we see another pattern of culture creation that does not depend on the founder's beliefs and values. It is similar to the Smithfield pattern except that it is the investors, functioning as owners, who decide when during the growth cycle to replace the founder with a professional manager. It is the new general manager who then begins to build the culture around the founding values of the technical entrepreneur who had been fired.

The culture that we eventually see in a mature organization may therefore be the result of the work of several leaders over a long period of time. Without knowing the history we would potentially make erroneous attributions, as the following examples illustrate.

Example 4: Steve Jobs and Apple

The story of Apple has by now been told many times in books and movies, but some of the cultural issues bear repeating. Apple was founded in 1976 by Steve Jobs and Steve Wozniak. Both grew up in the "revolutionary" era of the 1960s in the San Francisco area. Jobs was the one with the strongest sense of a mission, of revolutionizing how people would use computers, whereas Wozniak provided much of the technical talent. Their initial intention was to create products for children in the education market and products that would be fun and easy to use by "yuppies." Their base was clearly technical, as in the case of DEC, and this showed up in the aggressively individualistic "do your own thing" mentality that I encountered there when I did some consulting in the early 1990s.

From its founding until 1983 the company had two other CEOs—Michael Scott, an experienced manager from another company, and Mike Markkula, an early investor and friend. Still, Jobs was clearly the "moral compass" in having the strongest feelings about how the company culture should evolve. When Apple attempted to become more market oriented, Jobs agreed in 1983 to bring in John Scully from PepsiCo. Scully was not able to impose himself while Jobs was still there and insisted on firing Jobs in 1985.

Jobs, embittered but not cowed, started another computer company, NeXT, and became involved with Pixar, the computer-animated film company. Scully was initially successful but ended up in great difficulty, which led to his firing in 1993. It was said that Scully never earned the respect of the Apple technical community, suggesting that at the core of the Apple culture was technical creativity, simplicity, elegance, and aesthetic appeal, values that all seemed to derive from Steve Jobs.

Apple struggled with two more CEOs, Michael Spindler and Gilbert Amelio, but was near bankruptcy when the board decided to buy NeXT, thereby bringing Jobs back into the fold. He was installed as CEO in 1997, from which point the company rose to its imposing position today and was able to transition to its current CEO Tim Cook, an inside promotion.

Analytical Comments. The important culture question is, did Apple have the same culture throughout all this time, based essentially on the beliefs and values of its founders, even as it evolved through many other CEOs? It is significant that Apple eventually returned to its roots in bringing back Steve Jobs. If one observes the direction of Apple from 2009 on, one can see a return to those roots of creating products such as the smaller and lighter desktop and laptop computers, the iPhone, the iPod for music, and the iChat camera for video conferencing—products that are esthetically pleasing, easy to use, and fun. The attractive design of products and the proliferation of very attractive user-friendly stores to display them suggest that Apple now has very much a marketing orientation but that this orientation had to be combined with its technical skills, something that perhaps only Steve Jobs could push.

Apple now enjoys great business success, which has expressed itself in the decision to build a monumental circular headquarters building in Cupertino, CA. Apple is also now an old and very large company nested in a different and more complex international environment that will inevitably force its culture to evolve.

Example 5: IBM—Thomas Watson Sr. and His Son

Many people point out that IBM did much better in its efforts to revitalize its business in the 1990s by bringing in an outside marketing executive, Lou Gerstner. Why might this have worked better than Scully in Apple? Part of the answer is cultural. Where Apple had technical founders and a whole series of CEOs, IBM was founded by Tom Watson Sr., a salesman in the National Cash Register Company, and was managed for its first 50 years by that founder and his son Tom Watson Jr. (Watson and Petre, 1990).

The insight that cultural analysis provides is that IBM was not founded by a technical entrepreneur and never built an engineering-based organization in the first place. Tom Watson Sr. was a sales and marketing manager who thought like a salesman and marketer throughout his career, and his son, Tom Watson Jr., had the same kind of marketing mentality. Building a clear image with the public became an IBM hallmark, symbolized by its insistence on blue suits and white shirts, for all its salespeople. The sales organization met regularly and engaged in various kinds of bonding rituals including singing songs together and, in various other ways, forging a clear identity of who they were and why they were what they were.

Tom Watson Jr. clearly had the wisdom to become strong technically, but the deeper cultural assumptions were always derived more from sales and marketing. Is it any surprise, then, that an outstanding marketing executive would be accepted as an outsider to help the company regain its competitive edge and that he would succeed, not by really changing the culture but by reinvigorating it around its original identity (Gerstner, 2002).

Example 6: Hewlett and Packard

What of HP? Dave Packard and Bill Hewlett both came out of Stanford with the intention of building a technical business, initially in measurement and instrumentation technology (Packard, 1995). Computers were brought in only later as adjuncts to this core technology, and this led to the discovery that the kinds of people working in these technologies were different from each other, and to some degree incompatible. Ultimately this led to the splitting off of Agilent to pursue the original technology while HP evolved computers, printers, and various other related products.

HP's growth and success reflected an effective division of labor between Hewlett, who was primarily a technical leader, and Packard, who was more of a business leader. Their ability to collaborate well with each other was undoubtedly one basis for "teamwork" becoming such a central value in the "HP way." What we know of Packard's managerial style contrasts strongly with Ken Olsen's, in that HP formed divisions early on in its history, put much more public emphasis on teamwork and consensus, even though individual competition remained as the deeper covert assumption. HP became much more dogmatic about standardizing processes throughout the company and was much more formal and deliberate than DEC, which made the computer types at HP uncomfortable.

HP's and DEC's views of teamwork illustrate the importance of defining abstractions like "teamwork" very carefully in any cultural analysis. Teamwork in HP was defined as coming to agreement and not fighting too hard for your own point of view if the consensus was headed in a different direction In DEC, however, teamwork was defined as fighting for your own point of view until you either convinced others or truly changed your own mind. As I learned during some consulting with engineering managers in the computing arm of HP, the HP way required "being nice" and reaching consensus in group meetings, but "the decisions did not stick." Instead, one had to follow up after the meeting and make individual deals with each of the people on whom one was dependent. The espoused values were "the HP way," but the basic assumption was that as in other U.S. companies it was individual performance and competitive skill that produced results and that was, in the end, rewarded.

Subsequent to the splitting off of Agilent, the most significant event in the HP story is the introduction of an outsider, Carly Fiorina, as CEO. It appears that her strategy for making HP a successful global player in a variety of computer-related markets was to *evolve* the HP culture by the mega-merger with Compaq, acquiring in that process a large segment of DEC employees who had remained at Compaq. Because the computer market had become commoditized, becoming an efficient low-cost producer of commodities such as printers and ink became strategically advantageous but required the abandonment of some of the original values of the HP way.

One can speculate that Fiorina was brought in as an outsider to start the change process, but that her replacement after some years by homegrown executives reflected a desire to keep parts of the HP culture even as some elements evolved. Under current CEO Meg Whitman, a further splitting of the company has occurred, suggesting that we are now dealing not with a single HP corporate culture but a set of subcultures reflecting the different products and services that HP now offers.

Summary and Conclusions

The goal of this chapter is to introduce the broad concept of cultural beginnings by first showing a model of the basic issues that any new group has to deal with as it evolves its own culture, then showing how leaders in the role of founders start this process. Basically they impose some of their own beliefs, values, assumptions, and behavioral rules on their subordinates; if the organization is successful, they become taken for granted and a culture is born.

Founders are not likely to be conscious of the dynamic processes of group formation around the problems of authority and intimacy, but by the kinds of structures and processes they create, they are de facto dealing with those dynamics. In the following chapters we examine what happens with success, growth, and age.

Suggestions for Readers

1. Think of one or two organizations that interest you and look up their histories on the internet.
2. If there are biographies of founders listed, consider reading those to deepen your understanding of how cultures form.

Implications for Founders and Leaders

The above stories and what we now know about the many start-ups and new companies that have been created in the last few decades suggest some important lessons that budding entrepreneurs and founders need to learn from.

Your new ideas have to fit in with existing needs in the macro culture. Part of Ken Olsen's motivation derived from the cold-war need to develop interactive computing so that missiles that might have been fired by the Soviet Union could be tracked in real time. Steve Jobs sensed that computer users were frustrated by complex interfaces and set about to simplify them, something that was once called creating "toys for yuppies." Jeff Bezos created Amazon in a technological culture that was already rapidly evolving e-business and e-commerce, and in a consumer climate in which choice and rapid delivery were already high values.

Everything you say and do will be observed and will influence how the group will operate. Because a new group will be anxious, the members will be hypervigilant in observing your behavior. If you send conflicting signals, you will undermine the group's capacity to function in the future.

Every group has to go through the growth stages around inclusion, identity, authority, and intimacy. Provide enough opportunities for reflection, process analysis, and informal activities to allow these processes to occur before expecting total task engagement.

9

HOW EXTERNAL ADAPTATION AND INTERNAL
INTEGRATION BECOME CULTURE

Culture is defined by what a group has learned in solving its problems of external adaptation and internal integration. In the previous chapter I reviewed how founders begin their organization and what socio-psychological group issues they have to deal with whether or not they are aware of them. In this chapter we now turn to what founders have to be *explicitly* aware of in building an organization. Their purpose may or may not be to "create a culture," but in building the organization or business, they have to attend explicitly to certain issues that become eventually part of the culture. Why differentiate "external" from "internal"?

Groups and organizations of various sorts have been studied intensely since the 1940s, in part to better understand the events of World War II and partly to understand some of the anomalies of U.S. history such as slavery and racism. Parallel studies were going on in the U.K. in the Tavistock Institute and Clinic as that country reconstructed its ravaged industry after the world war. Both sets of studies reach the same basic conclusion, that all groups, whether small decision-making units or entire nations, have the same two fundamental problems: (1) how to organize themselves to deal with the environments in which they exist (what I have called the *external* problems of survival) and (2) how to organize themselves *internally* to deal with the inevitable human problems that arise in collective life.

Other terms and concepts that deal with the same dichotomy are "task and group maintenance," the "double bottom line," the "balanced score card," and "strategy and mission vs. structure and process" (Blake & Mouton, 1964; Kaplan & Norton, 1992). The cultural reality is, of course, that all of these tasks must be attended to and they are highly interconnected, which has led to the useful concept of "socio-technical systems" and looking at culture holistically. Understanding the consequences of how each of these issues is dealt with during the founding and growing period becomes crucial when later, in organizational midlife, change leaders find themselves trying to change elements of the culture and forget that all facets of how the organization operates externally and internally are now part of its culture and have come to be a pattern that hangs together—a socio-technical system.

In a sense these categories reflect what might be in a basic course on "organization design." In discussing them briefly in this chapter, I am trying to highlight those aspects of each category that have a special impact on culture formation. I will assume that the organization has now been founded and has created a culture, but I will identify the issues that arise culturally around the creation of each of the categories shown in the following text.

The Socio-Technical Issues of Organizational Growth and Evolution

External Adaptation

When reduced to their essence, the problems of external adaptation are

- **Mission:** Obtaining a shared understanding of core mission, primary task, and manifest and latent functions
- **Goals:** Developing consensus on goals, as derived from the core mission
- **Means:** Developing consensus on the means to be used to attain the goals, such as the organizational structure, division of labor, reward systems, and authority system
- **Measurement:** Developing consensus on the criteria to be used in measuring how well the group is fulfilling its goals, such as the information and control system
- **Correcting and repairing:** Developing consensus on the appropriate remedial or repair strategies to be used if goals are not being met

Internal Integration

When reduced to their essence, the problems of internal integration are

- **Language:** Creating a common language and conceptual categories
- **Identity and boundaries:** Defining group boundaries and criteria for inclusion
- **Authority:** Reaching consensus on the distributing power, authority, and status
- **Trust and openness:** Developing norms of relating to each other
- **Rewards and punishments:** Defining and allocating rewards and punishments
- **The unexplainable:** Developing concepts to explain the unexplainable

To discuss these issues we have to analyze them one at a time, but in reality as a founder builds an organization, he or she is dealing with both sets of issues all the time because the resolution for each issue is strongly embedded or nested in the macro cultures surrounding the new organization. Because a common language and common categories of thought derive initially from the country in which the new organization forms, language and thought must be our starting point.

Language and Categories of Thought

To interact at all, humans need a common language and shared categories for how to perceive and think about themselves and their environment. I explored this at the macro-cultural level in Chapter 6 and only need to point out here that when a founder launches an organization it is not enough to have a common macro language; the meanings of the terms used in the founder's vision also have to become shared. The young engineers hired by DEC had to learn what Ken Olsen meant by "do the right thing," and one of his later quips was completely misunderstood because of lack of context. Olsen was quoted as saying, "Who would want a computer in their home," which was taken to be a dismissal of the PC and other desktop computers. The context was that he made that comment when everyone was advocating extensive computer control of all the household appliances and, thereby, practically automating domestic life, something Olsen was indeed against. In fact, he had a personal computer at home that he used all the time.

Founders often develop special jargon and acronyms to distinguish their organization from others, all of which can be very confusing to newcomers, especially when the language of the organization's mission is itself obscured by ambiguous language.

Mission and Reason to Be

Every new group or organization must develop a shared concept of its ultimate survival problem, from which its most basic sense of core mission, primary task, or "reason to be" is usually derived. In most business organizations, this shared definition focuses on the issue of economic survival and growth, which in turn involves the maintenance of good relationships with the major stakeholders of the organization, including

- The investors and stockholders
- The suppliers of the materials needed to produce
- The managers and employees
- The community and government
- The customers willing to pay for the product or service

Many studies of organizations have shown that the key to long-range growth and survival is to keep the needs of these constituencies in some kind of balance, and that the mission of the organization, as a set of beliefs about its core competencies and basic functions in society, is usually a reflection of this balance (Donaldson & Lorsch, 1983; Kotter & Heskett, 1992; Porras & Collins, 1994; Christensen, 1997; O'Reilly and Tushman, 2016). It has been a mistake to think in terms of a total focus on any one of these constituencies, because all of them together make up the environment in which the organization must succeed.

In religious, educational, social, and governmental organizations, the core mission or primary task is clearly different, but the proposition that the

mission ultimately derives from a balancing of the needs of different stakeholders is the same. Thus, for example, the mission of a university must
balance the learning needs of the students (which include housing, feed-
ing, and often acting as *in loco parentis*), the needs of the faculty to teach
and conduct research to further knowledge, the needs of the community to
have a repository for knowledge and skill, the needs of the financial investors to have a viable institution, and, ultimately, even the needs of society
to have an institution to facilitate the transition of late adolescents into
the labor market and to sort them into skill groups.

Manifest and Latent Functions. Though core missions or primary tasks
are usually stated in terms of a single constituency, such as customers, a
more useful way to think about ultimate or core mission is to change the
question to "What is our function in the larger scheme of things?" or "What
justifies our continued existence?" Posing the question this way reveals that
most organizations have multiple functions reflecting multiple stakeholders. Some of these functions are public justifications or espoused values—
what have been called by sociologists "manifest functions," while others
are "latent functions" that are taken for granted but not publicly spoken of
(Merton, 1957).

For example, the manifest function of a school system is to educate,
but a close examination of what goes on in school systems suggests several
latent functions as well: (1) to keep children (young adults) off the streets
and out of the labor market until there is room for them and they have
some relevant skills, (2) to sort and group the next generation into talent
and skill categories according to the needs of the society, and (3) to enable
the various occupations associated with the school system to survive and
maintain their professional autonomy.

In examining the manifest and latent functions, it will be recognized
by the organization's leaders and members that to survive, the organization must to some degree fulfill all of these functions. We may then
find in a cultural analysis of a given organization that some of the most
important shared assumptions concern how to fulfill the *latent* functions
without publicly admitting the existence of those functions. For example,
Ken Olsen admitted that his strategy of dividing the units of DEC across
the four New England states was motivated, in part, by his recognition

that putting everything in one or two states would disadvantage the labor market in the other states, something he did not want to do but also could not publicly admit.

Identity and Latent Functions.   Some culture researchers have advocated that it is useful to think in terms of the organization's "identity," and to propose that survival and growth hinge on being able to connect this identity, "who we are and what is our purpose," with the market conditions, "what the customer needs, wants, and can afford" (Schultz, 1995; Hatch & Schultz, 2004, 2008). They propose that corporate survival depends very much on developing a "brand" that links the organization's basic competencies with market needs and provides, at the same time, a sense of purpose and engagement to employees. Being "in" the organization then is not only an employment contract but some kind of commitment by the employee to further the organization's sense of purpose.

The espoused values will, of course, emphasize the manifest functions, which leads to complexities of measurement as we will see subsequently. For example, universities are often criticized for not being cost-effective around their primary educational mission, but the critic is often not taking into account the cost of fulfilling various _latent_ functions that are also part of the mission. Core mission and public identity thus become complex multifunctional issues because some of the functions must remain latent to protect the manifest identity of the organization. For a university to announce publicly its babysitting, sorting, and professional autonomy functions would be embarrassing, but these functions often play an important role in determining the activities of the organization and become part of the DNA of the culture that will resist change. Note that when we assess an organization's culture, it is the taken-for-granted latent functions that will be the hardest to "measure."

Overall corporate culture dimensions will evolve around these issues, and subculture dimensions will show up in the subunits whose interests are involved in the latent functions. The importance of these latent functions may not surface until an organization is forced to contemplate closing or moving. Then subculture conflicts may erupt if the interests of some of these groups become threatened. The most common example is, of course, how the subcultures of labor organizations surface when companies find a need to downsize or move. For example, one possible explanation of why General Motors abandoned its successful Saturn car program was the need to maintain relations with its unions. What often seems like an irrational or even stupid decision by an organization becomes understandable when we examine what latent functions are being served by the decision.

Strategy Is Part of Culture. Mission relates directly to what organizations call "strategy." To fulfill its manifest and latent functions, the organization evolves shared assumptions about its "reason to be" and formulates long-range plans to fulfill those functions. That involves decisions about products and services and will reflect the "identity" of the organization. The shared assumptions about "who we are" become an important element of the organization's culture and *will limit the strategic options available to the organization*. Strategy consultants are often frustrated when their recommendations are not acted on. They forget that unless those recommendations are consistent with the organization's assumptions about itself, they will not make sense to the insiders and hence will not be implemented.

For example, at one stage in the evolution of Ciba-Geigy, I heard lengthy debates among top managers on the question of whether Ciba-Geigy should design and produce "any" product, provided it could be sold at a profit, or whether designs and products should be limited to what some senior executives believed to be "sound" or "valuable" products, based on their conception of what their company had originally been built on, and what their unique talents were. The debate focused on whether or not to keep Airwick, which made air fresheners to remove pet or other odors.

Airwick had been acquired in the firm's U.S. subsidiary to help Ciba-Geigy become more competent in consumer-oriented marketing. At one of the annual meetings of top management, the president of the U.S. subsidiary was very proudly displaying some TV ads for their new product "Carpet Fresh." I was sitting next to a senior member of the internal board, a Swiss researcher who had developed several of the company's key chemical products. He was visibly agitated by the TV ads and finally leaned over to me and loudly whispered, "You know, Schein, those things are not even *products*."

In subsequent debates about whether or not to sell Airwick (even though it was financially sound and profitable), I finally understood this comment when it was revealed that Ciba-Geigy could not stomach the image of being a company that produced something as seemingly trivial as an air freshener. Thus a major strategic decision to sell Airwick was made on the basis of the company's culture, not on marketing or financial grounds. Ciba-Geigy sold Airwick and thereby affirmed the assumption that they should only be in businesses that had a clear scientific base and that dealt with major global problems such as disease and starvation. This was articulated as a strategic principle that should and did govern future acquisitions.

In summary, one of the most central elements of any culture is the assumptions the members of the organization share about their identity and ultimate mission or functions. These are not necessarily very conscious but can surface if one probes the strategic decisions that the organization makes. Organizational analyses that show separate boxes for "culture" and "strategy" are making a fundamental conceptual error. Strategy is an integral part of the culture.

Issues around Goals Derived from the Mission

Consensus on the core mission and identity does not automatically guarantee that the key members of the organization will have common goals or that the various subcultures will be appropriately aligned to fulfill the mission. The basic subcultures in any organization may, in fact, be unwittingly working at cross purposes to some elements of the mission. The mission is often understood but not well articulated. To achieve consensus on goals, the group needs a common language and shared assumptions about the basic logistical operations by which one moves from something as abstract or general as a sense of mission to the concrete goals of designing, manufacturing, and selling an actual product or service within specified and agreed-on cost and time constraints. Clearly articulated goals become one of the key elements of the espoused part of the culture.

For example, in DEC there was a clear consensus on the mission of bringing out a line of technically sophisticated innovative products that would "win in the marketplace," but this consensus did not solve for senior management the problem of how to allocate resources among different product development groups, nor did it specify how best to market such products. Mission and strategy can be rather timeless, whereas goals have to be formulated for what to do next year, next month, and tomorrow. Goals concretize the mission and facilitate the decisions on means. In that process, goal formulation also often reveals unresolved issues or lack of sub-culture consensus around deeper issues.

In DEC, the debate around which products to support and how to support them revealed a deep lack of semantic agreement on how to think about "marketing." For example, one group thought that marketing meant better image advertising in national magazines so that more people would recognize the name of the company. Another group was convinced that marketing meant better advertising in technical journals. One group thought it meant developing the next generation of products, while yet another group emphasized merchandizing and sales support as the key elements of marketing.

Because operational goals have to be more precise, organizations typically work out their issues of mission and identity in the context of deciding annual or longer-range goals. To really understand cultural assumptions, one must be careful not to confuse these short-run assumptions about goals with assumptions about mission. Ciba-Geigy's concern with being only in businesses that make "science-based, useful products" did not become evident in its discussions about business goals until it hit a strategic issue such as whether or not to buy another company.

In fact, one way of looking at what we mean by "strategy" is to realize that strategy concerns the evolution of the basic mission, whereas operational goals reflect the short-run tactical survival issues that the organization identifies. Thus, when a company gets into basic strategy discussions, it is usually trying to assess in a more fundamental way the relationship between its sense of its mission and its operational goals. For example, Singapore's long-range strategy to become economically successful was converted into a variety of short-run goals such as keeping the city clean, building housing for everyone, creating a scholarship program, and so on.

In summary, goals can be defined at several levels of abstraction and in different time horizons. Is our goal to be profitable at the end of next quarter, to make 10 sales next month, or to call 12 potential customers tomorrow? Only as consensus is reached on such matters, leading to solutions that work repeatedly, can we begin to think of the goals of an organization as potential cultural elements. Once such consensus is reached, however, the assumptions about goals become a very strong element of that group's culture.

Issues around the Means: Structure, Systems, and Processes

Some of the most important and most invisible elements of an organizational culture are the shared basic assumptions that evolve about how things should be done, how the mission is to be achieved, how goals are to be met. Founding leaders usually *impose* structure, systems, and processes based on their own beliefs and values. If the organization is successful, they become shared and parts of the culture. And once those processes have become taken for granted they become the elements of the culture that may be the hardest to change.

The processes a group adopts reflect the national and occupational macro cultures in which it exists. A striking example occurred in our MIT Sloan Fellows program where young high-potential managers who came for a full-year master's degree program would be given an exercise to *build an organization*. Groups of about 15 were each made into a "company that was to produce two-line jingles to be put on greeting cards for birthdays and anniversaries." The products were "bought" by the exercise administrators, and the companies were measured on their output. Without fail every group immediately chose some executives, a sales manager, a marketing manager, proofreaders, supervisors, and, *finally*, a couple of writers. Only upon much reflection and analysis did it occur to any group that the best way to win was to have 15 writers. They all automatically fell into the typical hierarchical command and control structure that mirrored primarily the occupational macro culture of management that they came from.

The tendency to fall back on what one already knows does facilitate getting consensus quickly on the means by which goals will be met. Such consensus is important, because the means that are to be used have to do with day-to-day behavior and coordinated action. One can have ambiguous goals, but if anything is to happen at all, one must agree on how to structure the organization and how to design, finance, build, and sell the products or services. From the particular pattern of these agreements will emerge not only the "style" of the organization but the basic design of tasks, division of labor, reporting and accountability structures, reward and incentive systems, control systems, and information systems.

The skills, technology, and knowledge that a group acquires in its effort to cope with its environment then also become part of its culture if there is consensus on what those skills are and how to use them. For example, in his study of several companies that made the world's best flutes, Cook (1992) shows that for generations the craftsmen were able to produce flutes that artists would recognize immediately as having been made by a particular company, but neither management nor the craftsmen could describe exactly what they had done to make them so recognizable. It was embedded in the processes of manufacturing and reflected a set of learned skills that could be passed on for generations through an apprentice system yet was not formally describable.

In evolving the means by which the group will accomplish its goals, many of the internal issues that the group must deal with are partially settled. The external problem of division of labor will structure who will get to know whom and who will be in authority. The work system of the group will define its boundaries and its rules for membership. The particular beliefs and talents of the founders and leaders of the group will determine which functions become dominant as the group evolves and which occupations will acquire status. For example, engineers founding companies based on their inventions will create very different kinds of internal structures than venture capitalists creating organizations by putting technical and marketing talent under the direction of financially driven or marketing-oriented leaders.

In Ciba-Geigy the founders believed that solutions to problems resulted from hard thought, scientific research, and careful checking of that research in the marketplace. From the beginning this company had clearly defined research roles and distinguished them sharply from managerial roles.

In DEC a norm developed that the only turf one really owns is one's accountability for certain tasks and accomplishments. Budget, physical space, subordinates, and other resources were really seen as common organizational property over which one had only influence. Others in the organization could try to influence the accountable manager or his or her subordinates, but there were no formal boundaries or "walls."

In Singapore the leaders created a formal mechanism for implementation in creating the Economic Development Board, giving it the personal and financial resources it required and supporting its activities in whatever way that was needed, while at the same time using strong autocratic methods to create an internal environment that would support the strategy.

In summary, as cultural assumptions form around the means by which goals are to be accomplished, they will create the routines and behavioral regularities that will become some of the visible artifacts of the culture. Once these regularities and patterns are in place, they become a source of stability for members and are, therefore, strongly adhered to.

Issues around Measurement

All groups and organizations need to know how they are doing in attaining their goals and periodically need to check to determine whether they are performing in line with their mission. This process involves three areas in which the group needs to achieve consensus, leading to cultural dimensions that later drop out of awareness and become tacit assumptions. Consensus must be achieved on *what to measure, how to measure it, and what to do when corrections are needed.* The cultural elements that form around each of these issues often become the primary focus for what newcomers to the organization will be concerned about, because such measurements inevitably become linked to how each employee is doing his or her job. These issues become equally important to leaders because of the reality, as we will see in the following chapter, that what leaders pay attention to and measure becomes one of the primary mechanisms by which they embed cultural elements.

What and How to Measure. Once the group is performing, it must reach consensus on how to judge its own performance to know what kind of remedial action to take when things do not go as expected. Setting goals and agreeing on what kind of feedback is needed to check on goal progress becomes one of the most fundamental aspects of designing any task. Feedback is not any old comment or observation of "how things are going"; feedback is specific information on whether the results are on target or are deviating from the target. Measurement, therefore, has to be defined by the consensus on targets and goals. Such consensus need not be a formal quantitative measurement, however. For example, we have noted that early in DEC's history the evaluation of engineering projects hinged on whether certain key engineers in the company "liked" the product. The company assumed that internal acceptance was an acceptable surrogate for external acceptance. At the same time, if several competing engineering groups each liked what they were designing, the criterion shifted to "letting the market decide." These criteria could work in tandem as long as there were enough resources to support all the projects, because DEC was growing at a rapid rate.

At the Wellmade flute company, evaluation was done at each node in the production process, so that by the time an instrument reached the end of the line it was likely to pass inspection and to be acceptable to the artist. If a craftsman at a given position did not like what he felt or saw or heard, he simply passed the instrument back to the preceding craftsman; the norm was that it would be reworked without resentment. Each person trusted the person in the next position (Cook, personal communication, 1992).

Cook also found a similar process in a French brandy company. Not only was each step evaluated by an expert, but the ultimate role of "taster"—the person who makes the final determination of when a batch is ready—could be held only by a male son of the previous taster. In this company the last taster had no sons. Rather than pass the role on to the eldest daughter, it was passed on to a nephew, on the shared assumption that female taste preferences were in some fundamental way different from male taste preferences!

I was involved at one point in the 1980s with the exploration and production division management of the U.S. Shell Oil Company. My consulting assignment was to help them do a cultural analysis to develop better "measurements" of the division's performance. As we collectively began to examine the artifacts and espoused beliefs and values of this group, it immediately became apparent that the exploration group and the production group had completely different basic assumptions about how they wanted to be measured.

The *exploration* group wanted to be measured on finding evidence of oil, which they felt should be determined on a statistical basis over a long period of time because most wells proved to be "dry." In contrast, the *production* group, which was charged with safely removing oil from an active well, wanted to be measured on a short-term basis in terms of safe and efficient "production." For the exploration group, the risk was in not finding anything over a long period of time; for the production group, the risk was of an accident or fire, which could occur at any moment. In the end, because both groups wanted to contribute to the financial performance of the company, both the cost of exploration and the cost of safe production had to be factored in, but neither group wanted to be measured by a *general* criterion that did not fit its work.

Complex measurement issues arise over how to balance performance on the manifest versus the latent functions, which is well illustrated by current issues in the health care industry. The manifest function of hospitals and clinics is patient health and safety, but an important latent function has been to organize health care systems to meet the needs of the doctors. As health care costs climbed and it was discovered that many preventable medical errors occurred throughout the system, new measures of safety and of patient satisfaction emerged. Correcting medical errors and rude behavior by doctors toward nurses or patients had been handled latently by assuming that the occupation would measure and monitor itself. What is now emerging as a whole new measurement system is patient surveys along with complaint systems that enable special hospital committees to identify doctors who have problems and to require such doctors to accept "coaching."

Must Measurement Be Quantitative? I have already given several examples of various qualitative ways that production groups measure the quality of what they are doing. However, the cultures of management and finance promulgate the necessity to measure things quantitatively because it is more precise and "manageable." The occupational macro culture of management has always had a strong preference for quantitative measures, no doubt reflecting that it is always about finances and money, which can be quantitatively measured. As a consequence many organizations attempt to convert *everything* they measure into numbers, the best example being that individual career potential and performance is converted in many performance appraisal and career development systems into individual numbers.

For example, Exxon measured a manager's "ultimate potential" by requiring every manager to rank-order his or her subordinates on this criterion. These rankings were combined in a sophisticated statistical system for all managers across the company worldwide, resulting in a set of numbers that allowed one to locate for each category of work the person with the highest ultimate potential. When jobs had to be filled, it was the highest-ranking candidate who had to be offered the job. The ranking numbers were compiled into a highly secret document that came to be called "the green dragon," because everyone knew that it contained the most critical information for career advancement.

The cultural norm to use *ultimate potential* as the primary source of career advancement actually distorted the performance measurement system, as I found out in a project for Essochem Europe. An internal consultant and I were asked to find out why "performance dropped with age." The statistics clearly showed that for any given job, the older employees showed lower performance ratings. After extensive interviewing we discovered that a supervisor who rated an older subordinate as "high performance" but "low ultimate potential" was told by his superiors that this was "not possible." If one did not have "high ultimate potential" one could not have high performance. But, because ultimate potential was a sacred cow in the measurement system and had to be accurate, supervisors *lowered* the performance rating! The needs of the worldwide talent identification system actually overrode the needs for accurate performance management ratings. Of course, the actual performance of the older employees was not controlled by the ratings they eventually got, but it must certainly have affected their morale and their confidence in the credibility of management.

For our purposes the important message is to recognize that in a sociotechnical system, the cultural norms that revolve around the social needs of the system are sometimes stronger than the norms of the technical system. However, the technical system can introduce norms of measurement that make no sense in the social system as in the use of the bell curve for performance measurement. Most managers will aim to bring the performance of all of their subordinates to some minimum standard, yet the appraisal system will "force" them into percentage categories of high, medium, and low performers, even requiring that a certain percentage had to be designated to be fired. This kind of system, or its equivalent of "rank-ordering" all the subordinates, encourages ignoring the reality that different subordinates contribute in different ways and that it is fundamentally dehumanizing for people to think of themselves as merely a number (Level 1 relationship) rather than as a person (Level 2 relationship).

As is shown in Chapter 14, the same desire for quantitative measurement has overtaken the culture field as well, given the growth of surveys that turn individual opinions into numerical measurements of different cultural elements. The pros and cons of this are discussed in that chapter. In the health care arena, a similar phenomenon occurs around the measurement of patient satisfaction, with a strong bias toward using numbers based on questionnaires rather than qualitative information based on interviews of patients.

In summary, the methods an organization decides to use to measure its own activities and accomplishments, the criteria it chooses, and the information system it develops to measure itself become central elements of its culture as consensus develops around these issues. If consensus fails to develop and strong subcultures form around different assumptions, the organization will find itself in conflicts that can potentially undermine its ability to cope with its external environment. Inasmuch as organizations are socio-technical systems, the subcultures dealing with work design and performance can potentially clash with the subcultures that deal with people management per se, which are now typically called "human resources," were formerly called "personnel," and at Google are now called "people management."

Correction and Repair Strategies

The final area of consensus crucial for external adaptation concerns what to do if a change in course is required and how to make that change. If information surfaces indicating that the group is not on target—sales are off, market share is down, profits are down, product introductions are late, key customers complain about product quality, patient satisfaction scores decline, accident rates are up, and so on—by what process is the problem diagnosed and remedied?

Consensus is needed about how to gather external information, how to get that information to the right parts of the organization that can act on it, and how to alter the internal production processes to take the new information into account. Organizations can become ineffective if there is lack of consensus on any part of this information gathering and utilization cycle (Schein, 1980). For example, in General Foods the product managers used market research to determine whether or not the product they were managing was meeting sales and quality goals. At the same time, sales managers who were out in the supermarkets were getting information on how store managers were reacting to different products by giving them better or worse positions on the shelves. It was well established that shelf position was strongly correlated with sales.

Sales managers consistently attempted to get this information to the product managers, who consistently refused to consider it relative to their more "scientifically conducted" market research, thus unwittingly undermining their own performance. In the same vein, in the early days at DEC the person who knew the most about what competitors were doing was the purchasing manager, because he had to buy parts from competitor companies. Yet his knowledge was often ignored because engineers trusted their own judgment more than his information.

If information gets to the right place, where it is understood and acted on, there is still the matter of reaching consensus on what kind of action to take. For example, if a product fails in the marketplace, does the organization fire the product manager, reexamine the marketing strategy, reassess the quality of the research and development process, convene a diagnostic team from many functions to see what can be learned from the failure, or brush the failure under the rug and quietly move the good people into different jobs?

Macro-cultural elements come into play here just as they did with measurement biases. In individualistic cultures such as the United States, I often encountered what was called a "blame culture." When anything goes wrong, find out who is responsible and fire him or her. Even though the analysis of accidents has shown repeatedly that they are caused by multiple systemic events that may involve correct decisions by each party in the system, there is a strong desire to locate the one person who made the crucial mistake. For example, in the tragic shooting down of two helicopters in the Iraq "no fly zone" in 1994 that killed 26 diplomats, it was determined that the overall system of common radio frequencies covering both helicopters and the fighters monitoring the area had evolved into two systems, because the fighters needed different frequencies; that resulted on the fateful day of the inability to communicate with each other (Snook, 2000). The AWACS flying high above to monitor the area had both a new crew and a shared perception that helicopters are impossible to see on radar because they always dart into canyons, leading them to be less vigilant on that day and to say to the fighters that they did not see anything. The required visual identification of targets by the fighters failed because of the extra fuel tanks that had been attached to the helicopters to accommodate the larger number of people who would be on board, which, it turned out, made their silhouettes resemble the enemy ones. The pilots of the fighters had used all their checking routines and found ample cause to shoot them down! It was discovered to be a systemic failure even though initially the pilots were blamed for the immediate act of shooting down the helicopters.

Occupational macro cultures like medicine and architecture have been presumed to develop their own correction mechanisms when problems are found, but when the product of the occupation is a system, an operation, a building, or a bridge, society has chosen to add independent measurement and correction systems as well. At the societal level it comprises the entirety of policing, the courts, and the probation and prison systems. Government agencies and the military have their own inspector-general systems. However, cultural forces enter into how these systems function and the broader social values that influence them in the way in which policing, the courts, and the prison systems work in different societies.

This variation shows up at the organizational level. At DEC, both the diagnosis of the problem to be corrected and the proposed remedy were likely to result from widespread open discussion and debate among members at all levels of the organization, with more weight consistently being given to the technical people over the financial, marketing, or purchasing people. After discussion and debate, self-corrective action was often taken locally because people now recognized problems about which they could do something. Thus, by the time senior management ratified a course of action and announced it, most of the problem had already been dealt with. However, if the discussion led to proposals that violated some of Ken Olsen's assumptions or intuitions, he would step into the debate and attempt to influence thinking. If that did not work, he sometimes empowered different groups to proceed along different paths to "play it safe," to stimulate internal competition, and to "let the market decide." Though this process was at times haphazard, it was well understood and consensually agreed to as the way to get things done in the kind of dynamic marketplace that DEC found itself in.

At Ciba-Geigy, remedial action was taken locally, if possible, to minimize the upward delegation of bad news. However, if problems surfaced that were company wide, senior management went through a formal period of diagnosis, often with the help of task forces and other specific processes. Once a diagnosis had been made and remedial action decided on, the decision was formally disseminated through systematic meetings, memoranda, phone calls, and other formal means.

In Singapore, the corrective action depended very much on the degree to which the problem was perceived to undermine the strategy and goals, especially around the cleaning up of the urban environment. Even minor transgressions led to severe punishment. However, failure by the EDB to bring in an investment was carefully analyzed to discover how things could be handled more effectively. For example, the discovery that the EDB had no mechanisms for stimulating internal entrepreneurship led immediately to various programs to correct this lack.

"Corrective" processes are not limited to problem areas. If a company is receiving signals of success, it may decide to grow faster, to develop a careful strategy of controlled growth, or to take a quick profit and risk remaining small. Consensus on these matters becomes crucial to effectiveness, and the kind of consensus achieved is one of the determinants of the "style" of the company. Organizations that have not had periodic survival problems may not have a "style" of responding to such problems. However, organizations that have had survival crises often discovered in their responses to such crises what some of their deeper assumptions really were. In this sense an important piece of an organization's culture can be genuinely latent. No one really knows what response it will make to a severe crisis, yet the nature of that response will reveal deep elements of the culture. Crisis situations also reveal whether worker subcultures have developed around restriction of output and hiding ideas for improvement from management, or whether these subcultures support productivity goals.

Once remedial or corrective action has been taken, new information must be gathered to determine whether results have improved or not. Sensing changes in the environment, getting the information to the right place, digesting it, and developing appropriate responses is thus a perpetual learning cycle that will ultimately characterize how a given organization maintains its effectiveness.

Analytical Comment: Fixing versus Changing and Improving. Most of the examples have highlighted fixing something based on measurements indicating that something was not going right. With increasing complexity and with better models of how socio-technical systems work, it is often discovered that *fixing* has to be thought of more broadly as *changing* and *improving*. Information that something is not going right (what I call "disconfirmation") will reveal problems but not necessarily solutions. Managing change processes and finding ways to improve how something is done requires models of "change management" around which there is surprisingly little consensus. Even the improvement models (e.g., lean management, six sigma, re-engineering, and so on) disagree on the mechanics of the change-management process itself. These disagreements surface especially in the current climate of "culture change" in that the desire to change things far outruns the ability of organizations to actually make the changes.

Issues in Defining Group Boundaries and Criteria for Inclusion

As the founder builds the organization the issue of who is in and who is out becomes very important for its new members. As people are hired they are often given badges with numbers, and those numbers become a status symbol later on. In the process of building identity the founder may decide on providing a distinctive uniform that immediately identifies members. There may be different criteria for hiring such as in universities where it is crucial whether you are hired as "adjunct," "tenure track," "regular faculty but limited contract," or "part-time contract work." One of the immediate consequences of defining the initial "contract" is that differential treatment rules begin to be applied. Insiders are awarded special benefits, are trusted more, receive higher basic rewards, and, most important, acquire a sense of identity from belonging to a defined organization. Outsiders such as contract workers not only receive fewer of the various benefits and rewards but, more important, lose specific identity. They become part of a mass, labeled "outsiders," and they are more likely to be stereotyped and treated with indifference or hostility.

Who is in and who is out applies not only to the initial hiring decision but continues to have important symbolic meaning as an individual progresses in his or her career. Organizations have three dimensions of career movement: (1) lateral movement from one task or function to another, (2) vertical movement from one rank to another, and (3) inclusionary movement from outsider to insider (Schein, 1978; Schein & VanMaanen, 2013). Consensus forms around criteria both for promotion and for inclusionary movement. As people move farther "in," they become privy to some of the more secret assumptions of the organization. They learn the special meanings attached to certain words and the special rituals that define membership—such as the secret fraternity handshake—and they discover that one of the most important bases for status in the group is to be entrusted with group secrets. Such secrets involve historical accounts of how and why some of the things in the past really happened, who is really part of the dominant coalition or insider group, and what some of the latent functions of the organization are.

As organizations age and become more complex, the problem of defining clear external and inclusionary internal boundaries becomes more complex. More people—such as salespeople, purchasing agents, distributors, franchisees, board members, and consultants—come to occupy boundary-spanning roles. In some industries, economic circumstances have made it necessary for companies to reduce the size of their "permanent" workforce, causing an increase in the hiring of temporaries or contract workers, who can be laid off more easily if necessary. Macro cultures and organizations differ in their basic assumptions of what organizations and employees "owe each other."

We see in the United States as of 2016 both a macro-cultural change toward a sense of career freedom and a new kind of "paternalism" in organizations like Google that make work so attractive that employees will want to stay. Cultural assumptions then also come into bold relief when certain questions are raised from a policy perspective: What is a "temporary"? For how long can we keep people in that status? To what benefits if any are they entitled? How does an organization train them quickly in the essentials of the culture? How does the organization deal with the threat that temporaries pose to more permanent members of the organization (Kunda, 1992; Barley & Kunda, 2001).

In summary, defining the criteria for deciding who is in and who is out of an organization or any of its subunits is one of the best ways to begin to analyze a culture. Moreover, the very process by which a group makes those judgments and acts on them is a process of culture formation and maintenance that forces some integration of the external survival issues and the internal integration issues.

Issues in Distributing Power, Authority, and Status

In creating the structures and processes of the organization, it becomes obvious who and what are more important to achieving the goals. The founder has the biggest impact in how he or she distributes the key resources of money, time, space, and materials to different subordinates, thereby creating the basic *power* structure. By creating a division of labor, the essence of organization, the founder also creates the need for coordination, which eventually turns into some form of hierarchy that, in turn, creates an *authority* structure. The underlying technology (electrical engineering in DEC and chemistry in Ciba-Geigy) also plays a huge role in that certain kinds of knowledge become the basis of individual power. In knowledge-based organizations, that becomes the basis for the *status* structure, although, as in Ciba-Geigy, status can also come from family connections or other macrocultural criteria. It is important to recognize that inside the organization there may be clear consensus on who has power, who has authority, and who has status, but this may be by far the most difficult element to decipher for someone who is not an insider.

A correlated issue in any new group is how influence, power, and authority will be treated and what the rules will be for "deference and demeanor" (Goffman, 1967). The process of stratification in human systems is typically not as blatant as the dominance-establishing rituals of animal societies, but it is functionally equivalent in that it concerns the evolution of workable rules for managing aggression and mastery needs. Human societies develop pecking orders just as chickens do, but both the process and the outcome are, of course, far more complex and varied. In a new group the process of sorting out who will dominate or influence whom and in what way can be messy and unpredictable. But most organizations start with founders and leaders who have preconceptions about how things should be run and, therefore, impose rules that initially determine how authority is to be obtained and how aggressive behavior is to be managed.

Sociologists have shown very convincingly how manners and morals, politeness, and tact are not mere "niceties" of social life but essential rules for how to keep us from destroying each other socially (Goffman, 1959, 1967). Our functioning as human beings requires us to develop a self-image of who we are along with a degree of self-esteem—a sense that we have enough value to continue to function. The word "face" captures this publicly claimed value, and the rules of the social order are that we should protect each other's faces. If we offend or insult someone by not upholding their claims—laughing at something serious, humiliating or embarrassing the other—it is a loss of face for both parties. Not only has one party failed to uphold his or her claims, but the other party has behaved rudely, destructively, and irresponsibly.

Thus the most fundamental rule in all societies is that we must uphold each other's claims because our self-esteem is based on it. When we tell a joke, others laugh no matter how unfunny the joke; when someone breaks wind in public, we pretend not to have noticed no matter how loud the sound or bad the smell. Human society of any sort hinges on the cultural agreements to try to uphold each other's identities and illusions, even if that means lying. We compliment people to make them feel good even if we don't believe it; we teach little children not to say "Look at that fat lady over there," even though an obese person is clearly visible.

One reason why performance appraisal in organizations is emotionally resisted so strongly is that managers know full well they are violating the larger cultural rules and norms when they sit a subordinate down to give him or her "feedback." To put it bluntly, when we tell people what we "really think of them" in an aggressive way, this can be functionally equivalent to social murder. Someone who goes around doing this is viewed as unsafe to have around, and if the behavior persists, we often declare such a person mentally ill and lock him or her up. In his analysis of mental hospitals, Goffman showed brilliantly how "therapy" was in many cases teaching the patients the rules of polite society so that they could be let free to function in that society without making others too anxious (Goffman, 1961). In more traditional societies, the jester or the fool played the role of telling the truth about what was going on, and this worked only because the role could be publicly discounted and ignored.

Psychological Safety. In any hierarchy the subordinate is, by definition, more vulnerable than the superior. Authority systems differ most in how large the psychological distance is between higher and lower echelons, the dimension that Hofstede identified as "power distance." The manner in which founders create their organization and their personal behavior will have the biggest impact on how this dimension plays out and eventually becomes labeled in the culture. The more complex the task is, the greater the interdependency across hierarchical levels will be, and the greater the need will be to make the subordinate feel psychologically safe in speaking up and telling the truth upward (Edmondson, 2012; Schein, 2009a, 2013, 2016). Macro cultures differ enormously in the degree to which they encourage telling the boss what is wrong or when he or she is about to make a mistake. "Whistle blowing" in high-hazard industries is encouraged to identify unsafe practices, but the career of the whistle-blower is often destroyed. The burden ultimately falls on the higher level person to create an environment in which subordinates will feel encouraged to speak up and will be rewarded for doing so, but the manner in which this may work still depends on the prevailing norms in the macro culture.

To conclude, every group, organization, occupation, and macro culture develops norms around the distribution of influence, authority, and power. If those norms "work" in the sense of providing a system that gets external tasks done and leaves members in the group reasonably free of anxiety, these norms gradually become shared tacit assumptions and critical elements in the cultural DNA. As the world becomes more culturally interdependent, more organizations, projects, task forces, and joint ventures of various sorts will involve members from different nations, ethnicities, and occupations. In the efforts of those groups to develop a working consensus, it will be differences in the deep assumptions about authority that will be the most problematic. A special role for leaders will be to create cultural islands such as were described in Chapter 7, in which it will be possible for members to explore these differences to reach both mutual understanding and new rules for how to manage their own authority relationships.

Issues in Developing Norms of How to Relate to Each Other around Trust and Openness

Every new group must decide simultaneously how to deal with authority problems and how to establish workable peer relationships. Whereas authority issues derive ultimately from the necessity to deal with feelings of aggression, peer relationship and intimacy problems derive ultimately from the necessity to deal with feelings of affection, love, and sexuality. Thus, all societies develop clear sex roles, kinship systems, and rules for friendship and sexual conduct that serve to stabilize current relationships while ensuring procreation mechanisms and thereby the survival of the society. In most organizations, the rules around intimacy will be linked to the rules around authority in that newcomers learn quickly with whom they can joke and with whom they must be serious, whom they can trust with intimate personal details, and how appropriate it is to develop personal relationships with other employees, especially across status or rank lines.

In work organizations, the rules governing "intimacy" cover a broad range of issues—what to call each other, how much personal life to share, how much emotion to display, whom to ask for help and around what issues, how open to be in communicating, and whether or not sexual relationships with colleagues are condoned. I have put quotes around the word intimacy because in most macro cultures there are clear distinctions between the levels of social relationships that I described in Chapter 6. What I have called Level 1 transactional relationships, Level 2 personal relationships such as friendships, and Level 3 intimate relationships between lovers and close friends will be present but the boundaries may vary.

To recap, in Level 1 relationships we treat each other as "strangers" or in specific roles such as customer vis-à-vis salesperson or patient vis-à-vis doctor, and we learn the rules that govern those relationships. They are not emotionally intimate, but the doctor can ask very personal questions pertaining to the health issue under discussion. In Level 2 relationships we treat each other as full human beings and can then be more personal and intimate with each other as in friendships, but we would still not necessarily involve the deep emotional exchange of lovers and spouses that may involve sexual relations.

If we take these levels into work relationships, the question arises of whether or not they should remain at Level 1, in which case we maintain appropriate "professional distance" from superiors, subordinates, and team members, or whether complex work relationships should be at Level 2 to foster the right level of trust and openness (Schein, 2013, 2016). The greater the task interdependency, the more important it is to develop the trust and openness that Level 2 personal relationships imply. All the informal activities that have come to characterize "team building" are efforts to personalize relationships in the interest of trust and openness.

Rules regarding relationships interact powerfully with rules regarding task performance in new organizations, especially multicultural ones where the macro cultures may vary. The specific issue is whether the members of the culture believe that they must establish some Level 2 intimacy with colleagues before they can tackle the task effectively or whether they believe that tasks can be done immediately with Level 1 transactions. Stories abound of meetings where the members of one culture (usually the U.S. culture) wanted to get right to work while members of the other culture first wanted to "get to know each other through various informal activities" (often Asian or Latin cultures). Here again, the leadership role is to become aware of these differences and to create meetings and events where the issue can be confronted and accepted.

In summary, developing rules for how to get along with each other is critical to the functioning of any group and organization. Within a given culture such as the United States, there will be variations among organizations as to the degree of intimacy that is considered appropriate on and off the job. Still, as in the case of rules about authority relations, if future organizations will be more multicultural in terms of nations, ethnicities, and occupations, the potential for misunderstanding and offending each other will increase dramatically. Exploring these rules in a safe "cultural island" will become an essential component of developing organizations.

Issues in Allocating Rewards and Punishment

In a sense this is the human side of the technical problem of measurement and correction. Every group develops a system of sanctions for obeying or disobeying its norms and rules, most of which have to do with task performance but which also includes the important rules for how to get along with each other. It is violations of the rules for getting along with each other that often become the most critical elements of the culture. Those rules are also often the most difficult to learn because they are often implicit until violated. A new employee may be told by a friend, "You must *never* talk to the boss the way you just did. That was very disrespectful."

The subtlety of these rules derives from the fact that the founder may not be aware of the signals he or she is sending on what it is okay or not okay to do, and what is the right level of "respect." Older employees socialize younger ones and, thereby, embed the rules, thereby also making them harder to change if a new change leader wants to change the social environment. Deliberate changes in the reward and punishment system are the most difficult to bring about; they are also one of the quickest and easiest ways to begin to change overt behavior and thereby to *begin* to change some elements of the culture. Whether beliefs and values change as well depends on how well the new behavior works out in terms of adapting to the new external tasks.

Punishments, like rewards, have local meanings in different organizations. In several high-tech companies that have clear espoused values about not laying people off, people can lose the particular task they are working on and become "boat people" or "wander the halls" while looking for another job within the organization. They will be carried on the payroll indefinitely, but it is clear that they have been punished. Often the signals are subtle, but colleagues know when someone is in the "doghouse" or in the "penalty box." Actual loss of bonuses or the failure to get a raise may follow, but the initial punishment is clear enough already.

Some organizations develop a "blame culture," which implies that whenever something goes wrong, someone to blame is found and that person's career is damaged. One dramatic example was revealed in a cultural analysis of Amoco some years before it was acquired by British Petroleum. Amoco's managers and engineers explicitly called it a "blaming culture" in which the norm was that if something went wrong on a project, they had to identify who was responsible as quickly as possible. *Who* was more important than *why*. The person who was "blamed" was not necessarily punished in any overt way, and often was not even told that others considered him or her responsible. Instead, it was noted in the memory of senior managers as a reason to be less trustful of this person, leading to career limitation. People who were not given good assignments or promotions might never find out why. Consequently, employees viewed it as essential to distance themselves as quickly as possible from any project that might fail, lest they be "blamed" for the failure. This belief prevented Amoco from engaging in a joint venture with another company because if a project failed, any Amoco employees on the project felt vulnerable, even if it was clear that the failure was due to people in the other company.

Deciphering when a person has been rewarded and when a person has been punished is one of the most difficult tasks for newcomers in organizations because the signals are so often ambiguous from an outsider's point of view. Being yelled at by the boss may be a reward, while being ignored may be a punishment, and only someone farther along in the understanding of the culture can reassure the yelled-at newcomer that she or he was, in fact, doing well. As noted before, teamwork is usually touted as an important characteristic for promotion, but the definition of teamwork can vary all over the map.

What is rewarding or punishing varies with level in the organization. For junior employees, a raise or better assignment is a key reward, while for very senior managers, only a large promotion to a more responsible assignment or progress along the inclusionary dimension counts. Being told company secrets is a major reward, while being frozen out by not being told can be a major punishment that signals ultimate excommunication. Being no longer "in the loop" is a clear signal that the individual has done something wrong.

In summary, the reward and punishment system of an organization along with its assumptions about authority and intimacy forms the critical mass of the culture that determines how people will relate to each other, manage their anxieties, and derive meaning from their daily interactions. How you treat the boss, how you treat each other, and how you know whether you are doing things right or not all make up a kind of rock bottom of the cultural DNA. So here again, as organizations become more multicultural, we will see different systems clashing with each other leading to hurt feelings, offense, impatience, anxiety, and other dysfunctional behaviors until mutual explorations in a cultural-island setting produce understanding and new consensus.

Issues in Managing the Unmanageable and Explaining the Unexplainable

Every group inevitably faces some issues not under its control—events that are intrinsically mysterious and unpredictable and hence frightening. At the physical level, events such as natural disasters and threatening weather require explanation. At the biological and social level, events such as birth, growth, puberty, illness, and death require a theory of what is happening and why to avoid anxiety and a sense of meaninglessness.

In a macro culture heavily committed to reason and science, there is a tendency to treat everything as explainable; the mysterious is just not yet explained. But until science has demystified an event that we cannot control or understand, we need an alternative basis for putting what has happened into a meaningful context. Religious beliefs can provide such a context and can also offer justification for events that might otherwise seem unfair and meaningless. Superstitions explain the unexplainable and provide guidelines for what to do in ambiguous, uncertain, and threatening situations.

For example, in a study of the introduction of computerized tomography into hospital radiology departments, Barley (1984) observed that if the computer went down at an awkward time, such as when a patient was in the middle of a scan, the technicians tried all kinds of remedial measures, including the proverbial kicking of the machine. If the computer resumed operating, as it did occasionally, the technician carefully documented what he or she had just done. When engineering arrived on the scene, it was made very clear to the technicians that what they had done had "no conceivable connection" to the computer coming back up, yet this "knowledge" was carefully written down in a little notebook and passed on to new colleagues as part of their training. In a real sense, this was superstitious behavior, even in a realm in which logical explanation was possible.

Stories and myths are useful not only to explain the unexplainable but also to affirm the organization's picture of itself, its own theory of how to get things done, and how to handle internal relationships (Hatch & Schultz, 2004; Pettigrew, 1979; Wilkins, 1983). Many of the things we "know" are, ultimately, based on what I have called *social consensus*, which often makes them just as firm as superstitions.

Summary and Conclusions

In this chapter I have reviewed how cultural assumptions evolve around all the issues that founders face around external adaptation and internal integration as their organization grows and develops a culture. Ultimately all organizations are *socio-technical* systems in which the manner of external adaptation and the solution of internal integration problems are interdependent and intertwined and are occurring at the same time. The beliefs, values, and actions of the founder are the biggest determinants of how the culture will evolve, but the culture of the macro system in which the new organization evolves, the underlying technology, and the actual experiences of the organization are also important influences.

The most important conclusion to be derived from this analysis is that culture is a multidimensional, multifaceted phenomenon, not easily reduced to a few major dimensions. Culture fulfills the function of providing stability, meaning, and predictability in the present but is the result of functionally effective decisions in the group's past. As organizations become internally more multicultural, the problems of finding common language and meaning will require special efforts that take place in temporary cultural islands.

Suggestion for the Culture Analyst

How an organization handles the various cultural elements described in this chapter is a critical part of its cultural DNA and is therefore crucial to analyze when mergers, acquisitions, or other overall holistic pictures of the culture are desired. For each category in the chapter, one can develop interview questions to be brought to managers at various levels to arrive at a picture of the espoused beliefs and values. These can then be checked with observations to determine what might be the deeper assumptions.

Suggestion for the Manager and Leader

Take each of the categories of this chapter and ask yourself how your organization has resolved the issues that are described and how that has shaped your culture. Look for the tacit basic assumptions behind the way you do things.

10

HOW LEADERS EMBED AND TRANSMIT CULTURE

In the previous chapters we saw how founders of organizations start the culture-formation process by imposing their own beliefs, values, and assumptions about how things should be done on their followers and employees; we then reviewed all the external and internal issues that have to be addressed in creating an organization. A culture is now well on its way to being formed. If the founders or their successors believe that they are on the right track in how they have solved the external and internal issues, how do they consolidate and embed the new structures, processes, beliefs, and values? Founders and subsequently appointed or promoted leaders have available to them many mechanisms and processes to articulate and embed the culture they have created.

How will founders and formal leaders know whether or not to aggressively embed their beliefs, values, and assumptions? The main short-run criterion is the *external* one of whether or not the organization is succeeding. But many of the beliefs, values, and assumptions have long-range consequences. How should those be assessed? Should a leader who believes in teamwork impose team processes, team incentives, and team rewards? The primary *internal* criterion both for founding something new and then embedding it in the organization's structures and processes should be to examine the degree to which those beliefs, values, and assumptions are in alignment with the macro cultures in which the new organization must function.

Every culture is nested in some larger culture and can do only what the larger culture affords, tolerates, or supports. For example, I don't believe it is accidental that the communes that were created in the 1960s and 1970s all eventually failed because they were nested in a fundamentally non-communal culture. Religious groups like the Amish or the Hutterites succeed because they are nested in a larger religious macro culture and isolate themselves as much as possible from the immediate macro culture that would challenge some of their beliefs and values.

If the founder or leader does not consider how the new beliefs, values, and assumptions will fit into the macro culture, they will not be adopted. I witnessed a striking miscalculation along these lines in a large U.S. multinational that decided to adopt a performance improvement program that depended on regular, direct face-to-face feedback from the superior to the subordinate. Several years of training for managers at all levels were provided by the human resource (HR) department through its training arm. I happened to be at an executive development program in Hawaii that was attended by a team of managers from the Japanese subsidiary. One of the program's designated outside speakers was the head of international HR of this company. She had been invited to describe this program as an example of effective performance management. She not only described the program but used the occasion to announce with great pride that the face-to-face feedback component had now been officially accepted worldwide as a key element of the company's culture.

That evening I had dinner with several of the executives of the Japanese subsidiary and asked them whether they had had the training and how it was working out. They had all been trained, had politely pretended to go along, but as to doing it in Japan with their subordinates, they all said, "Of course we don't do that, it would not work in our culture, we have other ways of getting things across to our subordinates, *never* direct face-to-face!"

Assuming that the organization is succeeding and that the founder or new leader has considered the fit between the new culture and the macro culture in which it is nested, what are the primary mechanisms for embedding the new? The simplest explanation of how leaders get their message across is that they do it through "charisma," that mysterious ability to capture the subordinates' attention and to communicate major assumptions and values in a vivid and clear manner (Bennis & Nanus, 1985; Conger, 1989; Leavitt, 1986). Charisma is an important mechanism of culture creation, but it is not, from the organization's or society's point of view, a reliable mechanism of embedding or socialization because leaders who have it are rare and their impact is hard to predict.

Historians can look back and say that certain people had charisma or had a great vision. It is not always clear at the time, however, how they transmitted the vision. However, leaders of organizations without charisma have many ways of getting their message across. and it is these other ways that form the focus of this chapter. Exhibit 10.1 shows 12 embedding mechanisms divided into primary and secondary sections to highlight the difference between the most powerful daily behavioral things that leaders do and the more formal but less powerful mechanisms that support and reinforce the primary messages.

Exhibit 10.1

How Leaders Embed Their Beliefs, Values, and Assumptions

Primary Embedding Mechanisms

- What leaders pay attention to, measure, and control on a regular basis
- How leaders react to critical incidents and organizational crises
- How leaders allocate resources
- Deliberate role modeling, teaching, and coaching
- How leaders allocate rewards and status
- How leaders recruit, select, promote, and excommunicate

Secondary Reinforcement and Stabilizing Mechanisms

- Organizational design and structure
- Organizational systems and procedures
- Rites and rituals of the organization
- Design of physical space, façades, and buildings
- Stories about important events and people
- Formal statements of organizational philosophy, creeds, and charters

---

Primary Embedding Mechanisms

The six primary embedding mechanisms shown in Exhibit 10.1 are the major "tools" that leaders have available to them to teach their organizations how to perceive, think, feel, and behave based on their own conscious and unconscious convictions. They are discussed in sequence, but they operate simultaneously. They are visible artifacts of the emerging culture and they directly create what would typically be called the "climate" of the organization (Schneider, 1990; Ashkanasy et al., 2000; Ehrhart et al., 2014).

What Leaders Pay Attention to, Measure, and Control on a Regular Basis

The most powerful mechanisms that founders, leaders, managers, and parents have available for communicating what they believe in or care about is what they systematically pay attention to. This can mean anything from what they notice and comment on to what they measure, control, reward, and in other ways deal with *systematically*. Even casual remarks and questions that are consistently geared to a certain area can be as potent as formal control mechanisms and measurements.

If leaders are aware of this process, then being systematic in paying attention to certain things becomes a powerful way of communicating a message, especially if leaders are totally consistent in their own behavior. However, if leaders are not aware of the power of this process or they are inconsistent in what they pay attention to, subordinates and colleagues will spend inordinate time and energy trying to decipher what a leader's behavior really reflects and will even project motives onto the leader where none may exist. This mechanism is well captured by the phrase "you get what you settle for."

It is the consistency that is important, not the intensity of the attention. To illustrate, at a recent conference on safety in industrial organizations, the speaker from Alcoa pointed out that one of the company's former CEOs, Paul McNeill, wanted to get across to workers how important safety was and did this by insisting that the first item on *every* meeting agenda was to be a discussion of safety issues. In the Alpha Power Company that I will be discussing subsequently, supervisors start every job with a job briefing that includes a discussion of the safety issues they might encounter that day. The organization has many safety programs, and senior managers frequently announce the importance of safety, but it is the questions they ask on a daily basis that get the message across.

Douglas McGregor (1960) tells of a company that wanted him to help install a management-development program. The president hoped that McGregor would propose exactly what to do and how to do it. Instead, McGregor asked the president whether he really cared about identifying and developing managers. On being assured that he did, McGregor proposed that the president should build his concern into the reward system and set up a consistent way of monitoring progress; in other words, he should start to pay attention to it. The president agreed and announced to his subordinates that henceforth 50 percent of each senior manager's annual bonus would be contingent on what he or she had done to develop his or her immediate subordinates during the past year. He added that he himself had no specific program in mind, but that *in each quarter he would ask each senior manager what had been done*.

One might think that the bonus was the primary incentive for the senior managers to launch programs, but far more important was the fact that they had to report regularly on what they were doing. The senior managers launched a series of different activities, many of them pulled together from work that was already going on piecemeal in the organization. A coherent program was forged over a two-year period and has continued to serve this company well. The president continued his quarterly questions and once a year evaluated how much each manager had done for development. He never imposed any program, but by paying consistent attention to management development and by rewarding progress, he clearly signaled to the organization that he considered management development to be important.

At the other extreme, some DEC managers illustrated how inconsistent and shifting attention causes subordinates to pay less and less attention to what senior management wants, thereby empowering the employee by default. For example, a brilliant manager in one technical group would launch an important initiative and demand total support, but two weeks later he would launch a new initiative without indicating whether or not people were supposed to drop the old one. As subordinates two and three levels down observed this seemingly erratic behavior, they began to rely more and more on their own judgment of what they should actually be doing.

Some of the most important signals of what founders and leaders care about are sent during meetings and in other activities devoted to planning and budgeting, which is one reason why planning and budgeting are such important managerial processes. In questioning subordinates systematically on certain issues, leaders can transmit their own view of how to look at problems. The ultimate content of the plan may not be as important as the learning that goes on during the planning process.

Leader Emotional Outbursts.   An even more powerful signal than regular questions is a visible emotional reaction—especially when leaders feel that one of their important values or assumptions is being violated. Emotional outbursts are not necessarily very overt, because many managers believe that one should not allow one's emotions to become too involved in the decision-making process. But subordinates generally know when their bosses are upset and many leaders do allow themselves to get overtly angry and use those feelings as messages.

Subordinates find their bosses' emotional outbursts painful and try to avoid them. In the process, they gradually come to condition their behavior to what they perceive the leader to want, and if, over time, that behavior produces desired results they adopt the leader's assumptions. For example, Olsen's concern that line managers stay on top of their jobs was originally signaled most clearly in an incident at an executive committee meeting when the company was still very young. A newly hired chief financial officer (CFO) was asked to make his report on the state of the business. He had analyzed the three major product lines and brought his analysis to the meeting. He distributed the information and then pointed out that one product line in particular was in financial difficulty because of falling sales, excessive inventories, and rapidly rising manufacturing costs. It became evident in the meeting that the vice president (VP) in charge of the product line had not seen the CFO's figures and was somewhat embarrassed by what was being revealed.

As the report progressed, the tension in the room rose because everyone sensed that a real confrontation was about to develop between the CFO and the VP. The CFO finished, and all eyes turned toward the VP. The VP said that he had not seen the figures and wished he had had a chance to look at them; because he had not seen them, however, he had no immediate answers to give. At this point Olsen (CEO) blew up, but to the surprise of the whole group he blew up not at the CFO but at the VP. Several members of the group later revealed that they had expected Olsen to blow up at the CFO for his obvious grandstanding in bringing in figures that were new to everyone. However, no one had expected Olsen to turn his wrath on the product-line VP for not being prepared to deal with the CFO's arguments and information. Protests that the VP had not seen the data fell on deaf ears. He was told that if he were running his business properly he would have known everything the CFO knew, and he certainly should have had answers for what should now be done.

Suddenly everyone realized that there was a powerful message in Olsen's outburst. He clearly expected and assumed that a product-line VP would always be totally on top of his own business and would never put himself in the position of being embarrassed by financial data. The fact that the VP did not have his own numbers was a worse sin than being in trouble. The fact that he could not respond to the troublesome figures was also a worse sin than being in trouble. The Olsen blowup at the line manager was a far clearer message than any amount of rhetoric about delegation, accountability, and the like would have been.

If a manager continued to display ignorance or lack of control of his own situation, Olsen would continue to get angry at him and accuse him of incompetence. If the manager attempted to defend himself by noting that his situation either was the result of actions on the part of others over whom he had no control or resulted from prior agreements made by Olsen himself, he would be told emotionally that he should have brought the issue up right away to force a rethinking of the situation and a renegotiation of the prior decision. In other words, Olsen made it very clear, by the kinds of things to which he reacted emotionally, that poor performance could be excused but not being on top of one's own situation and not informing others of what was going on could never be excused.

Olsen's deep assumption about the importance of always telling the truth was signaled most clearly on the occasion of another executive committee meeting, when it was discovered that the company had excess inventory because each product line, in the process of protecting itself, had exaggerated its orders to manufacturing by a small percentage. The accumulation of these small percentages across all the product lines produced a massive excess inventory, which the manufacturing department disclaimed because it had produced only what the product lines had ordered. At the meeting in which this situation was reviewed, Olsen said that he had rarely been as angry as he was then because the product-line managers had *lied*. He stated flatly that if he ever caught a manager exaggerating orders again, it would be grounds for instant dismissal no matter what the reasons. The suggestion that manufacturing could compensate for the sales exaggerations was dismissed out of hand because that would compound the problem.

The prospect of one function lying while the other function tried to figure out how to compensate for it totally violated Olsen's assumptions about how an effective business should be run.

Both Steinberg and Olsen shared the assumption that meeting the customer's needs was one of the most important ways of ensuring business success, and their most emotional reactions consistently occurred whenever they learned that a customer had not been well treated. In this area the official messages, as embodied in company creeds and the formal reward system, were completely consistent with the implicit messages that could be inferred from founder reactions. In Sam Steinberg's case, the needs of the customer were put ahead even of the needs of the family, and one way that a family member could get in trouble was by mistreating a customer.

Inferences from What Leaders Do Not Pay Attention To.   Other powerful signals that subordinates interpret for evidence of the leader's values are what leaders do *not* react to. For example, in DEC, managers were frequently in actual trouble with cost overruns, delayed schedules, and imperfect products, but such troubles rarely caused comment if the manager had displayed evidence that he or she was in control of the situation. Trouble was assumed to be a normal condition of doing business; only failure to cope and regain control was unacceptable. In DEC's product design departments, one frequently found excess personnel, very high budgets, and lax management with regard to cost controls, none of which occasioned much comment. Subordinates correctly interpreted this to mean that it was far more important to come up with a good product than to control costs.

Inconsistency and Conflict.   If leaders send inconsistent signals in what they do or do not pay attention to, this creates emotional problems for subordinates, as was shown in the Steinberg case. Sam Steinberg valued high performance but accepted poor performance from family members, causing many competent non-family members to leave. Ken Olsen wanted to empower people but he also signaled that he wanted to maintain "paternal" centralized control. Once some of the empowered engineering managers developed enough confidence in their own decision-making ability, they were forced into a kind of pathological insubordination—agreeing with Olsen during the meeting but then telling me as we were walking down the hall after the meeting that "Ken no longer is on top of the market or the technology so we will do something different from what he wants." A young engineer coming into DEC would also find an organizational inconsistency in that the clear concern for customers coexisted with an implicit arrogance toward certain classes of customers because the engineers often assumed that they knew better what the customer would like in the way of product design. Olsen implicitly reinforced this attitude by not reacting in a corrective way when engineers displayed such arrogance.

The fact that leaders may be unaware of their own conflicts or emotional issues and therefore may be sending mutually contradictory messages leads to varying degrees of culture conflict and organizational pathology (Kets de Vries & Miller, 1987; Frost, 2003; Goldman, 2008). Both Steinberg's and DEC were eventually weakened by their leaders' unconscious conflicts between a stated philosophy of delegation and decentralization and a powerful need to retain tight centralized control. Both intervened frequently on very detailed issues and felt free to go around the hierarchy. Subordinates will tolerate and accommodate contradictory messages because, in a sense, founders, owners, and others at higher levels are always granted the right to be inconsistent or, in any case, are too powerful to be confronted.

The emerging culture will then reflect not only the leader's assumptions but also the complex internal accommodations created by subordinates to run the organization in spite of or around the leader. The group, sometimes acting on the assumption that the leader is a creative genius who has idiosyncrasies, may develop compensatory mechanisms, such as buffering layers of managers, to protect the organization from the dysfunctional aspects of the leader's behavior. In those cases the culture may become a defense mechanism against the anxieties unleashed by inconsistent leader behavior. In other cases the organization's style of operating will reflect the very biases and unconscious conflicts that the founder experiences, thus causing some scholars to call such organizations "neurotic" (Kets de Vries & Miller, 1984, 1987). At the extreme, subordinates or the board of directors may have to find ways to move the founder out altogether, as has happened in a number of first-generation companies.

In summary, what leaders consistently pay attention to, reward, control, and react to emotionally communicates most clearly what their own priorities, goals, and assumptions are. If leaders pay attention to too many things or if their pattern of attention is inconsistent, subordinates will use other signals or their own experience to decide what is really important, leading to a much more diverse set of assumptions and many more subcultures.

Leader Reactions to Critical Incidents and Organizational Crises

When an organization faces a crisis, the manner in which leaders and others deal with it reveals important underlying assumptions and often creates new norms, values, and working procedures. Crises are especially significant in culture creation and transmission because the heightened emotional involvement during such periods increases the intensity of learning. Crises heighten anxiety, and the need to reduce anxiety is a powerful motivator of new learning. If people share intense emotional experiences and collectively learn how to reduce anxiety, they are more likely to remember what they have learned and to ritually repeat that behavior to avoid anxiety.

For example, a company almost went bankrupt because it over-engineered its products and made them too expensive. The company survived by hitting the market with a lower-quality, less expensive product. Some years later the market was ready for a more expensive, higher-quality product, but this company was not able to produce such a product because it could not overcome the anxiety based on its memories of almost going under with the more expensive high-quality product.

What is defined as a crisis is, of course, partly a matter of perception. There may or may not be actual dangers in the external environment, and what is considered to be dangerous is itself often a reflection of the culture. For purposes of this analysis, a crisis is what is perceived to be a crisis and what is defined as a crisis by founders and leaders. Crises that arise around the major external survival issues are the most potent in revealing the deep assumptions of the leaders.

A story told about Tom Watson Jr. highlights his concern for people and for management development. A young executive had made some bad decisions that cost the company several million dollars. He was summoned to Watson's office, fully expecting to be dismissed. As he entered the office, the young executive said, "I suppose after that set of mistakes you will be wanting to fire me." Watson was said to have replied, "Not at all, young man, we have just spent a couple of million dollars educating you."

Innumerable organizations have faced the crisis of shrinking sales, excess inventories, technological obsolescence, and the subsequent necessity of laying off employees to cut costs. How leaders deal with such crises reveals some of their assumptions about the importance of people and their view of human nature. Ouchi (1981) cites several dramatic examples in which U.S. companies faced with layoffs decided instead to go to short workweeks or to have all employees and managers take cuts in pay to manage the cost reduction without staff reduction. We have seen many examples of this sort during the economic crisis of 2009.

The DEC assumption that "we are a family who will take care of each other" came out most clearly during periods of crisis. When the company was doing well, Olsen often had emotional outbursts reflecting his concern that people were getting complacent. When the company was in difficulty, however, Olsen never punished anyone or displayed anger; instead, he became the strong and supportive father figure, pointing out to both the external world and the employees that things were not as bad as they seemed, that the company had great strengths that would ensure future success, and that people should not worry about layoffs because things would be controlled by slowing down hiring.

However, Steinberg displayed his lack of concern for his own young managers by being punitive under crisis conditions, sometimes impulsively firing people only to have to try to rehire them later because he realized how important they were to the operation of the company. This gradually created an organization built on distrust and low commitment, leading good people to leave when a better opportunity came along.

Crises around issues of internal integration can also reveal and embed leader assumptions. I have found that a good time to observe an organization very closely is when acts of insubordination take place. So much of an organization's culture is tied up with hierarchy, authority, power, and influence that the mechanisms of conflict resolution have to be constantly worked out and consensually validated. No better opportunity exists for leaders to send signals about their own assumptions about human nature and relationships than when they themselves are challenged.

For example, Olsen clearly and repeatedly revealed his assumption that he did not feel that he knew best through his tolerant and even encouraging behavior when subordinates argued with him or disobeyed him.

He signaled that he was truly depending on his subordinates to know what was best and that they should be insubordinate if they felt they were right. In contrast, a bank president with whom I have worked publicly insisted that he wanted his subordinates to think for themselves, but his behavior belied his overt claim. During an important meeting of the whole staff, one of these subordinates, in attempting to assert himself, made some silly errors in a presentation. The president laughed at him and ridiculed him. Though the president later apologized and said he did not mean it, the damage had been done. All the other subordinates who witnessed the incident interpreted the outburst to mean that the president was not really serious about delegating to them and having them be more assertive. He was still sitting in judgment of them and was still operating on the assumption that he knew best.

How Leaders Allocate Resources

How budgets are created in an organization reveals leader assumptions and beliefs. For example, a leader who is personally averse to being in debt will bias the budget-planning process by rejecting plans that lean too heavily on borrowing and favoring the retention of as much cash as possible, thus undermining potentially good investments. As Donaldson and Lorsch (1983) show in their study of top-management decision making, leader beliefs about the distinctive competence of their organization, acceptable levels of financial crisis, and the degree to which the organization must be financially self-sufficient strongly influence their choices of goals, the means to accomplish them, and the management processes to be used. Such beliefs function not only as criteria according to which decisions are made but as constraints on decision making in that they limit the perception of alternatives.

Olsen's budgeting and resource allocation processes clearly revealed his belief in the entrepreneurial bottom-up system. He always resisted letting senior managers set targets, formulate strategies, or set goals, preferring instead to stimulate the engineers and managers below him to come up with proposals, business plans, and budgets that he and other senior executives would approve if they made sense. He was convinced that people would give their best efforts and maximum commitment only to projects and programs that they themselves had invented, sold, and were accountable for.

This system created problems as the DEC organization grew and found itself increasingly operating in a competitive environment in which costs had to be controlled. In its early days the company could afford to invest in all kinds of projects whether they made sense or not. In the late 1980s one of the biggest issues was how to choose among projects that sounded equally good but there were insufficient resources to fund them all. The effort to fund everything resulted in several key projects being delayed, and this became one of the factors in DEC's ultimate failure as a business (Schein, 2003).

Deliberate Role Modeling, Teaching, and Coaching

Founders and new leaders of organizations generally seem to know that their own visible behavior has great value for communicating assumptions and values to other members, especially newcomers. Olsen and some other senior executives made videotapes that outlined their explicit philosophy, and these tapes were shown to new members of the organization as part of their initial training. However, there is a difference between the messages delivered by videos or from staged settings, such as when a leader gives a welcoming speech to newcomers, and the messages received when that leader is observed informally. The informal messages are the more powerful teaching and coaching mechanism.

Sam Steinberg, for example, demonstrated his need to be involved in everything at a detailed level by his frequent visits to stores and the minute inspections he made once he got there. When he went on vacation, he called the office every day at a set time and asked detailed questions about all aspects of the business. This behavior persisted into his semiretirement, when he would call every day from his retirement home thousands of miles away. Through his questions, his lectures, and his demonstration of personal concern for details, he hoped to show other managers what it meant to be highly visible and on top of one's job. Through his unwavering loyalty to family members, Steinberg also trained people in how to think about family members and the rights of owners. Olsen made an explicit attempt to downplay status and hierarchy in DEC by driving a small car, dressing informally, and spending many hours wandering among the employees at all levels, getting to know them personally.

How Leaders Allocate Rewards and Status

Members of any organization learn from their own experience with promotions, from performance appraisals, and from discussions with the boss what the organization values and what the organization punishes. Both the nature of the behavior rewarded and punished and the nature of the rewards and punishments themselves carry the messages. Leaders can quickly get across their own priorities, values, and assumptions by consistently linking rewards and punishments to the behavior they are concerned with.

I am referring here to the actual practices—what really happens—not what is espoused, published, or preached. For example, product managers in General Foods were each expected to develop a successful marketing program for their specific product and then were rewarded by being moved to a better product after about 18 months. Because the results of a marketing program could not possibly be known in 18 months, what was really rewarded was the performance of the product manager in creating a "good" marketing program, as measured by the ability to sell it to the senior managers who approved it, not by the ultimate performance of the product in the marketplace.

The implicit assumption was that only senior managers could be trusted to evaluate a marketing program accurately; therefore, even if a product manager was technically accountable for his or her product, it was, in fact, senior management that took the real responsibility for launching expensive marketing programs. What junior managers learned from this was how to develop programs that had the right characteristics and style from senior management's point of view. If junior-level managers developed the illusion that they really had independence in making marketing decisions, they had only to look at the relative insignificance of the actual rewards given to successful managers. They received a better product to manage, they might get a slightly better office, and they received a good raise, but they still had to present their marketing programs to senior management for review, and the preparations for and dry runs of such presentations took four to five months of every year even for very senior product managers. An organization that seemingly delegated a great deal of power to its product managers was, in fact, limiting their autonomy very sharply and systematically training them to think like senior managers.

To reiterate the basic point, if the founders or leaders are trying to ensure that their values and assumptions will be learned, they must create a reward, promotion, and status system that is consistent with those assumptions. Although the message initially gets across in the daily behavior of the leader, it is judged in the long run by whether the important rewards such as promotion are allocated consistently with that daily behavior.

Most organizations espouse a variety of values, some of which are intrinsically contradictory, forcing new employees to figure out for themselves what is really rewarded: customer satisfaction, productivity, safety, minimizing costs, or maximizing returns to the investors. Only by observing the actual behavior of senior managers and experiencing actual promotions and performance reviews can newcomers figure out what the underlying assumptions are by which the organization works.

How Leaders Select, Promote, and Excommunicate

One of the subtlest yet most potent ways through which leader values get embedded and perpetuated is the process of selecting new members. For example, Olsen assumed that the best way to build an organization was to hire very smart, articulate, tough, independent people and then give them lots of responsibility and autonomy. Ciba-Geigy, however, hired very well-educated, smart people who would fit into the more structured culture that had evolved over a century.

This cultural embedding mechanism is subtle because in most organizations it operates unconsciously. Founders and leaders generally find attractive those candidates who resemble present members in style, assumptions, values, and beliefs. They are perceived to be the best people to hire and are assigned characteristics that will justify their being hired. Unless someone outside the organization is explicitly involved in the hiring, there is no way of knowing how much the current implicit assumptions are dominating recruiters' perceptions of the candidates. "Fitting in" becomes a value in its own right.

Some Concluding Observations. These embedding mechanisms all interact and tend to reinforce each other if the leader's own beliefs, values, and assumptions are consistent. By breaking out these six categories, I am trying to show the many different ways by which leaders can and do communicate their assumptions. Most newcomers to an organization have a wealth of data available to them to decipher the leader's real assumptions. Much of the socialization process is, therefore, embedded in the organization's normal working routines. It is not necessary for newcomers to attend special training or indoctrination sessions to learn important cultural assumptions. They become quite evident through the daily behavior of the leaders.

Secondary Reinforcement and Stabilizing Mechanisms

In a young organization, design, structure, architecture, rituals, stories, and formal statements are both culture creators and culture reinforcers. Once an organization has matured and stabilized, these same mechanisms come to be constraints on future leaders. In a growing organization these six mechanisms are secondary because they work only if they are consistent with the primary mechanisms discussed previously. When they are consistent, they begin to build organizational ideologies and thus to formalize much of what is informally learned at the outset. If they are inconsistent, they will either be ignored or will be a source of internal conflict. Such internal conflict will often be the primary source of subcultures that are not aligned with the organizational culture and thereby produce difficult integration problems for leaders, as we shall see.

All these secondary mechanisms can be thought of as cultural artifacts that are highly visible but may be difficult to interpret without insider knowledge obtained from observing leaders' actual behaviors. When an organization is in its developmental phase, the driving and controlling assumptions will always be manifested first and most clearly in what the leaders demonstrate through their own behavior, not in what is written down or inferred from visible designs, procedures, rituals, stories, and published philosophies. However, as we shall see later, these secondary mechanisms can become very strong in perpetuating the assumptions even when new leaders in a mature organization would prefer to change them.

Organization Design and Structure

How founders and early leaders design their organizations usually reveals high levels of passion and prejudice but not too much clear logic. The requirements of the primary task—how to organize to survive in the external environment—seem to get mixed up with powerful assumptions about internal relationships and with theories of how to get things done that derive more from the founder's background than from current analysis. If it is a family business, the structure must make room for key family members or trusted colleagues, cofounders, and friends. Even in publicly held companies, the organization's design is often built around the talents of the individual managers rather than the external task requirements. The management theories in which the founders are nested often dominate how the founder wants to organize rather than the requirements of the task.

Founders also have strong theories about how to organize for maximum effectiveness based on their own history and experience. Some assume that only they can ultimately determine what is correct; therefore, they build a tight hierarchy and highly centralized controls. Others assume that the strength of their organization is in their people and therefore build a highly decentralized organization that pushes authority down as low as possible. Still others, like Olsen, believe that their strength is in negotiated solutions; they hire strong people but then create a structure that forces such people to negotiate their solutions with each other, creating in the process a matrix organization.

Some leaders believe in minimizing interdependence to free each unit of the organization; others believe in creating checks and balances so that no one unit can ever function autonomously. Lee Kuan Yew believed in creating departments like the EDB and giving it simultaneously "complete independence" and the requirement to "coordinate its activities with the other government departments" so that the investor would experience Singapore as a "one-stop shop" that produced reliable information, made commitments, and "never broke its promises."

Beliefs also vary about how stable a given structure should be, with some leaders seeking a solution and sticking with it, while others, like Olsen, were perpetually redesigning their organization in a search for solutions that better fit the perceived problems of the ever-changing external conditions. The initial design of the organization and the periodic reorganizations that companies go through thus provide ample opportunities for the founders and leaders to embed their deeply held assumptions about the task, the means to accomplish it, the nature of people, and the right kinds of relationships to foster among people.

Some leaders are able to articulate why they have designed their organization the way they have; others appear to be rationalizing and are not really consciously aware of the assumptions they are making, even though such assumptions can sometimes be inferred from the results. In any case, the organization's structure and design can be used to reinforce leader assumptions but rarely does it provide an accurate initial basis for embedding them, because structure can usually be interpreted by the employees in a number of different ways in that any given hierarchical relationship can vary from total domination to intimate collaboration. It is the quality of the relationship that ultimately makes the difference, especially whether the leader defines his or her relationship with subordinates as a transactional, emotionally distant, Level 1 role relationship, or attempts to create a more personal Level 2 relationship that is designed to be more open and trusting.

Organization Systems and Procedures

The most visible parts of life in any organization are the daily, weekly, monthly, quarterly, and annual cycles of routines, procedures, reports, forms, and other recurrent tasks that have to be performed. The origins of such routines are often not known to participants or, sometimes, even to senior management. But their existence lends structure and predictability to an otherwise vague and ambiguous organizational world. The systems and procedures thus serve a function quite similar to the formal structure in that they make life predictable and thereby reduce ambiguity and anxiety. Though employees often complain of stifling bureaucracy, they need some recurrent processes to avoid the anxiety of an uncertain and unpredictable world.

Given that group members seek this kind of stability and anxiety reduction, founders and leaders have the opportunity to reinforce their assumptions by building systems and routines around them. For example, Olsen reinforced his belief that truth is reached through debate by creating many different kinds of committees and attending their meetings. Steinberg reinforced his belief in absolute authority by creating review processes in which he would listen briefly and then issue peremptory orders. Ciba-Geigy reinforced its assumptions about truth deriving from science by creating formal research studies before making important decisions. Alpha Power reinforced its assumptions about the inherent danger of delivering electricity, gas, and steam by writing hundreds of procedures for how to do things and constant training and monitoring to ensure compliance. Lee Kuan Yew supported his belief that only the best and the brightest should be in government by creating a scholarship program that sent the brightest to the best overseas universities but then required them to enter government service for a period of years.

Systems and procedures can formalize the process of "paying attention," thus reinforcing the message that the leader really cares about certain things. This is why the president who wanted management-development programs helped his cause immensely by formalizing his quarterly reviews of what each subordinate had done. Formal budgeting or planning routines are often adhered to less to produce plans and budgets but more to provide a vehicle to remind subordinates what to pay attention to.

If founders or leaders do not design systems and procedures as reinforcement mechanisms, they open the door to the evolution of inconsistencies in the culture or subcultures that conflict with the CEO's primary values. Olsen believed that line managers should be in full control of their own operation but refused to allow them to become divisions. He allowed strong centralized corporate financial, engineering, manufacturing, and sales organizations to evolve; at the same time he expected the product-line managers to be on top of their jobs. This resulted in much more expensive product lines because they wanted their own engineering, manufacturing, and finance people as liaisons. As the organization matures, subcultures will develop in each function that may or may not be aligned with each other or with the overall corporate culture. If those groups end up fighting each other, it will be the direct result of the initial inconsistency in design logic, not the result of the personalities or the competitive drives of the managers of those functions.

Rites and Rituals of the Organization

Some students of culture view the special organizational processes of rites and rituals as central to the deciphering as well as to the communicating of cultural assumptions (Deal & Kennedy, 1982, 1999; Trice & Beyer, 1984, 1985). Rites and rituals are symbolic ways to formalize certain assumptions and are, therefore, important artifacts to observe. However, their lessons are not always easy to decipher; hence I do not consider them to be primary embedding mechanisms. Instead, they might be considered to be important reinforcers of key cultural assumptions if those assumptions are made clear by the primary embedding mechanisms.

In DEC, for example, the monthly "Woods meetings" devoted to important long-range strategic issues were always held off-site in highly informal surroundings that strongly encouraged informality, status equality, and dialogue. The meetings usually lasted two or more days and involved some joint physical activity such as a hike or a mountain climb. Olsen strongly believed that people would learn to trust each other and be more open with each other if they did enjoyable things together in an informal setting. As the company grew, various functional groups adopted this style of meeting as well, to the point where periodic off-site meetings became corporate rituals with their own various names, locales, and informal procedures.

In Ciba-Geigy, the annual meeting always involved the surprise athletic event that no one was good at and that would therefore equalize status. The participants would let their hair down, try their best, fail, and be laughed at in a good-humored fashion. It was as if the group were trying to say to itself, "We are serious scientists and business people, but we also know how to play." During the play, informal messages that would not be allowed in the formal work world could be conveyed, thus compensating somewhat for the strict hierarchy.

In Alpha Power the values of teamwork, especially in environmental, health, and safety activities, were symbolized by monthly "way we work" special lunches attended by three or four teams that had been nominated for outstanding achievements by senior management. Each team was asked to tell the entire group what they had accomplished and how they had done it. Group photographs then published in the house organ served as additional reward and publicity. In addition, the company had all kinds of prizes for safety performance.

One can find examples of ritualized activities and formalized ritual events in most organizations, but they typically reveal only very small portions of the range of assumptions that make up the culture of an organization. Therein lies the danger of putting too much emphasis on the study of rituals. One can perhaps decipher one piece of the culture correctly, but one may have no basis for determining what else is going on and how important the ritualized activities are in the larger scheme of things.

Design of Physical Space, Façades, and Buildings

Physical design encompasses all the visible features of the organization that clients, customers, vendors, new employees, and visitors would encounter. The messages that can be inferred from the physical environment, as in the case of structure and procedures, potentially reinforce the leader's messages, but only if they are managed to accomplish this (Steele, 1973, 1986; Gagliardi, 1990). If they are not explicitly managed, they may reflect the assumptions of architects, the organization's planning and facilities managers, local norms in the community, or other subcultural assumptions. Often the architecture also reflects macro culture assumptions in that buildings have to fit the style of the community in which they exist.

DEC chose to locate itself initially in an old woolen mill to emphasize frugality and simplicity. What the visitor experienced visually in this organization was an accurate reflection of deeply held assumptions, and one indicator of this depth was that the effects were reproduced in the offices of this organization all over the world.

Ciba-Geigy strongly valued individual expertise and autonomy. But because of its assumption that the holder of a given job becomes the ultimate expert on the area covered by that job, it physically symbolized turf by giving people privacy. In both companies physical arrangements were not incidental or accidental physical artifacts. They reflected the basic assumptions of how work gets done, how relationships should be managed, and how one arrives at truth.

The current trend toward open areas, cubicles, and mixed-use space is very vivid but not easy to decipher. Is it about reducing costs, stimulating certain kinds of interaction, making employees more visible to managers, creating flexible designs that can easily be altered, or combinations of these things? Without getting into the organization to reconstruct the history of the decision process, we don't know what to infer about the culture.

Stories about Important Events and People

As a group develops and accumulates a history, some of this history becomes embodied in stories about events and leadership behavior (Allan, Fairtlough, & Heinzen, 2002; Martin & Powers, 1983; Neuhauser, 1993; Wilkins, 1983). Thus, the story—whether it is in the form of a parable, legend, or even myth—reinforces assumptions and teaches values to newcomers. However, because the message to be found in the story is often highly distilled or even ambiguous, this form of communication is somewhat unreliable. Leaders cannot always control what will be said about them in stories, though they can certainly reinforce stories that they feel good about and perhaps can even launch stories that carry desired messages. Leaders can make themselves highly visible to increase the likelihood that stories will be told about them, but sometimes attempts to manage the message in this manner backfire because the story may reveal inconsistencies and conflicts in the leader.

Efforts to decipher culture from collecting stories encounter the same problem as the deciphering of rituals: unless one knows other facts about the leaders, one cannot always correctly infer what the point of the story is. If one understands the culture, then stories can be used to enhance that understanding and make it concrete, but it is dangerous to try to achieve that understanding in the first place from stories alone.

For example, let's revisit the story told about Ken Olsen that when he first saw the IBM PC he said, "Who would ever want a computer in their home?" and "I would fire the engineer who designed that piece of junk." This story sends strong messages about Olsen's prejudices, but it turns out that only one of the messages is correctly interpreted. Olsen did think the PC was less elegant than what he would have wanted to produce, but his remark about computers in the home was made at a time when people were advocating computers as a way of *controlling* everything in the home. This remark was made at a time when fears of computers taking over all functions in our lives was very real, as viewers of the film *2001: A Space Odyssey* will recall. Olsen welcomed and used computers in his home as work and play stations but not as mechanisms for organizing and controlling daily activities. Unfortunately, the story was often told to show that Olsen did not perceive the growing use of home computers, even as he also said that he felt that DEC had actually invented the personal computer because DEC was the first company to provide desktop interactive capabilities.

Formal Statements of Organizational Philosophy, Creeds, and Charters

The final mechanism of articulation and reinforcement to be mentioned is the formal statement—the attempt by the founders or leaders to state explicitly what their values or assumptions are. These statements typically highlight only a small portion of the assumption set that operates in the group and, most likely, will highlight only those aspects of the leader's philosophy or ideology that lend themselves to public articulation. Such public statements have a value for the leader as a way of emphasizing special things to be attended to in the organization, as values around which to rally the troops, and as reminders of fundamental assumptions not to be forgotten.

Issuing formal statements can be crucial to articulating the identity that the organization wants to convey to its investors, customers, and employees, but it cannot be viewed as a way of defining the organization's whole culture. At best, formal statements cover a small, publicly relevant segment of the culture—those aspects that leaders find useful to publish as an ideology or focus for the organization. I have called such statements part of the espoused values, noting that how well aligned they are with the deeper basic assumptions has to be determined by looking at all the primary indicators mentioned previously.

Lessons for Leaders and Researchers

- **Culture is a complex system.** When founders create a new organization, it is the totality of their own thinking that gets transmitted into the new organization through all these mechanisms. This reminds us that culture is an interconnected set of assumptions, not isolated elements of how groups work.

- **New cultures must be aligned with macro cultures.** The new culture is nested in occupational and national macro cultures and will not survive if it is not aligned with the assumptions of the macro cultures.

- **Founder conflicts and inconsistencies create subcultures and culture conflict.** Most subcultures form around the differentiation of the subtasks that organizations have to perform. If the leader sends conflicting signals, that will stimulate subcultures that can become countercultures and create organizational conflict that will be hard to explain and manage until the conflicted leader leaves or is ousted.

- **Many of the second set of embedding mechanisms are artifacts and cannot be reliably used to infer a founder's basic assumptions.**

- **During the growth period the culture is the organization's identity, and it will be fiercely defended if it is perceived to be the source of the organization's success.**

- **Founders must be aware that they are creating culture, whether or not they explicitly intend to and whether or not they are aware of their impact.** It is this point that is missed when managers in a mature organization launch culture-change programs without seriously examining the culture they already have, based on the founder's activities and the history of learning by the group.

Summary and Conclusions

The purpose of this chapter is to examine how leaders embed the beliefs, values, and assumptions that they hold, thereby creating the conditions for culture formation, stabilization, and evolution. Six of the mechanisms discussed are powerful primary means by which founders or leaders are able to embed their own assumptions in the ongoing daily life of their organizations. Through what they pay attention to and reward, through the ways in which they allocate resources, through their role modeling, through the manner in which they deal with critical incidents, and through the criteria they use for recruitment, selection, promotion, and excommunication, leaders communicate both explicitly and implicitly the beliefs, values, and assumptions they actually hold even if they cannot articulate them clearly. If they are conflicted, the conflicts and inconsistencies are also communicated and become a part of the culture or become the basis for subcultures and countercultures.

Less powerful, more ambiguous, and more difficult to control are the messages embedded in the organization's structure, its procedures and routines, its rituals, its physical layout, its stories and legends, and its formal statements about itself. These six secondary mechanisms can provide powerful reinforcement of the primary messages if the leader is able to control them. The important point to grasp is that all these mechanisms do communicate culture content to newcomers. Leaders do not have a choice about whether or not to communicate. They only have a choice about how to manage what they communicate.

At the organization's early growth stage, the secondary mechanisms of structure, procedures, rituals, and formally espoused values are only supportive, but as the organization matures and stabilizes, they will become institutionalized and become important primary maintenance mechanisms. The more effective they are in making the organization successful, the more they become the filter or criteria for the selection of new leaders. "This is the way we do things around here" becomes the explicit definition of the culture. As a result, the likelihood of new leaders becoming cultural change agents declines as the organization matures. The socialization process then begins to reflect what has worked in the past, not what may be the primary agenda of a new leader coming in. The dynamics of the "midlife" organization are, therefore, quite different from those of the young and emerging organization, as is shown in the following chapters.

Questions for Researchers, Students, and Employees

1. Visit a local supermarket or bank, find someplace to sit, and observe the interactions of employees and managers for as long as you are comfortable. Note especially the interactions with managers, and try to infer what kind of rules are operating around hierarchical boundaries. Watch how employees deal with each other, and see what you can infer about relationships. Are they Level 1 or Level 2?

2. Ask a friend who works in a large company, how he or she knows what is acceptable in that organization in dealing with the boss? How open can you be? How does the boss respond to bad news? What can you infer from what your friend tells you about whether or not you would want to work in that organization?

11

THE CULTURE DYNAMICS OF ORGANIZATIONAL GROWTH, MATURITY, AND DECLINE

If an organization is successful in fulfilling its mission, it will mature and grow. The founders and their early followers will age or die and will be replaced by new leaders who have been promoted from within the organization or have been brought in from the outside. Ownership by founders or founding families will evolve into public ownership and governance by boards of directors. The decision whether or not to retain private ownership or "go public" may appear to be primarily a financial decision, but it has enormous cultural consequences.

With private ownership, the leaders can continue to enforce their own values and assumptions through all of the mechanisms cited in the previous chapter. After governance has shifted to a promoted CEO and a board of directors, the leadership role becomes more diffuse and transient, because CEOs and board members usually have limited terms of office and are more accountable to stockholders.

At the same time, the culture that the organization has evolved thus far will be perceived as the source of the organization's success and will, therefore, limit the choice of new CEOs to individuals who adhere to the basic assumptions of that culture. Whereas leadership created culture in the founding stage, that culture now creates criteria and boundaries within which promoted leaders need to function, unless the board brings in a "turnaround CEO" whose primary job is to *change the culture*.

The new CEO may gradually erode elements of the existing culture and attempt to bring in new cultural elements, but major culture change at the basic-assumption level will occur only if the new CEO gets rid of the culture carriers, the senior management that has grown up with the existing culture. Otherwise, the existing management and employees will want to preserve their culture and limit the new CEO's options or undermine the changes he or she might want to make.

Apart from this basic point that leadership in a mature company is culturally constrained, let's examine what kinds of issues arise in the normal cultural evolution that accompanies success, growth, and age. These issues involve some general effects of age and size as well as the specific effects of differentiation into subgroups that create their own subcultures, which may or may not be aligned.

General Effects of Success, Growth, and Age

To fully understand the impact of growth and age, we have to analyze the systemic effects that are not immediately connected to leadership or culture but that have enormous consequences for the primary challenges that leaders face.

Face-to-Face Communication and Personal Acquaintance Is Lost

With growth it becomes physically less and less possible to "know" everyone that one has to work with and supervise. Getting around to "seeing everyone" becomes harder because people are spread apart more, leading to more electronic communication. When it shifts away from phoning, there is even the loss of tone of voice, pacing, and other cues that are needed to sense emotion in communication.

"Functional Familiarity" Is Lost

With growth, fewer people know what others are doing and how to relate to them. When DEC was small all the different engineering and support units were run by people who were friends who knew what to expect of each other. With growth, the "others" became names and roles who could not always be predicted or counted on. Personal commitments and promises become "contracts" with strangers, which heightens impersonality and formality. Those contracts evolve into job descriptions for the different roles and a set of procedural rules for how roles have to relate to each other; these then are labeled "bureaucracy" and are increasingly viewed as a "problem" that slows things down and makes relationships less reliable. During the early growth, Level 2 personal relationships are natural; with size many of these turn into Level 1 transactions and newcomers find themselves primarily in Level 1 "stranger" roles.

Coordination Methods Change

Integration and alignment of functions and groups change from interpersonal to intergroup processes that require more formal and impersonal communication processes.

Measurement Mechanisms Change

What is measured and how it is measured now have to be made consistent across the many functions and units, which may seem logical and fair to some but not to others.

Pressures for Standardization Increase

As more units need to be coordinated and measured, it becomes more expensive to use different systems in each unit, increasing the pressure to find standard ways of doing things that may affect different units differently.

Standardized Methods Become More Abstract and Potentially Irrelevant

As the number of different units doing different things increases, the standards that apply to all inevitably become more abstract and distant from the actual work being done. In businesses, that process inevitably leads to measuring everything in quantitative terms because numbers are easier to standardize and compare. The ultimate effect of this process is that the performance and potential of individual employees are reduced to numbers and ranking.

The Nature of Accountability Changes

Accountability comes to mean "meeting the numbers" rather than finding out why the numbers were not met. From measuring the credibility of an individual manager's explanation of results or problems, the process changes to finding appropriate formal metrics that can be applied equitably across groups and units. This process often results in managers looking only at the numbers for their subordinates, leading to complaints that "my people are not accountable" when the numbers don't meet the targets. This process reinforces the depersonalization from Level 2 to formal Level 1 distant "professional" relationships.

Strategic Focus Becomes More Difficult

With growth, there is a proliferation of products, services, and markets, which makes it more and more difficult to allocate resources equitably and appropriately when each unit is fighting for "its fair share" while strategy calls for allocating resources differentially. Deciding which things to shut down ("eating one's own children") becomes very difficult.

The Role of Central Functions and Services Becomes More Controversial

With growth it becomes more difficult to decide whether each unit should have its own services or such services should be centralized. Which ones should be centralized and how they should be connected to their counterparts in the units become very complex systemic dilemmas.

Growth of Responsibility for Others Increases

With age and experience managers in growing companies acquire subordinates for whom they are now responsible. Failure in doing one's job now means not only losing one's own job but jeopardizing the jobs and livelihoods of potentially countless others.

Decision Making Becomes Biased by Responsibility for Others

This process was clearest in DEC, where the same people who argued passionately from their own logical premises when the company was small became managers of larger units, which led them to "sound logical" but actually to argue for protection of their own units. This bias is strongly influenced by the recognition that losing a "project" may mean having to fire large numbers of people.

Family Feeling Is Lost

A small unit can maintain the illusion that "we are a family" (or at least a community), but with growth it becomes clear that most of the others are "strangers" with whom it is difficult to identify.

A Common Culture Is Harder to Maintain

The term "corporate culture" begins to have more meaning as the growing organization differentiates into many units that develop their own subcultures. The management of those subcultures then becomes the major culture issue in the large, older organization. In the rest of this chapter we focus on the more specific cultural issues that differentiation creates.

All of these effects are systemic results of growth and age. To fully understand why they happen and what the consequences are for leadership and culture, we have to look more closely at differentiation and integration issues in systems.

Differentiation and the Growth of Subcultures

All organizations undergo a process of differentiation as they age and grow. This is variously called division of labor, functionalization, divisionalization, or diversification. The common element, however, is that as the number of people, customers, goods, and services increases, it becomes less and less efficient for the founder to coordinate everything. If the organization is successful, it inevitably creates smaller units that begin the process of culture formation on their own with their own leaders. The major bases on which such differentiation occurs are as follows:

- Functional or occupational differentiation
- Geographical decentralization
- Differentiation by product, market, or technology

- Divisionalization
- Differentiation by hierarchical level

Functional or Occupational Differentiation

The forces creating functional subcultures derive from the technology and occupational culture of the function. The production department hires people trained in manufacturing and engineering, the finance department hires economics and finance types, the sales department hires sales types, research and development hires technical specialists, and so on. Even though these newcomers to the organization will be socialized into the corporate culture, they will bring with them other cultural assumptions derived from their education and from association with their occupational community (Van Maanen & Barley, 1984). Such differences arise initially from personality differences that cause people to choose different occupations and from the subsequent education and socialization into an occupation (Holland, 1985; Schein, 1971, 1978, 1987c; Van Maanen & and Schein, 1979).

The cultures of different occupations, in the sense of the shared assumptions that members of that occupation hold, will differ because of the core technology that is involved in that occupation. Thus engineers, doctors, lawyers, accountants, and so on will differ from each other in their basic beliefs, values, and tacit assumptions because they are doing fundamentally different things, have been trained differently, and have acquired a certain identity in practicing their occupation. Therefore, in each functional area, we will find a blend of the founder's assumptions and the assumptions associated with that functional or occupational group.

For example, a powerful occupational subculture based on technology is information technology (IT). The IT professional subculture is a prime example of an "engineering culture," dedicated primarily to improvement and innovation. IT assumes the following:

- Information can be packaged into bits and transmitted electronically.
- More information is always better than less.
- The more quantifiable information is, the better.
- Information can be captured and frozen in time on the computer screen.

- A paperless office is possible and desirable.
- Technology leads, and people should adapt.
- People can and should learn the language and methods of IT.
- Management will give up hierarchy if IT provides better coordination mechanisms.
- The more fully connected an organization is, the better it will perform.
- People will use information responsibly and appropriately.
- Anything that can be standardized, routinized, and made people-proof should be instituted.

By way of contrast, employees and nontechnical managers might assume the following:

- Information relevant to operations must include face-to-face human contact to be accurately understood.
- Information must be extracted from raw data and is meaningful only in a particular context that is itself perpetually changing.
- Meaning derives only from complex patterns, not individual data bits.
- The costs associated with speed may not be worth it.
- Too much connectivity produces information overload.
- The more information you have, the more you need; therefore, sometimes having less information is better.
- Certain kinds of information, such as personal feedback in a performance appraisal, should not be quantitative and should not be computerized.
- Not everything should be "paperless"; the ability to see and manipulate paper is intrinsic to many kinds of tasks.
- Technology should adapt to people and be user friendly.
- Hierarchy is intrinsic to human systems and is a necessary coordination mechanism, no matter how efficient networked communications are.
- Control of information is a necessary *management* tool and the only way of maintaining power and status.
- Standardization can inhibit innovation in a dynamic environment.

Note that in many ways these assumption sets are in direct conflict with each other, which explains why IT implementations are often so strongly resisted by employees. If the IT subculture and the other subcultures are not recognized and acknowledged as cultures that must be aligned, the organization will flounder. However, if a CEO understands the different assumptions of these subcultures, he or she can create a "cultural island" in which employees and IT professionals can work together to decide how best to implement a new system. Of necessity, managing potential subculture problems and conflicts becomes one of the critical functions of leadership in a mature organization.

With organizational growth and continued success, functional subcultures become stable and well articulated. Organizations acknowledge this most clearly when they develop rotational programs for the training and development of future leaders. When a young manager is rotated through sales, marketing, finance, and production, she or he is learning both the technical skills in each of these functions and the point of view, perspective, and underlying assumptions of that subculture. Such deeper understanding is thought to be necessary to doing a good job as a general manager later in the career.

In some cases, the communication barriers between functional subcultures become so powerful and chronic that organizations have had to invent new boundary-spanning functions or processes. The clearest example is "production engineering," a function whose major purpose is to smooth the transition of a product from engineering into production. Engineering often designs for elegance and with the belief that production can build anything that they design, while production perceives engineering to be unrealistic, lacking in cost consciousness, and too concerned with product elegance instead of the practicalities of how to build the product.

In summary, functional subcultures bring into the organization the diversity that is associated with the occupational communities and technologies that underlie the functions. This diversity creates the basic problem of general management, in that the leader now has to bring into alignment organizational members who have genuinely different points of view based on their education and experience in the organization. If these problems are anticipated, the leader can either avoid organizing by function or bring the different functions together in dialogues that stimulate mutual understanding of each other's taken-for-granted assumptions. To facilitate such communication across subcultural boundaries requires cultural humility from the leader and the ability to perceive subcultural differences and to respect them.

Geographic Decentralization

As the organization grows geographically, it becomes necessary to create local units for the following reasons:

- Customers in different regions require different goods and services.
- Local labor costs are lower in some geographical areas.
- It is necessary to get closer to where raw materials, sources of energy, or suppliers are located.
- If products are to be sold in a local market, they may have to be produced in that market area as well.

With geographical differentiation, the question inevitably arises as to whether the corporate culture can be strong enough to assert itself in the different regions. If the corporate leadership feels strongly about perpetuating and extending its core assumptions, it sends senior managers from the home country into the regions. Alternatively, if it selects local managers, it puts them through an intensive socialization process. Recall the example of my meeting in Singapore an Australian who had just been named head of Hewlett-Packard's local plant there. Though he had been hired in Australia and was to spend most of his career in Singapore, he was a dedicated HPer. When I asked him why, he explained that shortly after being hired, he had been flown to California, where he had immediately been met by Mr. Packard himself and then spent six hours with all the top managers. In the following two weeks, he was given a thorough indoctrination in the "HP way" and was encouraged to visit headquarters often. What impressed him most was senior management's willingness to spend time with him to really get to know and perpetuate the central values embodied in the HP way.

In DEC, the senior managers responsible for large regions and countries were based in those countries, but they spent two to three days of every month in meetings with Olsen and other senior managers at headquarters, so the basic assumptions under which DEC operated were constantly reinforced, even though most of the employees were locals. The local offices all resembled each other and used the same tools and procedures to do their work.

However, the local national macro culture inevitably shapes the geographic subculture as well. A different blend of assumptions can be found in each geographical area, reflecting the local national culture as well as the business conditions, customer requirements, and the like. The process of local influence becomes most salient where business ethics are involved, as when giving money to suppliers or local government officials is defined in one country as a bribe or kickback and is deemed illegal and unethical, whereas in another country the same activity is not only legal but is considered an essential and normal part of doing business.

As organizations mature, the geographical units may take over more and more of the functions. Instead of being just local sales or distribution units, they may evolve into integrated divisions, including engineering and manufacturing. In those divisions, the additional subcultural difficulty of alignment across functional boundaries becomes evident. For example, DEC's various European units, typically organized by country, found that the customers in different countries wanted different versions of the basic products, leading to the question of where the engineering for the local needs should be done. On the one hand, it was important to maintain common engineering standards worldwide; on the other hand, those common standards made the product less attractive in a given geographical region. The local units then had to develop their own engineering to customize the product for the country in which they were selling.

Differentiation by Product, Market, or Technology

As organizations mature, they typically differentiate themselves in terms of the basic technologies they employ, the products this leads to, and the types of customers they ultimately deal with. Founders and promoted leaders in older companies must recognize and decide at what point it is desirable to differentiate products, markets, or technologies, knowing that this will create a whole new set of cultural alignment problems down the line. For example, Ciba-Geigy started out as a dyestuffs company, but its research on chemical compounds led it into pharmaceuticals, agricultural chemicals, and industrial chemicals. Though the core culture was based on chemistry, as described previously, subcultural differences clearly reflected the different product sets.

The forces that created such subcultural differences were of two kinds. First, different kinds of people with different educational and occupational origins were attracted into the different businesses. Second, the interaction with the customer required a different mindset and led to different kinds of shared experiences. Remember that at one point Basel headquarters suggested a marketing program that would cut across the divisions and learned that it was shot down when a divisional marketing executive from pharmaceutical said, "Do we really think an educated salesman who deals all day with doctors and hospital administrators has anything in common with an ex-farm boy slogging around in manure talking farmers into buying the newest pesticide?"

Alpha Power primarily delivers electricity to its city, but it also has a gas unit and a steam unit that use different technologies in delivering their services. In addition, the company has geographical regions within its urban environment, leading to a large number of sub-organizations that have developed their own subcultures. These are labeled as "silos" in the organization and are viewed as problematic for total corporate safety and environmental programs because local conditions often require modifications of the programs.

Divisionalization

As organizations grow and develop different markets, they often "divisionalize" in the sense of decentralizing most of the functions into product, market, or geographical units. This process has the advantage of bringing all the functions closer together around a given technology, product set, or customer set, allowing for more alignment among the subcultures. To run an integrated division requires a strong general manager, and that manager is likely to want a fair amount of autonomy in the running of his or her division. As that division develops its own history, it will begin to develop a divisional subculture that reflects its particular technology and market environment, even if it is geographically close to the parent company.

Strong divisional subcultures would not be a problem to the parent organization unless the parent wants to implement certain common practices and management processes. An example from my own experience highlights this issue. I was asked to work with the senior management of the Swedish government–owned conglomerate of organizations to help headquarters decide whether or not it should work toward developing a "common culture." This conglomerate included ship building, mining, and, at the other extreme, consumer products such as Ramlosa bottled water. We spent two days examining all of the pros and cons and finally decided that the only two activities that required a common perspective were financial controls and human resource development. In the financial area, the headquarters staff had relatively little difficulty establishing common practices, but in the human resource area, they ran into real difficulty.

From the point of view of headquarters, it was essential to develop a cadre of future *general* managers, requiring that divisions allow their high-potential young managers to be rotated across different divisions and headquarters functional units. But the division subcultures differed markedly in their assumptions about how to develop managers. One division considered it essential that all of its people be promoted from within because of their knowledge of the business, so its members rejected out of hand the idea of cross-divisional rotation of any sort. In another division, cost pressures were so severe that the idea of giving up a high-potential manager to a development program was unthinkable. A third division's norm was that an individual rose by staying in functional "stovepipes"; as a result, managers were rarely evaluated for their generalist potential. When the development program called for that division to accept a manager from another division in a rotational developmental move, it rejected the candidate outright as not knowing enough about the division's business to be acceptable at any level. The divisional subcultures won out, and the development program was largely abandoned.

Implementing information technology systems across divisions is commonly cited as a major problem. For example, in the evolution of medical practice, the introduction of electronic records keeping is now encountering resistance; many doctors are refusing to learn to use keyboards because it takes too much time away from maintaining close eye-to-eye contact with their patients. Many feel that it depersonalizes the relationship with the patient at a time when the macro norms of medical practice argue for closer personal relationships with patients to improve the overall "patient experience."

One of the significant facts about DEC's evolution is that it did create product lines but never divisions, which allowed central functions such as sales and engineering to remain dominant. In contrast, HP divisionalized very early in its history. Many managers within DEC speculated that the failure to divisionalize was one of the major reasons for DEC's ultimate economic difficulties.

With globalization, a growing problem will be the imposition of common human resource processes. The assumptions of the parent organization may be that everyone should be treated the same way with respect to pay and benefits, but the realities in other macro cultures may make that impossible. In the United States, we believe that people should be paid for their skills regardless of formal rank or family connections (status is gained through achievement); however, many other countries consider it appropriate to hire and pay family members regardless of level of achievement. U.S. companies give out bonuses and stock options, but many non-U.S. companies stick to very strict salary guidelines.

Differentiation by Hierarchical Level

As the number of people in the organization grows, it becomes increasingly difficult to coordinate their activities. One of the simplest and most universal mechanisms that all groups, organizations, and societies use to deal with this problem is to create additional layers in the hierarchy so that the span of control of any given manager remains reasonable. Of course, what is defined as reasonable will itself vary from 5 to 50; nevertheless, it is clear that every organization, if it is successful and grows, will sooner or later differentiate itself into more and more levels.

The interaction and shared experience among the members of a given level provide an opportunity for the formation of common assumptions—a subculture based on rank or status (Oshry, 2007). The strength of such shared assumptions will be a function of the relative amount of interaction and the intensity of the shared experience that the members of that level have with each other as contrasted with members of other levels.

Promoted managers will sometimes tell poignant tales of how their managerial style had to change as they rose through the hierarchy. One senior executive of a supermarket chain described how he first became a store manager and succeeded by knowing all of his employees personally. When he was promoted to district manager over three stores, he still tried to maintain this contact by visiting all the stores and spending as much time as he could with store and department managers. When he was promoted to regional manager over 10 districts he realized that he could no longer visit stores because he was now "a stranger whose visits occasioned sprucing up the store and kow-towing to the high-level boss."

He now had to begin to manage by rules and policies and could be personal only with his immediate 10 district managers. As he moved into national headquarters he realized he now had to find ways to develop his regional managers and help them develop their subordinates but that his performance was now measured by the financial returns of each region. More and more of his time was spent on looking over financial results and justifying them to the CEO and the board. He also realized that all of this time he was losing "functional familiarity" not only with the people but with the work itself. He was becoming more and more dependent on the organization below him because he knew less and less about how things actually worked.

The recognition by managers that they know less and less about how things actually work in the trenches is one of the main consequences of success, growth, and age. Another consequence is that the designers of the organization, the engineers who create the new ideas and processes, also fall into the trap of not knowing what is going on, but they have an additional cultural handicap: their own occupational culture, which puts less value on human effort and more value on elegant design. What this means from a subculture point of view is that every mature organization has a potential disconnect between the executives, the engineers and designers, and the actual operators who do the daily work of the organization.

The Need for Alignment between Three Generic Subcultures: Operators, Designers, and Executives

In every organization in the public or private sector, three generic subcultures must be identified and managed to minimize misalignment or destructive conflict. Such conflicts are often misdiagnosed as political interdepartmental fights, power maneuvers, or personality conflicts. What can be missed in that perception is that these different groups may have evolved genuinely different subcultures because they have different functions, face different environmental problems, and are often based on different occupational macro cultures. In a young organization they are blended and held together by the founders, but in a mature organization they will have evolved into different basic assumptions about themselves and their role, which creates potential conflicts. Each of these "macro functions" is needed for organizational effectiveness, which means that one of the critical functions of leadership is to ensure that these subcultures are aligned toward shared organizational goals.

The Subculture of the Operator Function

All organizations have some version of what has been called "the line" as opposed to the "the staff," referring to those employees who produce and sell the organization's products or services. I call these the "operators" to identify the employees who feel they run the place. They are distinguished from the designers of the work, the "engineers," and from the top executives whose function is to maintain the financial health of the organization. Some of the basic assumptions of the operators in all organizations are shown in Exhibit 11.1.

This subculture is the most difficult to describe because it evolves locally in organizations and within operational units. Thus, you can identify an operator subculture in a nuclear plant, in a chemical complex, in an auto manufacturing plant, in the cockpit, and in the office, but it is not clear what elements make this culture broader than the local unit. To get at this issue, we must consider that the operations in different industries reflect the broad technological trends within those industries.

Exhibit 11.1   Assumptions of the Operator Subculture

- The action of any organization is ultimately the action of people. We are the critical resource; we run the place.
- The success of the enterprise therefore depends on our knowledge, skill, learning ability, and commitment.
- The knowledge and skills required are "local" and are based on the organization's core technology and our specific experience.
- No matter how carefully engineered the production process is or how carefully rules and routines are specified, we know that we will have to deal with unpredictable contingencies.
- Therefore, we have to have the capacity to learn, to innovate, and to deal with surprises.
- Most operations involve interdependencies between separate elements of the process, so we must be able to work as a collaborative team in which communication, openness, mutual trust, and commitment are highly valued.
- We depend on management to give us the proper resources, training, and support to get our jobs done.

At some fundamental level, how someone does things in a given industry reflects the core technologies that created that industry. And as those core technologies themselves evolve, the nature of operations changes. For example, as Zuboff (1984) has persuasively argued, information technology has made manual labor obsolete in many industries, replacing it with conceptual tasks. In a chemical plant making paint, the worker no longer walks around observing, smelling, touching, and manipulating. Instead he or she sits in a control room and infers the conditions in the plant from the various indexes that come up on the computer screen. But what defines this subculture across all of these examples is the sense these employees have that they really run things, that they are the key to the functioning of the organization, the "front line."

The operator subculture is based on human interaction, and most line units learn that high levels of communication, trust, and teamwork are essential to getting the work done efficiently. Operators also learn that no matter how clearly the rules are specified of what is supposed to be done under different operational conditions, the world is to some degree unpredictable and they must be prepared to use their own innovative skills to deal with it. If the operations are complex as in a nuclear plant, operators learn that they are highly interdependent and that they must work together as a team, especially when unanticipated events have to be dealt with. Rules and hierarchy often get in the way under unpredicted conditions. Operators become highly sensitive to the degree to which the production process is a system of interdependent functions all of which must work together to be efficient and effective. These points apply to all kinds of "production processes" whether we are talking about a sales function, a clerical group, a cockpit, or a service unit.

The operators know that to get the job done effectively, they must adhere to most of the assumptions stated previously, but because conditions are never quite the same as what their training had shown, all operators learn how to deviate from formal procedures, usually to get the job done but sometimes to subvert what they may regard as unreasonable demands from management. One of the most effective variations of this process is to "work to rule," which means to do everything very precisely and slowly, thus making the organization very inefficient. An example that most travelers have experienced is when airline traffic controllers can practically paralyze the system by working strictly to rule.

The general phenomenon of adapting the formal work process to the local situation and then normalizing the new process by teaching it to newcomers has been called "practical drift," and is an important characteristic of all operator subcultures (Snook, 2000). It is the basic reason why sociologists who study how work is actually done in organizations always find sufficient variations from the formally designated procedures to talk of the "informal organization" and to point out that without such innovative behavior on the part of employees the organization might not be as effective (Dalton, 1959; Hughes, 1958; Van Maanen, 1979). The cultural assumptions that evolve around the way work is actually done are often the most important parts of an organizational culture.

For example, as all observers of production units have learned, employees rarely work to their full capacity except under crisis conditions. More typically, norms develop of "a fair day's work for a fair day's pay," and workers who work harder than this are defined as "rate busters" and are in danger of being ostracized. To fully understand how things work in a mature organization, you must, therefore, observe the informal culture within operations.

The Subculture of the Engineering and Design Function

In all organizations, there is a group that represents the basic design elements of the technology underlying the work of the organization, and this group has the knowledge of how that technology is to be used. Within a given organization, they function as a subculture, but what makes this group significant is that their basic assumptions are derived from their occupational community and their education. Though engineer designers work within an organization, their occupational identification is much broader and cuts across nations and industries. In technically based companies, the founders are often engineers in this sense and create an organization that is dominated by these assumptions. DEC was such an organization, and, as we will see subsequently, the domination of the engineering subculture over other business functions is part of the explanation of DEC's economic success as well as its failure (Kunda, 1992; Schein, 2003). The basic assumptions of the engineering subculture are listed in Exhibit 11.2.

Exhibit 11.2   Assumptions of the Engineering Subculture (Global Community)

- The ideal world is one of elegant machines and processes working in perfect precision and harmony without human intervention.
- People are the problem—they make mistakes and therefore should be designed out of the system wherever possible.
- Nature can and should be mastered: "That which is possible should be done" (proactively optimistic).
- Solutions must be based on science and available technology.
- Real work involves solving puzzles and overcoming problems.
- Work must be oriented toward useful products and outcomes.

The shared assumptions of this subculture are based on common education, work experience, and job requirements. The education reinforces the view that problems have abstract solutions, and those solutions can, in principle, be implemented in the real world with products and systems that are free of human foibles and errors. "Engineers," using this label in the broadest sense, are designers of products and systems that have utility, elegance, permanence, efficiency, safety, and, maybe, as in the case of architecture, even aesthetic appeal.

However, those products are basically designed to require standard responses from their human operators or, ideally, to have no human operators at all.

In the design of complex systems such as jet aircraft or nuclear plants, the engineer prefers a technical routine to ensure safety rather than relying on a human team to manage the contingencies that might arise. Engineers recognize the human factor and design for it, but their preference is to make things as automatic as possible because of the basic assumption that it is ultimately humans who make mistakes. Ken Olsen, the founder of DEC, would become furious if someone said there was a "computer error," pointing out that the machine does not make mistakes, only humans do. Safety is built into the designs themselves. I once asked an Egyptian Airlines pilot whether he preferred Russian or U.S. planes. He answered immediately that he preferred U.S. planes and gave as his reason that Russian planes have only one or two back-up systems while U.S. planes have three back-up systems. In a similar vein, I overheard two engineers saying to each other during a landing at the Seattle airport that the cockpit crew was totally unnecessary. The plane could easily be flown and landed by computer.

In other words, one of the key themes in the subculture of engineering is the preoccupation with designing humans out of the systems rather than into them. Recall that the San Francisco Bay Transit Authority known as BART was designed to run with totally automated trains. In this case, it was not the operators but the customers who objected to this degree of automation, forcing management to put human operators back onto each train even though they had nothing to do except to reassure people by their presence. Automation and robotics are increasingly popular because of the lower cost and greater reliability of systems that have no humans in them. But, as has been pointed out, humans are needed when conditions change and innovative responses are needed.

I have focused on engineers in technical organizations, but their equivalent exists in all organizations. In medicine, it would be the doctors who are developing new surgical techniques; in law offices, the designers of computerized systems for creating necessary documents; in the insurance industry, the actuaries and product designers; and in the financial world, the designers of new and sophisticated financial instruments. Their job is not to do the daily work but to design new products, new structures, and new processes to make the organization more effective. It is not entirely clear how "software engineering" should be perceived. Is it design, operations, or both?

Both the operators and the engineers often find themselves out of alignment with a third critical culture, the culture of executives.

The Executive Subculture

A third generic subculture that exists in all organizations is the executive subculture based on the fact that top managers in all organizations share a similar environment and similar concerns. This subculture is usually represented by just the CEO and his or her executive team. The executive worldview is built around the necessity to maintain the survival and financial health of the organization; it is fed by the preoccupations of boards, of investors, and of the capital markets. Whatever other preoccupations executives may have, they cannot get away from having to worry about and manage the financial issues of the survival and growth of their organization. In private enterprises, the executives have to worry specifically about profits and return on investments, but financial issues around survival and growth are just as salient in the public and nonprofit enterprise. The essence of this executive subculture is described in Exhibit 11.3.

Exhibit 11.3   Assumptions of the Executive Subculture (Global Community)

Financial Focus

- Without financial survival and growth, there are no returns to shareholders or to society.
- Financial survival is equivalent to perpetual war with competitors.

Self-Image Focus: The Embattled Lone Hero

- The economic environment is perpetually competitive and potentially hostile; "in a war you cannot trust anyone."
- Therefore, the CEO must be "the lone hero," isolated and alone, yet appearing to be omniscient, in total control, and feeling indispensable.
- You cannot get reliable data from below because subordinates will tell you what they think you want to hear; therefore, the CEO must trust his or her own judgment more and more (i.e., lack of accurate feedback increases the leader's sense of rightness and omniscience).
- Organization and management are intrinsically hierarchical; the hierarchy is the measure of status and success and is the primary means of maintaining control.
- Though people are necessary, they are a necessary evil not an intrinsic value; people are a resource like other resources to be acquired and managed, not ends in themselves.
- The well-oiled machine organization does not need whole people, only the activities they are contracted for.

For example, the executive level has been shown in a study by Donaldson and Lorsch (1983) to make all decisions through a "dominant belief system" that translated all the needs of their major constituencies—the capital markets from which they must borrow, the labor markets from which they must obtain their employees, the suppliers, and, most important, the customers—into financial terms. Executives had complex mental equations by which they made their decisions. There was clearly an executive culture that revolved around finance. If culture forms around common experience then one could also postulate that there will be in most organization a middle management subculture, because they have neither the power nor the autonomy and so must learn how to live in this ambiguous authority environment. Similarly, first-line supervisors have often been identified as a distinct subculture because they are identified with both the rank-and-file and management.

The basic assumptions of the executive subculture apply particularly to CEOs who have risen through the ranks and have been promoted to their jobs. Founders of organizations or family members who have been appointed to these levels exhibit different kinds of assumptions and often can maintain a broader, more humanistic focus (Schein, 1983). The promoted CEO tends to adopt the exclusively financial point of view because of the nature of the executive career. As managers rise higher and higher in the hierarchy, as their level of responsibility and accountability grows, they have to become more preoccupied with financial matters and they also discover that it becomes harder and harder to observe and influence the basic work of the organization. They discover that they have to manage at a distance, and that discovery inevitably forces them to think in terms of control systems and routines, which become increasingly impersonal.

Because accountability is always centralized and flows to the tops of organizations, executives feel an increasing need to know what is going on while recognizing that it is harder and harder to get reliable information. That need for information and control drives them to develop elaborate information systems alongside the control systems and to feel increasingly alone in their position atop the hierarchy.

Paradoxically, throughout their career, managers have to deal with people and surely recognize intellectually that it is people who ultimately make the organization run. First-line supervisors, especially, know very well how dependent they are on people. However, as managers rise in the hierarchy, two factors cause them to become more "impersonal."

First, they become increasingly aware that they are no longer managing *operators* but other *managers* who think like they do, thus making it not only possible but likely that their thought patterns and worldview will increasingly diverge from the worldview of the operators. Second, as they rise, the units they manage grow larger and larger until it becomes impossible to know everyone personally who works for them. At some point, they recognize that they cannot manage all the people directly and therefore have to develop systems, routines, and rules to manage "the organization." People increasingly come to be viewed as "human resources" and are treated as a cost rather than a capital investment. The immediate subordinates also pose a problem in that they are people, but they are competing for the CEO's job and therefore have to be treated impersonally to avoid accusations of favoritism.

The executive subculture thus has in common with the engineering subculture a predilection to see people as impersonal resources that generate problems rather than solutions. Another way to put this point is to note that in both the executive and engineering subcultures, people and relationships are viewed as means to the end of efficiency and productivity, not as ends in themselves. Both of these subcultures also have in common their occupational base outside the particular organization in which they work. Even if a CEO or engineer has spent his or her entire career inside a given organization, he or she still tends to identify with the occupational reference group outside the organization. For example, when conducting executive programs for CEOs, CEOs will attend only if other CEOs will be there. Similarly, design engineers count on being able to go to professional conferences where they will learn of the latest technologies from their outside professional colleagues.

I have highlighted these three subcultures because they are often working at cross purposes with each other, and we cannot understand the organizational culture if we do not understand how these conflicts are dealt with in the organization. Many problems that are attributed to bureaucracy, environmental factors, or personality conflicts among managers are in fact the result of the lack of alignment between these subcultures. So when we try to understand a given organization, we must consider not only the overall corporate culture but also the identity of the various subcultures and assess their alignment with each other.

The Unique Role of the Executive Function: Subculture Management

I have described the executive subculture and its biases. What remains to be said, however, is that the executive function in most public and private organizations has, in addition, the unique role of having to manage the other functions and, therefore, to deal with the other subcultures. It is for this reason that executives, the formal leaders of organizations, have to understand and manage cultural dynamics for the organization to function well.

As is shown in the following chapters on culture evolution and managed change, the worst examples of culture mismanagement are organizations where the leaders turn over the responsibility for culture management to the human resource function or to consultants. Subcultures cannot coordinate themselves. Leaders create culture, and it is leaders who have to manage cultures that are in organizational midlife and beyond if environmental, technological, economic, or political changes create the threat of organizational decline (O'Reilly & Tushman, 2016). The culture of the organization that has been built on past success may become, to varying degrees, dysfunctional, requiring what the leader comes to perceive as a need for "culture change." Such change varies all the way from just adapting to normal evolutionary processes, steering those processes without changing cultural DNA, or confronting the need for more fundamental culture change, as is described in the following several chapters.

Summary and Conclusions

Organizational success usually produces the need to grow; with growth and aging, organizations need to differentiate themselves into functional, geographic, product, market, or hierarchical units. One of the critical functions of leadership in this process is to recognize the cultural consequences of different ways of differentiating. New subgroups will eventually share enough experience to create subcultures based on occupational, national, and uniquely historical experiences. After such differentiation has taken place, the leader's task is to find ways of coordinating, aligning, and integrating the different subcultures.

Growth and age also produce general problems of loss of personal relationships and the gradual replacement of face-to-face methods of coordinating, measuring, holding accountable, and maintaining strategic focus with standardized routines, contracts, impersonal communication mechanisms, and what ends up being negatively labeled as bureaucracy.

Leaders should not be surprised when they find that different functions seem to be talking completely different languages, when geographically isolated managers do not interpret headquarters memos accurately, or when the concerns of senior management about costs and productivity are not shared by employees. Building an effective organization is ultimately a matter of meshing the different subcultures by encouraging the evolution of common goals, common language, and common procedures for solving problems.

It is essential that leaders recognize that such cultural alignment requires cultural humility on the leader's part along with skills in bringing different subcultures together into the kind of dialogue that will maintain mutual respect and create coordinated action. This increasingly requires the design of cultural islands and dialogic problem solving inside the organization of the sort I described in Chapter 7 for macro culture management.

Suggestions for the Reader

1. Think of an organization that you are interested in and contrast the activities of the designers and engineers, the operators, and the executives.

2. For each of these groups, figure out the environment they are nested in and how that affects their culture.

3. See if you can identify lack of alignment between the cultures of the three groups.

12

NATURAL AND GUIDED CULTURAL EVOLUTION

This chapter deals with the natural processes by which culture evolves and changes as organizations grow and age and also discusses how change leadership can influence those processes. Such influence can come about by deliberately redesigning the structure of the organization to give subgroups different environments, changing some of the organizational processes and thereby "coercing" new kinds of behavior that may or may not lead to new beliefs and values, or taking advantage of natural events such as disasters or scandals that force new behavior among organization members. These changes are generally not planned and are not usually preceded by formal cultural diagnoses or assessments. Rather, they result from how change leaders' react to emergent events.

In the following chapters we take up the cases in which change leadership perceives a specific problem to be addressed and launches a *managed*-change process that will inevitably involve culture in some manner. Leaders need to understand the normal evolutionary change processes to be able to steer them.

The mechanisms and processes by which culture can and does evolve depend on the stage at which the organization finds itself. These mechanisms are cumulative in the sense that at a later stage, all the prior change mechanisms are still operating, but additional ones are becoming relevant.

Understanding how these mechanisms work is especially important for formal leaders, because the best kinds of change programs are often those where the leader enhances a normal evolutionary process rather than going against what may turn out to be the most stable elements in the cultural DNA. Resistance based on cultural DNA is especially likely if we consider the fact that an organization from one macro culture may be nested in a different macro culture with its own DNA. For example, a corporation from a country in which bribing officials is normal procedure would find its attempts to do that in the United States to be either fruitless or dangerous.

Founding and Early Growth

In the first stage—the founding and early growth of a new organization—the main cultural thrust comes from the founders and their assumptions as was described in Chapter 8. The cultural paradigm that becomes embedded becomes that organization's distinctive competence, the basis for member identity, and the psychosocial "glue" that holds the organization together. The emphasis in this early stage is on differentiating the organization from its environment and from other organizations; the organization makes its culture explicit, integrates it as much as possible, and teaches it firmly to newcomers (or selects them for initial compatibility).

The implications for change at this stage are clear. The culture in a young and successfully growing company is likely to be strongly adhered to because (1) the primary culture creators are still present, (2) the culture helps the organization define itself and make its way into a potentially hostile environment, and (3) many elements of the culture have been learned as defenses against anxiety as the organization struggles to build and maintain itself.

It is therefore likely that proposals to deliberately change the culture from either inside or outside will be totally ignored or strongly resisted. Instead, dominant members or coalitions will attempt to preserve and enhance the culture. The only force that might influence such a situation would be an external crisis of survival in the form of a sharp drop in growth rate, loss of sales or profit, a major product failure, the loss of some key people, or some environmental event that cannot be ignored. If such a crisis occurs, the founder may be discredited and a new senior manager may be brought into the picture. If the founding organization itself stays intact, so will the culture. How then does culture evolve in the early growth phase of an organization?

Incremental Change through General and Specific Evolution

If the organization is not under too much external stress and if the founder or founding family stays around for a long time, the culture evolves in small increments by continuing to assimilate what works best over the years. Such evolution involves two basic processes: general evolution and specific evolution (Sahlins & Service, 1960).

General Evolution. General evolution toward the next stage of development involves diversification, growing complexity, higher levels of differentiation and integration, and creative syntheses into new and more complex forms. The growth of subcultures, diversification into other macro cultures, the gradual aging and retirement of the founding group, going from private to public ownership, and merging with or acquiring other companies all create the need for new structures, new systems of governance, and new cultural alignments. Although there are a number of models that have been proposed for such evolution, it has been my experience that we still need to see many more cases before any of these models can really be validated (Adizes, 1990; Aldrich & Ruef, 2006; Chandler, 1962; Gersick, 1991; Greiner, 1972; Tushman & Anderson, 1986).

The general principle of this evolutionary process is that the overall corporate culture will adapt to changes in its external environment and internal structure. Basic assumptions may be retained, but the form in which they appear may change, creating new behavior patterns that ultimately change the character of the basic assumptions. For example, in DEC the assumptions that a person must find "truth through debate" and always "do the right thing" evolved from debate based on pure logic to debate based on protecting one's turf, one's organization.

Specific Evolution. Specific evolution results from the adaptation of specific parts of the organization to their particular environments and the impact of increasing macro-cultural diversity on the core culture. This is the mechanism that causes organizations in different industries to develop different *industry* cultures and causes subgroups to develop different subcultures. Thus, a high-technology company will develop highly refined research and development (R&D) skills, whereas a consumer products company in foods or cosmetics will develop highly refined marketing skills. In each case, such differences will come to reflect important underlying assumptions about the nature of the world and the actual growth experience of the organization.

If the subculture is occupationally based it will also acquire the values of that occupation *as the occupation itself changes.* For example, the personnel function in most companies was originally very locally nested in the company culture, but as the occupation grew into a more "professional" cosmopolitan occupation, more managers in that function began to advocate the values and beliefs of the *profession* even if that deviated from the corporate culture. In many organizations "human resources" began to wield power, began to change some of the rules to fit the profession, and began to be less aligned with the original cultural DNA.

This lack of alignment between the ideals of the corporate culture and the practices of a subculture is one of the main forces leading to "managed culture evolution" as the organization matures (personal communication, Cook, 2016). In the early stage, those differences will be tolerated and efforts will be made to minimize them. For example, it was clear that the service organization at DEC was run more autocratically, but this was tolerated because everyone recognized that a service organization required more discipline if the customers were to get timely and efficient service. The higher-order principle of "do the right thing" justified all kinds of managerial variations within the various functions. However, it is the lack of alignment between the company culture and the subculture that becomes a primary force for change in midlife and beyond.

Self-Guided Evolution through Insight

A young organization is usually highly aware of its culture, even if it does not call its way of doing things "our culture." In some organizations (e.g., DEC), the culture became a focus of attention and was perceived as a source of strength. DEC managers realized that their culture was an important motivator and integrative force, so they created "boot camps" to help newcomers gain insight and published many internal documents in which the culture was explicitly articulated and touted as a strength. They also recognized that cultural assumptions and the norms that they created could be used as a powerful control mechanism (Kunda, 1992; O'Reilly & Chatman, 1996).

Managed Evolution through Hybrids

The preceding mechanisms serve to preserve and enhance the culture as it exists, but changes in the environment often create disequilibria that force more adaptive change—change that challenges some of the deeper assumptions of the cultural paradigm. How can a young organization highly committed to its identity make such changes? One mechanism of gradual and incremental change is the systematic promotion of insiders whose own assumptions are better adapted to the new external realities. Because they are insiders, they accept much of the cultural core and have credibility. But because of their personalities, their life experiences, or the subculture in which their career developed, they hold assumptions that are to varying degrees different from the basic paradigm and thus can move the organization gradually into new ways of thinking and acting. When such managers are put into key positions, they often elicit the feeling from others, "We don't like what this person is doing in the way of changing the place, but at least he (or she) is one of us."

For this mechanism to work, some of the most senior leaders of the company must first have insight into what needs to be changed and what in their culture is missing or is inhibiting the change. They can obtain such insight by engaging in formal cultural assessment activities, by stimulating their board members and consultants to raise questions, or through educational programs at which they meet other leaders. What all of these activities have in common is to compel the leader to step partially outside his or her culture to be able to look at it more objectively. If leaders then recognize the need for change, they can begin to select "hybrids" for key jobs by locating insiders who have a bias toward the new beliefs and values that they want to introduce or enhance. For example, as the computer industry moved away from hardware innovation to software development, change leaders could put more software-oriented managers into key positions in product development. Because DEC needed to become more disciplined in its operations as it grew, it put more people from manufacturing into key product-line jobs because they had learned to be more disciplined in their function.

Transition to Midlife: Problems of Succession

Organizational midlife can be defined structurally as the stage at which founder owners have relinquished the control of the organization to promoted or appointed general managers. They may still be owners and remain on the board, but operational control is turned over to a second generation of general managers. This stage can occur slowly or rapidly and can happen when the organization is very small or very large, so it is best to think of it structurally rather than temporally. Many start-up companies reach midlife very quickly, whereas an organization such as IBM reached it only when Tom Watson Jr. relinquished the reins. The Ford Motor Company is perhaps still in the transition phase in that a family member, William Clay Ford, is still the chair of the board.

The succession from founders and owning families to midlife under general managers often involves many stages and processes. The first and often most critical of these processes is the relinquishing of the CEO role by the founder. Even if the new CEO is the founder's son or daughter or another trusted family member, it is in the nature of founders and entrepreneurs to have difficulty giving up what they have created (Dyer, 1986, 1989; Schein, 1978; Watson & Petre, 1990). During the transition phase, conflicts over which elements of the culture employees like or do not like become surrogates for what they do or do not like about the founder, because most of the culture is likely to be a reflection of the founder's personality.

Battles develop between "conservatives" who like the founding culture and "liberals" or "radicals" who want to change the culture, partly because they want to enhance their own power position. The danger in this situation is that feelings about the founder are projected onto the culture, and in the effort to displace the founder, much of the culture comes under challenge. If members of the organization forget that the culture is a set of learned solutions that have produced success, comfort, and identity, they may try to change the very things they value and depend on.

What is often missing in this stage is an understanding of what the organizational culture is and what it is doing for the organization, regardless of how it came to be. Change leaders among the investors and board members should therefore design succession processes that enhance those parts of the culture that provide identity, distinctive competence, and protection from anxiety. The new leaders not only should have the competence to bring the organization into maturity but should have beliefs and attitudes that will be compatible with the culture or they will fail, as happened to John Sculley and several other outside CEOs that Apple tried out. Figuring out what is the DNA of the existing culture and what is the DNA of the macro cultures in which the organization is nested become critical tasks for a change leader.

The preparation for succession is psychologically difficult, both for the founder and for potential successors, because entrepreneurs typically like to maintain high levels of control. They may officially be grooming successors, but unconsciously they may be preventing powerful and competent people from functioning in those roles. Or they may designate successors but prevent them from having enough responsibility to learn how to do the job—the "Prince Albert" syndrome, remembering that Queen Victoria did not permit her son many opportunities to practice being king. This pattern is particularly likely to operate with a father-to-son transition as was the case in IBM (Watson & Petre, 1990).

When the founder or founding family finally relinquishes control, an opportunity arises to change the direction of the cultural evolution if the successor is the right kind of hybrid and represents what is needed for the organization to survive. If the right kind of hybrid is not found, the organization sometimes reverts to former members who have become hybrids by evolving their own career outside their original organization. For example, after Scully had been fired by Apple, several outside CEOs were brought in, but none were able to revitalize the organization. It was only when they brought back Steve Jobs, who had created and run NeXT and presumably had learned some valuable new things to bring to the organization he founded, that Apple regained its momentum.

In midlife, the most important elements of the culture will have become embedded in the structure and major processes of the organization. Hence, consciousness of the culture and the deliberate attempt to build, integrate, or conserve the culture have become less important. The culture that the organization has acquired during its early years now comes to be taken for granted. The only elements that are likely to be conscious are the credos, dominant espoused values, company slogans, written charters, and other public pronouncements of what the company wants to be and claims to stand for—its philosophy and ideology, which may or may not be consistent with its cultural DNA.

A number of change mechanisms come into play in connection with these transition processes. They may be launched by the outgoing founder or owner or by the new CEO or may occur spontaneously. In midlife organizations, these mechanisms will operate *in addition* to the ones previously mentioned.

Taking Advantage of Subculture Diversity

The strength of the midlife organization lies in the diversity of its subcultures. Leaders can therefore evolve midlife organizations culturally by assessing the strengths and weaknesses of different subcultures and then biasing the corporate culture toward one of those subcultures by systematically promoting people from that subculture into key positions of power. This is an extension of the previously mentioned use of hybrids but has a more potent effect in midlife because preservation of the corporate culture is not as big an issue as it was in the young and growing organization. Also, the midlife organization is led by general managers who are not as emotionally embedded in the original culture and are therefore better able to assess needed future directions. Where product or market changes are involved, as was the case with Ciba-Geigy moving toward pharmaceuticals, I observed that several of the most important corporate-level general management positions were usually filled by executives from the pharma division.

Whereas the diversity of subcultures is a threat to the young organization, in midlife it can be a distinct advantage if the environment is changing. Diversity increases adaptive capacity. The only disadvantage to this change mechanism is that it is very slow. If the pace of culture change needs to be increased because of crisis conditions, more systematic planned change projects must be launched.

Changes in Technology

Culture elements, even at the basic-assumption level, are sometimes forced to evolve in midlife when a new technology is brought in "disruptively" by competitors or by the leaders themselves through mergers, acquisitions, or their own R&D units (Christensen, 1997; O'Reilly & Tushman, 2016). New technologies require new behavior of employees and managers that may or may not be compatible with their talents and preferences. As Zuboff (1984) showed so powerfully, when information technology and numbers in the control room displaced the reliance on employee sensory data in the manufacture of paint, many employees could not make the transition and had to leave what became a "new" culture for them. Doctors who are now required to fill in electronic data on patients and no longer use handwriting for prescriptions experience these changes as major cultural shifts, which many of them resent and refuse to adopt.

Interestingly, I recently experienced yet another iteration in this changing technology as my doctor was wearing GoogleGlasses, which allowed him to look directly at me and dictate everything that he used to have to enter into a computer. Changes in technology do not influence culture directly, but they coerce all kinds of new behavior, which gradually leads to new skills, beliefs, and attitudes. When desktop computers first became available, many organizations mandated that all managers would start to use them, just as medicine is beginning to coerce doctors to use them for medical records and prescriptions. The insightful change leader will realize that if beliefs and values are to follow, the manner in which such new technologies are introduced influences the likelihood of their successful acceptance. Instead of just giving in to the coercive force of the new technology, many change leaders created more *managed-change* programs of the kind that are discussed in the following chapters.

As a preliminary to managed-change programs, companies have used "educational interventions" to introduce a new social technology as part of an organization-development program, with the avowed purpose of creating some common concepts and language in a situation where they perceive a lack of shared assumptions—for example, Blake's managerial grid (Blake & Mouton, 1969; Blake, Mouton, & McCanse, 1989), "systems dynamics" and "the learning organization" as presented in Senge's *The Fifth Discipline* (1990), and Scharmer's *Theory U* (2007), total quality management, and the Toyota production system, commonly known as "lean" (Womack, Jones, & Roos, 1990).

The growing practice of introducing personal computers and related networking information technology, the mandatory attendance at training courses, the introduction of expert systems to facilitate decision making, and the use of various kinds of groupware to facilitate meetings across time and space barriers all clearly constitute another version of what might best be called technological "seduction," though perhaps unintended by the original architects (Gerstein, 1987; Grenier & Metes, 1992; Johansen, et al., 1991; Savage, 1990; Schein, 1992). The assumption underlying this strategy is that a new common language and concepts in a given cultural area, such as "how people relate to subordinates" or "how people define reality in terms of their mental models," will gradually force organization members to adopt a common frame of reference that will eventually lead to new shared assumptions.

An unusual example of technological seduction was provided by a manager who took over a British transportation company that had grown up with a royal charter 100 years earlier and had developed strong traditions around its blue trucks with the royal coat of arms painted on their sides. The company was losing money because it was not aggressively seeking new concepts of how to sell transportation. After observing the company for a few months, the newly appointed CEO abruptly and without giving reasons ordered that the entire fleet of trucks be painted solid white. Needless to say, there was consternation. Delegations urging the president to reconsider, protestations about loss of identity, predictions of total economic disaster, and other forms of resistance arose. All of these were patiently listened to, but the president simply reiterated that he wanted it done, and soon. He eroded the resistance by making the request nonnegotiable.

After the trucks were painted white, the drivers suddenly noticed that customers were curious about what they had done and inquired what they would now put on the trucks in the way of new logos. These questions got the employees at all levels thinking about what business they were in and initiated the market-oriented focus that the president had been trying to establish in the first place. Rightly or wrongly, he assumed that he could not get this broader focus just by requesting it. He had to seduce the employees into a situation in which they had no choice but to rethink their identity.

Beyond these intra-organizational processes, we have to acknowledge that the broader IT revolution is at least as powerful as the introduction of the automobile in creating sweeping world-wide changes even in the concept of "organization" and "occupational community." As Tyrell (2000) puts it in his summary of these impacts: "the development and deployment of rapid interactive communications technologies (especially . . . the Internet, intranets, EDI, and the World Wide Web) has produced new environments that give many people unprecedented access to specialized communities of interest" (p. 96). Since those words were written, we have acquired Facebook, LinkedIn, Twitter, and other new technologies that are already making even email potentially obsolete.

If the boundaries of organizations and occupational communities become fluid, the whole question arises of how culture as shared assumptions can form and operate in a group of people who interact only electronically (Baker, 2016). Some of the most fundamental aspects of culture deal with how people manage their interactions; in the electronic age, new forms of social contract must evolve to deal with authority and intimacy issues. For example, many professional service firms now consist of a very small headquarters organization and a vast network of geographically dispersed relevant experts (lawyers, consultants, doctors) who are "on call" but are not employees of the organization except on a contract basis. As various employment contracts change, the concept of what is a "career" changes as well, leading to further cultural evolution in the macro-cultural domain (Schein & Van Maanen, 2013).

Culture Change through Infusion of Outsiders

Shared assumptions can be changed by changing the composition of the dominant groups or coalitions in an organization—what Kleiner in his research has identified as "the group who really matters" (2003). The most potent version of this change mechanism occurs when a board of directors brings in a new CEO from outside the organization, or when a new CEO is brought in as a result of an acquisition, merger, or leveraged buyout. The new CEO usually brings in some of his or her own people and gets rid of people who are perceived to represent the old and increasingly ineffective way of doing things. In effect, this destroys the hierarchical subculture that was the originator of the corporate culture and starts a process of new culture formation. If there are strong functional, geographic, or divisional subcultures, the new leaders usually have to replace the leaders of those units as well. Dyer (1986, 1989) has examined this change mechanism in several organizations and found that it follows certain patterns:

- The organization develops a sense of crisis because of declining performance or some kind of failure in the marketplace, and concludes it needs new leadership.

- Simultaneously, there is a weakening of "pattern maintenance" in the sense that procedures, beliefs, and symbols that support the old culture break down.

- A new leader with new beliefs and values is brought in from the outside to deal with the crisis.

- Conflict develops between the proponents of the old assumptions and the new leadership.

- If the crisis is eased and the new leader is given the credit, he or she wins the conflict, and the new beliefs and values begin to be embedded and reinforced by a new set of pattern maintenance activities.

The extreme version of this is called "turnaround" management, which drastically changes structures and processes and espouses new beliefs and values, but this can happen to varying degrees. Employees may feel, "We don't like the new approach, but we can't argue with the fact that it made us profitable once again, so maybe we have to try the new ways." Members who continue to cling to the old ways are either forced out or leave voluntarily, because they no longer feel comfortable with where the organization is headed and how it does things.

The new leader can fail in three ways—improvement does not occur, the new leader is not given credit for the improvement that does occur, or the new leader's assumptions threaten too much of the core of the culture that is still embodied in the founder's traditions. If any of these three conditions apply, the new leader will be discredited and forced out as happened with Scully at Apple (it is said that he was never accorded the respect of the technical community within Apple, yet that was Apple's core, no pun intended). This situation occurs frequently when an outsider is brought into young companies in which the founders or owning families are still powerful. In those situations, the probability is high that the new leader will violate the owners' assumptions and will be forced out by them.

Culture change is sometimes stimulated by systematically bringing outsiders into jobs below the senior-management level and allowing them gradually to educate and reshape senior management's thinking. This is most likely to happen when those outsiders take over subgroups, reshape the cultures of those subgroups, become highly successful, and thereby create a new model of how the organization can work. Probably the most common version of this process is to bring in a strong outsider or an innovative insider to manage one of the more autonomous divisions of a multidivisional organization. If that division becomes successful, it generates a new model for others to identify with and creates a cadre of managers who can be promoted into more senior positions and can thereby influence the main part of the organization. As O'Reilly & Tushman (2016) have shown this is also the way organizations can cope with disruptive technological or market changes by creating their own subunits of disruption and fostering their growth alongside the original culture.

For example, the Saturn division of General Motors and the NUMMI (New United Motor Manufacturing, Inc.) plant—a joint venture of GM and Toyota—were deliberately given freedom to develop new assumptions about how to involve employees in the design and productions of cars and thus learn some new assumptions about how to handle human relationships in a manufacturing plant context. GM also acquired EDS (Electronic Data Systems) as a technological stimulus to organizational change. Each of these units became successful and created different cultures; they could thus become a model for change in the parent organization, but the GM "experiment" showed that if an innovative subculture is nested within a strong macro culture, the larger culture does not necessarily adopt the new culture. GM closed down Saturn and NUMMI in spite of its need to make major changes, because the DNA of the innovators clashed too much with the basic assumptions that had driven GM and that persisted even after GM went through bankruptcy procedures some years later.

Organizational Maturity and Potential Decline

Continued success creates two organizational phenomena that make culture change more complicated: (1) Many basic assumptions become more strongly held, and (2) organizations develop espoused values and ideals about themselves that are increasingly out of line with the actual assumptions by which they operate. If the internal and external environments remain stable, strongly held assumptions could be an advantage. However, if there is a change in the environment, some of those shared assumptions can become liabilities precisely because of their strength.

As an organization matures, it also develops a positive ideology and a set of myths about how it operates. The organization develops a self-image, an organizational "face" so to speak, that will be built around the best things it does and did in the past. Because organizations, like individuals, have a need for self-esteem and pride, it is not unusual for them to begin to claim to be what they aspire to be or were at one time, while their actual practices are more responsive to the realities of accomplishing their primary task. Espoused values therefore come to be, to varying degrees, out of line with the actual assumptions that have evolved out of successful daily practices and with some of the assumptions that evolved in the various subcultures.

The best examples of such myths can be seen around the issue of "safety" in high-hazard industries such as oil companies, power companies, airlines, hospitals, and other organizations that espouse concern for the safety of its employees and the public. Each of these industries and individual companies espouses that "safety is our primary concern," but its practices are almost always driven by various tradeoffs around cost, productivity, schedules, and political considerations (Amalberti, 2013). The two major accidents experienced by NASA with the *Challenger* and *Columbia* space shuttles both involved overriding concerns by some employees that there were safety issues. The BP Texas City deaths resulted from employee houses being built too close to dangerous chemical processes. The failure to cap the well in the Gulf of Mexico was the result of having only one instead of two back-up systems because of cost pressures. The ultimate irony of that case was that on the day of the explosion, employees were getting awards for safety performance because the number of "slips, trips, and falls" had gone down.

If nothing happens to expose these incongruities, myths grow up that support the espoused values, thus even building up reputations that are out of line with reality. The most common example in the 1990s was the myth in many companies that they would never lay off anybody, and in 2009 the myth that the banks, the financial companies, and related industries could survive the consequences of the bursting of the housing bubble. It is the growing strength of culture and the illusion that the espoused values are actually how the organization operates that makes managed culture change so difficult in a mature company. Most executives will say that nothing short of a "burning platform" or some major crisis will motivate a real assessment and subsequent change process.

Culture Change through Scandal and Explosion of Myths

Where incongruities exist between espoused values and basic assumptions, scandal and myth explosion become the primary mechanisms of culture change. Nothing motivates an assessment and subsequent change program until there is a major accident, usually involving loss of life, which produces consequences that cannot be hidden, avoided, or denied and thus creates a public and visible scandal. Disastrous accidents, such as the near-meltdown at Three Mile Island, the losses of the *Challenger* and *Columbia* space shuttles, the Bhopal chemical explosion, the BP Texas City refinery explosion and the oil spill in the Gulf, the Fukushima nuclear plant destruction by the tsunami, quickly lead to a cry to "examine the culture that could allow such a thing to happen." In the health care industry the equivalent is a "wrongful death" that reveals a failure in the hospital's safety programs.

In all of these cases, it is usually discovered that the assumptions by which the organization was operating had drifted toward what was economical and practical to get the job done, and those practices came to be in varying degrees different from what the official ideology claimed (Gerstein, 2008; Snook, 2000). Often there have been employee complaints identifying such practices, but because they are out of line with what the organization wants to believe about itself, they are ignored or denied, sometimes leading to the punishment of the employees who brought up the information. When an employee feels strongly enough to "blow the whistle," a scandal may result, and practices then may finally be reexamined, though the whistleblower's career may be ruined (Gerstein, 2008).

Public scandals force senior executives to examine norms and practices and assumptions that had been taken for granted and had operated out of awareness. Disasters and scandals do not *automatically* cause culture change, but they are a powerful disconfirming force that cannot be denied and that therefore start some kind of public self-assessment and change program. In the United States, this kind of public reexamination started with respect to the occupational culture of finance through the public scandals involving Enron and various other organizations that have evolved questionable financial practices. Government oversight practices were reviewed in the wake of the Bernie Madoff scandal, and even some of the more fundamental assumptions of the capitalist system of free enterprise were reexamined because of the deep recession of 2009. These reexaminations sometimes lead to new practices, but they do not automatically create new cultures, because the new practices may not result in greater external success or internal comfort. Scandals create the conditions for new practices and values to come into play but they become new cultural elements only if they produce better results.

After a scandal or crisis has brought basic assumptions into consciousness and has been assessed as dysfunctional, the basic choices are between some kind of "turnaround," a more rapid transformation of parts of the culture to permit the organization to become adaptive once again, or destruction of the organization and its culture through a process of total reorganization via a merger, acquisition, a turnaround process with outside leaders, or bankruptcy proceedings (or all of the above). In any case, strong new change leaders are likely to be needed to unfreeze the organization and launch the change program that will actually change the cultural DNA (Kotter & Heskett, 1992; Tichy & Devanna, 1987). The important point to note is that when myths are exploded, it provides an opportunity for change leaders to steer the organization in a new direction.

Culture Change through Mergers and Acquisitions

When one organization acquires another organization or when two organizations are merged for financial or marketing reasons, or in various kinds of joint ventures, there is inevitable culture clash because it is unlikely that two organizations will have the same cultures. The leadership role is then to figure out how best to manage this clash. The two cultures can be left alone to continue to evolve in their own way. A more likely scenario is that one culture will dominate and gradually either convert or excommunicate the members of the other culture. A third alternative is to blend the two cultures by selecting elements of both cultures for the new organization, either by letting new learning processes occur or by deliberately selecting elements of each culture for each of the major organizational processes (Salk, 1997, Schein, 2009b).

For example, in the merger of Hewlett–Packard with Compaq, though many felt that it was really an acquisition that would lead to domination by HP, in fact the merger-implementation teams examined each business process in both organizations, chose the one that looked better, and imposed it immediately on everyone. Elements of both cultures were imported by this means, which accomplished the goal of eliminating those elements that the HP leadership felt had become dysfunctional in the HP culture.

An interesting variation of this approach was reported in the takeover by General Electric of Pignone, an old Italian company in 1994, an acquisition that Jack Welch later announced as a key step in GE's "globalization" (Busco, Riccaboni, & Scapens, 2002). Needless to say, the GE and Pignone culture differed on many dimensions but the GE approach to the takeover was to impose only its accounting system and, thereby, focus everything on the numbers, even as the GE executives exhorted the Pignone managers "not to pay attention to the numbers, but concentrate on the vision." Numbers, being more objective and manageable, not only became the prime focus but also enabled Pignone to improve its own management processes significantly. The authors report that what then happened was that Pignone, which had initially resisted being taken over by the GE culture, began to get very interested in how GE did things and voluntarily began to adopt many other elements of the GE culture!

Culture Change through Destruction and Rebirth

This dramatic title reflects the fact that bringing in outside executives because there are no hybrids that can evolve the culture strategically is the last resort when a mature company finds itself in a serious survival crisis. If the board or the investors bring in a strong outsider to "fix" the situation, what has come to be called a "turnaround manager," it is likely that this new leader will find it necessary to bring in his or her own team and basically get rid of the managers who adhere to the old cultural basics. In other words, when you remove the key culture carriers, usually the old-timers at the senior levels, you can destroy the culture because you are destroying the group.

When a company is acquired, a similar process can take place in that the acquiring company can impose its culture by replacing all of the key people in the acquisition with its own people. A third version of such destruction often occurs through bankruptcy proceedings. During such proceedings, a board can bring in entirely new executives, decertify a union, reorganize functions, bring in new technologies, and in other ways force real culture change. A new organization then begins to function and begins to build its own new culture. This process is traumatic and therefore not typically used as a deliberate strategy, but it may be necessary if economic survival is at stake. In the recession of 2009, many financial organizations and auto companies went through such destructive proceedings, but it is not always predictable in what form "rebirth" did or will occur. Historical research on past transformations in industry shows that sometimes even with crises only small changes occur, while at other times, changes are truly transformational (Gersick, 1991; Tushman & Anderson, 1986).

Summary and Conclusions

I have described various mechanisms and processes by which culture changes in a natural way but have also noted that those changes can be steered by change leaders. As was noted, different functions are served by culture at different organizational stages, and the change issues are therefore different at those stages. In the formative stage of an organization, the culture is most often a positive growth force, which needs to be elaborated, developed, and articulated. In organizational midlife, the culture becomes diverse in that many subcultures have formed. Deciding which elements need to be changed or preserved then becomes one of the tougher strategic issues that leaders face, but at this time leaders also have more options for changing beliefs and values by differentially rewarding different subcultures. In the maturity-and-decline stage, the culture often becomes partly dysfunctional and can be changed only through more drastic processes such as scandals that lead to mergers, acquisitions, bankruptcy, and turnarounds.

Culture evolves through the entry into the organization of people with new assumptions and from the different experiences of different parts of the organization. Leaders have the power to enhance diversity and encourage subculture formation, or they can, through selection and promotion, reduce diversity and thus manipulate the direction in which a given organization evolves culturally. The more turbulent the environment, the more important it is for the organization to maximize diversity, thereby maximizing its chances of being able to adjust to whatever new challenges the environment creates by having a wider selection of hybrids available.

Questions for Readers

1. What changes, if any, have resulted from the financial scandals of recent years?

2. What changes have resulted from the BP oil spill in the Gulf of Mexico?

3. Can you think of any major changes in recent years that have resulted without a scandal or crisis of some sort?

Part Four

ASSESSING CULTURE AND LEADING PLANNED CHANGE

What I have tried to provide thus far is a descriptive analysis of what culture is, how it works, and how to think about and understand it. When and how you would *assess* the culture would depend entirely on your reasons. For example, you might want to assess the culture of an organization that has offered you a job, and you wonder whether or not you would fit in there. You might be a leader who is considering acquiring another company and might want to know how your culture and the new company's culture might mesh. You might be a manager who is trying to reduce conflict between two departments under you and wonder about the cultures of those two departments. You might be a human resources executive who has been asked by your CEO whether employees are engaged enough in their jobs; he also wants you to "create a culture of engagement." Or you might be a hospital executive who is worried about too many wrongful deaths or high rates of infection and has heard about the concept of "safety culture" in high-hazard industries.

My point is that each of these and many other possible reasons for assessing a culture might lead to different diagnostic and change processes, using different kinds of tools and models of change. What we will do in this

253

part of the book is to provide as best we can some of the generic issues of assessment and change and describe the kinds of cultural assessment tools and change processes that are most appropriate for each of these generic issues. In Chapter 13 we review the broad problem of assessment when it's involved with as complex a concept as *culture*. In Chapters 14 and 15 we focus on the two main methods of assessment that have evolved in relation to culture-*change* programs, and in Chapter 16 we provide a general change model for change leaders to consider.

Our final chapter will consider what is involved now and might be in the future in the creation and management of culture. What should leaders be and do to deal with this complex area?

13

DECIPHERING CULTURE

Organizational culture can be studied in various ways. The method should be determined by the purpose. Just deciphering a culture for curiosity is as vague an enterprise as just assessing personality or character in an individual. Assessment makes more sense when there is some problem to be illuminated or some specific issue about which we need information. As we will see, how we perform the assessment and what tools we use very much depend on our purpose. If we think about all of the cultural dimensions that have just been reviewed in the previous chapters, we will realize that deciphering a culture to the level of its basic assumptions can be a formidable task. This chapter describes the general issues that are encountered when we try to decipher something as complex as culture.

Why Decipher Culture?

There are several quite different reasons for wanting to decipher or assess an organizational culture. At one extreme is pure academic research where the researcher is trying to present a picture of a culture to fellow researchers and other interested parties to develop a theory or to test some hypothesis. This covers most anthropologists who go to live in a culture to get an insider's view and then present the culture in written form for others to get a sense of what goes on there (e.g., Dalton, 1959; Kunda, 1992; Van Maanen, 1973).

At the other extreme is the student's need to assess the culture of an organization to decide whether or not to work there, or the need of an employee or manager to understand his or her organization better to improve it. In between is the consultant's and change agent's need to decipher the culture to facilitate some change program that the organization has launched to solve a business problem. What differs greatly in these cases is the focus and level of depth involved in the deciphering and who needs to know the results. At the end of this chapter, we also discuss the ethical issues and risks involved in each of these approaches.

Deciphering from the Outside

It is not only the ethnographer or researcher who needs to decipher an organization's culture. The job applicant, the customer, and the journalist all have the need from time to time to figure out what goes on inside a particular organization. They do not need to know the totality of a given culture, but they do need to know some of its essences in relation to their goal. The most common version of this need is the college graduate who wants to know whether or not to go to work in a particular organization. Thus he or she might

- Visit and observe
- Identify artifacts and processes that are puzzling
- Ask insiders why things are done that way
- Identify espoused values that are appealing and ask how they are implemented within the organization
- Look for inconsistencies and ask what really determines day-to-day behavior

The essential point is not to get too involved with the deep content of the culture until you have experienced it at the artifact level. That means visiting the public spaces, taking tours, asking to see inside areas, and reading whatever literature the organization makes available. The first cut at thinking about content areas should come out of the things that puzzle you. Why are the offices (or cubicles or tables) laid out the way they are, why is it so quiet or noisy, why are there no pictures on the walls, and so on? Your personal needs and interests should guide this process, not some formal checklist. To give yourself some content focus, try to observe how the insiders behave toward each other in terms of the critical issues of authority and intimacy.

You will have met some insiders in the process—recruiters, customer representatives, tour guides, friends who work there, or friendly strangers with whom you can strike up a conversation. When you interact with insiders, the culture will reveal itself in the way that the insiders deal with you. Culture is best revealed through interaction. Ask insiders about the things you have observed that puzzle you. To your surprise, they may be puzzled as well, because insiders do not necessarily know why their culture works the way it does. But being jointly puzzled begins to give you some insight into the layers of the culture, and you can ask the same question of other insiders, some of whom may be more insightful as to what is going on. If you have read all about the organization and have heard its claims about its goals and values, look for evidence that they are or are not being met and ask insiders how those goals and values are met. If you discover inconsistencies, ask about them. Whenever you hear a generalization or an abstraction such as "we are a team here," ask for some specific behavioral examples.

This process of deciphering cannot be standardized, because organizations differ greatly in what they allow the outsider to see. Instead you have to think like the anthropologist, lean heavily on observation, and then follow up with various kinds of inquiry. The reason for focusing on things that puzzle you is that it keeps the inquiry pure. If you start with trying to verify your assumptions or stereotypes of the organization, you will be perceived as threatening and will elicit inaccurate defensive information. If you display genuine puzzlement, you will elicit efforts on the part of insiders to help you understand. In that regard, the best form of inquiry may be to reveal something that puzzles you and then say, "Help me to understand why the following things are happening."

Deciphering in a Researcher Role Is an Intervention

If you are a researcher trying to decipher what is going on in relation to a particular research question, your first issue is getting entry. In the process of contacting the organization, negotiating what you need and what you can offer them in return, you will go through all of the preceding steps with the insiders whom you have already met. You will acquire a great deal of superficial but potentially very relevant cultural knowledge. Depending on your research goals, you then have to decide what additional information to gather to get a deeper understanding of the culture.

You must realize that gathering valid data from a complex human system is intrinsically difficult, involves a variety of choices and options, and *is always an intervention into the life of the organization.* The most obvious difficulty in gathering valid cultural data is the well-known phenomenon that when human "subjects" are involved in research, there is a tendency for the subjects either to resist and hide data that they feel defensive about or to exaggerate to impress the researcher or to get cathartic relief—"Finally someone is interested enough in us to listen to our story." The need for such cathartic relief derives from the fact that even the best of organizations generate "toxins"—frustrations with the boss, tensions over missed targets, destructive competition with peers, scarce resources, exhaustion from overwork, and so on (Frost, 2003; Goldman, 2008).

In the process of trying to understand how the organization really works, you may find yourself listening to tales of woe from anxious or frustrated employees who have no other outlet. To get any kind of accurate picture of what is going on in the organization, you must find a method that encourages the insiders to "tell it like it is" rather than trying to impress you, hide data, or blow off steam. It may well be that the best way to do this is to volunteer to help in some way or to become an intern, ask if there are chores that you could do part time or in some other way indicate that you are willing to help and are not there just to gather data.

If you have made any kind of contact with the organization, even if it is only getting permission to observe silently, the human system has been perturbed in unknown ways. The employees being observed may view you as a spy or as an opportunity for catharsis, as noted earlier. Motives will be attributed to management as to why you are there. You may be seen as a nuisance, a disturbance, or an audience to whom to play. But you have no way of knowing which of the many possible reactions you are eliciting and whether or not they are desirable either from a data-gathering or ethical point of view. For this reason, you should examine carefully the broad range of data-gathering interventions available and choose carefully which method to use.

The many possible ways of gathering data are shown in the following list in terms of the degree to which the "researcher" will be involved with the organization being studied and how involved the members of the organization will become in the data-gathering process. I put researcher in quotes because with human systems there is no way to be "just a researcher" unless you literally study only the products of the organization or its demographics. *The ethical issues of doing the research therefore have to be considered at the outset and have to override the needs of the researcher for reliable and valid data.*

- Demographics: measurement of "distal variables"
- Content analysis of documents and organizational products such as stories, myths, rituals, symbols, and other artifacts
- Ethnography or participant observation: asking to hang around, shadowing selected participants, sitting quietly to observe but avoiding getting involved even if asked
- Participation in a volunteer or helping role
- Asking members to fill in questionnaires, ratings, objective tests, scales as individuals and anonymously, with scoring done by outsiders
- Educational interventions, projective tests, assessment centers, and interviews
- Action research or organizationally initiated contract research
- Incidental clinical inquiry as part of a helping or consulting process
- Total involvement in improvement processes such as statistical quality control or "lean" process redesign
- Take a regular job for some time to fully experience the culture

Experiments are usually not possible for ethical reasons, but surveys and questionnaires are often used, with the limitations that are discussed in detail in the following chapter. If you recognize that the interpretation of cultural data may require interaction with the subjects, you could use semi-structured interviews, projective tests, or standardized assessment situations, but these methods again raise the ethical issues of whether you are intervening in their system beyond what they might have agreed to and are influencing the culture through the data-gathering process itself.

In an interview, you can ask broad questions such as the following:

- What was it like to come to work in this organization?
- What did you notice most as being important to getting along?
- How do bosses communicate their expectations?

The main problem with this approach is that it is very time-consuming, and it may be hard to put data from different individuals together into a coherent picture; each person may see things differently even though he or she uses the same words. The dilemma for you, then, is how to get access to groups in which the deeper cultural assumptions reveal themselves. The answer is that you must somehow motivate the organization to want to reveal itself to you because it has something to gain. That brings us to the concepts of *action research* and *clinical research*. Action research is generally thought of as a process whereby the members of the organization being studied become involved in the gathering of data and especially in the interpretation of what is found. If the motivation for the project is to help the researcher gather valid data, the action-research label is appropriate. However, if the project was initiated by the organization to solve a problem, we move to what I have called "clinical research or inquiry" (Schein, 1987a, 2001, 2008).

Clinical Inquiry: Deciphering in a Helper or Consultant Role

The methodology that I have used most in cultural deciphering is to learn from my own experience as a helper, either as a volunteer or as a paid consultant. This level of analysis can be achieved if the organization needs some kind of help from you and if you are trying to help the organization understand itself better to make changes. Your deeper insight into the culture is then a byproduct of your helping; it is likely to be deeper, because in the helper role you can ask questions that the insiders might normally consider intrusive. The critical distinguishing feature of this inquiry model is that the data come voluntarily from the members of the organization, either because they initiated the process and have something to gain by revealing themselves to you, the outsider, or, if you initiated the project, because they feel they have something to gain from cooperating with you. In other words, no matter how the contact was initiated, the best cultural data will surface if the members of the organization feel they are getting some help from you.

If you are an ethnographer or researcher, you must analyze carefully what you may genuinely have to offer the organization and work toward a psychological contract in which the organization benefits in some way or in effect becomes a client. This way of thinking requires you to recognize from the outset that your presence will be an intervention in the organization and that the goal should be to make that intervention useful to the organization.

Ethnographers tell stories of how they were not "accepted" until they became helpful to the members of the organization in some way, either by doing a job that needed to be done or by contributing in some other way (Barley, 1984; Kunda, 1992). The contribution can be entirely symbolic and unrelated to the work of the group being studied. For example, Kunda (1992) reports that in his work in an engineering group, he was "permitted" to study the group, but they were quite aloof, which made it hard to inquire about what certain rituals and events in the group meant. However, Kunda was a very good soccer player and was asked to join the lunchtime games. He made a goal for his team one day and from that day forward, he reports, his relationship to the group changed completely. He was suddenly "in" and "of" the group, and that made it possible to ask about many issues that had previously been off limits.

Barley (1984), in his study of the introduction of computerized tomography into a hospital radiology department, offered himself as a working member of the team and was accepted to the extent that he actually contributed in various ways to getting the work done. The important point is to approach the organization with the intention of helping, not just gathering data. Alternatively, a consultant may be invited into the organization to help with some problem that has been presented that initially has no relationship to culture. In the process of working on the problem, the consultant will discover culturally relevant information, particularly if the process-consultation model is used, given its emphasis on inquiry and helping the organization to help itself (Schein, 1999a, 2009a, 2016).

If you are in the helper role, you are licensed to ask all kinds of questions that can lead directly into cultural analysis, thereby allowing the development of a research focus as well. Both you and the "client" become fully involved in the problem-solving process, and the search for relevant data becomes a joint responsibility. It is then in the client's interest to say what is really going on instead of succumbing to the potential biases of hiding, exaggerating, or blowing off steam. In this clinical helping role, you are not limited to the data that surface around the client's specific issues. There will usually be many opportunities to hang around and observe what else is going on, allowing you to combine some of the best elements of the clinical and the participant-observer ethnographic models. In fact, the ethnographic model (where the ethnographer comes to be seen as a helper) and the helper model as just described converge and become one and the same.

How Valid Are Clinically Gathered Data?

How can you judge the "validity" of the data gathered by this clinical model? The validity issue has two components: (1) factual accuracy based on whatever contemporary or historical data you can gather and (2) interpretative accuracy in terms of your representing cultural phenomena in a way that communicates what members of the culture really mean rather than projecting into the data your own interpretations (Van Maanen, 1988). To fully understand cultural phenomena requires at least a combination of history and clinical research, as some anthropologists have argued persuasively (Sahlins, 1985). Factual accuracy can be checked by the usual methods of triangulation, multiple sources, and replication. Interpretative accuracy is more difficult, but three criteria can be applied. First, if the cultural analysis is "valid," an independent observer going into the same organization should be able to see the same phenomena and interpret them the same way. Second, if the analysis is valid, you should be able to predict the presence of other phenomena and anticipate how the organization will handle future issues. In other words, predictability and replication become the key validity criteria. Third, the members of the organization should feel comfortable that what you have depicted makes sense to them and helps them to understand themselves.

The clinical model makes explicit two fundamental assumptions: (1) it is not possible to study a human system without intervening in it, and (2) we can fully understand a human system only by trying to change it (Lewin, 1947). This conclusion may seem paradoxical in that we presumably want to understand a system as it exists in the present. This is not only impossible because our very presence is an intervention that produces unknown changes, but if we attempt to make helpful changes, we will enable the system to reveal both its goals and its defensive routines, the essential parts of its culture. For this process to work, the intervention goals must be jointly shared by the outsider and insider. If the consultant tries to change the organization in terms of his or her own goals, the risk of defensiveness and withholding of data rises dramatically. If the consultant is helping the organization to make some changes that it wants, the probability rises that organization members will reveal what is really going on. A more detailed analysis of how such a managed-change process works is provided in Chapters 15 and 16.

Ethical Issues in Deciphering Culture

Deciphering culture has some inherent risks that both the insider and the outsider should assess before proceeding. The risks differ, depending on the purpose of the analysis, and they are often subtle and unknown. Therefore, the desire to go ahead and the organization's permission to do so may not be sufficient to warrant proceeding. The outside professional, whether consultant or ethnographer, must make a separate assessment and sometimes limit his or her own interventions to protect the organization.

Risks of an Analysis for Research Purposes

An organization can be made vulnerable by having its culture revealed to outsiders. The obvious solution is always to disguise the organization in published accounts, but if the intent is to communicate accurately to outsiders, the data are much more meaningful if the organization and the people are identified. Naming the organizations, as I have done in most of the examples used in this book, makes it possible to gain a deeper understanding of cultural phenomena and also makes it possible for others to check for accuracy and replicate the findings.

However, if a correct analysis of an organization's culture becomes known to outsiders because it either is published or is simply discussed among interested parties, the organization or some of its members may be put at a disadvantage because data that would ordinarily remain private now may become public. For various reasons, the members of the organization may not want their culture laid bare for others' viewing. If the information is inaccurate, potential employees, customers, suppliers, and any other categories of outsiders who deal with the organization may be adversely influenced.

Cases used in business schools are rarely disguised, even though they often include revealing details about an organization's culture. If the organization fully understands what it is revealing and if the information is accurate, no harm is done. But if the case reveals material that the organization is not aware of, such publication can produce undesirable insight or tension on the part of members and can create undesirable impressions on the part of outsiders. If the information is not accurate, both insiders and outsiders may get wrong impressions and may base decisions on incorrect information.

For example, when I was teaching at the Centre d'Etudes Industrielles in Geneva in the early 1980s, they were using a case about DEC that was outdated and gave an entirely incorrect impression of what was going on in DEC, yet students were influenced by this case in terms of whether or not they would apply for jobs at DEC. Furthermore, most such cases are only a slice through the organization at a particular time and do not consider historical evolution. The case material about DEC may have been accurate at one point in time but was presented as a general picture.

Researchers often attempt to avoid this danger by providing their analysis to the members of the organization before it is published. This step has the advantage of also testing, to some degree, the validity of the information. However, it does not overcome the risk that the members of the organization who "clear" the data for publication might not be aware of how the analysis might make others in the organization more vulnerable. Nor does it overcome the risk that the members of the organization who review the material may want to play it safe and forbid the publication of anything that names the organization. The ultimate ethical responsibility therefore falls to the researcher. Whenever a researcher publishes information about an individual or organization, he or she must think carefully about the potential consequences. Where I have named organizations in this book, I have either been given permission or have decided that the material can no longer harm the organizations or individuals. In my original edition I was still involved with DEC and Ciba-Geigy so I labeled them the Action Co. and the Multi Co. Neither company exists today, which justifies in my mind naming them. The same logic applied to my naming Steinberg's.

Risks of an Internal Analysis

If an organization is to understand its own strengths and weaknesses, if it wants to learn from its own experience and make informed strategic choices based on realistic assessments of external and internal factors, it must at some point study and understand its own culture (Bartunek & Louis, 1996; Coghlan & Brannick, 2005). This process is not without its problems, risks, and potential costs, however. Basically, two kinds of risks must be assessed: (1) the analysis of the culture could be incorrect or (2) the organization might not be ready to receive feedback about its own culture.

If decisions are made on the basis of incorrect assumptions about the culture, serious harm could be done to the organization. Such errors are most likely to occur if culture is defined at too superficial a level—if espoused values or data based on questionnaires are taken to be an accurate representation of the underlying assumptions without conducting group and individual interviews that specifically dig for deeper assumptions and patterns. This is the major risk in the use of typologies and surveys; it is discussed further in the following chapter.

The second risk is that the analysis may be correct, but insiders other than those who made the analysis may not be prepared to digest what has been learned about them. If culture functions in part as a set of defense mechanisms to help avoid anxiety and to provide positive direction, self-esteem, and pride, reluctance to accept certain cultural truths about one's culture is a normal human reaction. Psychotherapists and counselors constantly must deal with resistance or denial on the part of patients and clients. Similarly, unless an organization's personnel recognize a real need to change and unless they feel psychologically safe enough to examine data about the organization, they will not be able to hear the cultural truths that inquiry may have revealed. Even worse, they may lose self-esteem because some of their myths or ideals about themselves may be destroyed by the analysis.

Another risk is that some members will achieve instant insight and automatically and thoughtlessly attempt to produce changes in the culture that (1) some other members of the organization may not want, (2) some other members may not be prepared for and therefore may not be able to implement, or (3) may not solve the problem.

Therefore, the culture analyst should make the client system fully aware that there are consequences to having elements of culture laid bare, so to speak. Consultants are often called in by insiders to reveal what some insiders know but feel they cannot say for various reasons. The risk in agreeing to do this is that the organization may not like to hear the consultant's analysis of its culture. I have had more than one experience where my analysis was praised by some insiders and rejected by others, which has led me to the general conclusion that it is better to help the organization to figure out its own culture and not to become an outside expert on something that is so intrinsically systemic and so infused with insider meaning that outsiders may never grasp. The outsider should never lecture insiders on their own culture, because the outsider cannot know where the sensitivities will lie and cannot overcome his or her own subtle biases.

Professional Obligations of the Culture Analyst

If the foregoing risks are real, then who should worry about them? Is it enough to say to an organization that we will study your culture and let you know what we find and that nothing will be published without your permission? If we are dealing with surface manifestations, artifacts, and publicly espoused values, then the guideline of letting members clear the material seems sufficient. However, if we are dealing with the deeper levels of the culture, the basic assumptions and the patterns among them, the insiders clearly may not know what they are getting into, and the obligation shifts to the outsider as a professional to make the client genuinely aware of what the consequences of a cultural analysis might be. The principle of informed consent does not sufficiently protect the client or research subject if he or she cannot initially appreciate what will be revealed.

The analyst of a culture undertakes a professional obligation to understand fully what the potential consequences of an investigation are. Such consequences should be carefully spelled out before the relationship reaches a level at which there is an implied psychological contract that the outsider will give feedback to the insiders on what has been discovered about the culture, either for inside purposes of gaining insight or for clearing what may eventually be published. For all of these reasons, deciphering and reporting on a culture works best and is psychologically safest when the organization is motivated to make changes that may involve the culture.

As should be evident by now, there is no simple formula for gathering cultural data. Artifacts can be directly observed; espoused values are revealed through the questions the researcher or consultant asks of whomever is available and through the organization's published materials; and shared tacit assumptions have to be inferred from a variety of observations and further inquiry around inconsistencies and puzzlements.

Because culture is a shared group phenomenon, the best way to gather systematic data is to bring representative groups of 10 to 15 people together and ask them to discuss artifacts, values, and the assumptions behind them. A detailed way to do this is described in one of the cases presented in Chapter 15. If the researcher is simply trying to gather information for his or her own purposes and if problems of reliability and validity can afford to be ignored, the various culture-content categories described in the previous chapters are perfectly adequate guidelines for what to ask about. The actual questions around each of the content areas should be constructed by the researcher in terms of the goals of the research, bearing in mind that culture is broad and deep. To capture a whole culture is probably impossible, so the researcher must have some more specific goal in mind before a set of questions for the groups can be designed.

Summary and Conclusions

There are many ways of deciphering or "assessing" cultural dimensions, which can be categorized in terms of the degree to which the researcher is directly involved with the organization and the degree to which organization members become directly involved in the research process. For purposes of academic research or theory building, it is important to learn what is really going on, which requires real entry into and involvement with the organization beyond what questionnaires, surveys, or even individual interviews can provide. The researcher must create a relationship with the organization that permits him or her to become a researcher-helper to ensure that reliable and valid data will be forthcoming because it is in the organization's own interest to provide data.

If the consultant is helping leaders to manage a change process, he or she may design a culture-assessment process and may learn some things about the culture, but it is only the insiders who must understand their own culture. I have been in many situations where insiders achieved clarity about essential elements of their culture while I went away from the project not really understanding their culture at all, and this was fine. In either case, the deeper cultural data will reveal themselves only if the researcher or consultant establishes a helping relationship with the organization such that the organization members feel they have something to gain by revealing what they really think and feel to the researcher. Such a "clinical-inquiry" relationship is the minimum requirement for obtaining valid cultural data, but the outsider researcher can go beyond helping the organization and gather additional data relevant to his or her research purpose.

The process of deciphering a culture, whether for the purposes of an insider or for the purposes of describing that culture to outsiders, has a set of associated risks and potential costs. These risks are internal in the sense that the members of the organization may not want to know or may not be able to handle the insights into their own culture; they are external in that the members of the organization may not be aware of the manner in which they become vulnerable once information about their culture is made available to others.

The implication for leaders is "be careful." Cultural analysis can be very helpful if you know what you are doing and why. By this I mean that there must be some valid purpose to a cultural analysis and there must be a clear understanding of the different consequences of using different methods. An assessment is an intervention into the organization. If it is done for its own sake, the risks of either wasting time or doing harm increase. However, the potential for insight and constructive action is tremendous if it is done with a responsible facilitator from either inside or outside the organization.

Questions for the Reader

1. Why are you reading this book? What is your interest in culture?

2. Have you given some thought to your own cultural history and how you would decipher the various cultures you have come from: family, peer group, school, jobs, community?

3. What culture-deciphering issue do you face, and what is your plan for culture assessment?

14

THE DIAGNOSTIC QUANTITATIVE APPROACH TO ASSESSMENT AND PLANNED CHANGE[1]

In the previous chapter we discussed the broad issues of deciphering culture. In this chapter we zero in on the change leader who wants to know about culture because he or she has a change agenda. Without a precise and concrete notion of the kind of change the leader wants to make, there is no point in assessing the culture. But once the change leader has clearly defined the problem in future-behavior terms, it is time to assess the culture to see how it will aid or hinder the change process. This can be done in two ways:

- Seeking insight by measuring specific dimensions of culture or looking for various typological models of culture—what we call the *diagnostic quantitative* approach, as illustrated in this chapter
- Seeking insight by using internally focused observations combined with individual or group interviews—what we call the *dialogic qualitative* approach, as will be described in the following chapter

Many of the diagnostic typologies and profiles that have been proposed by various authors are based on questionnaires or surveys of members of the organization. We will therefore discuss typologies both as theoretical constructs and as labels derived from factor analyzing a lot of perceptual data. The fact that there are a number of different models built around questionnaires requires us to consider how to evaluate the relative validity and utility of such models. Before reviewing some of them, we need to understand what role typologies play in trying to understand an abstract concept such as organizational culture and what the advantages and disadvantages are of using them.

---

[1] This chapter is based in part on research conducted by Peter Schein and was written jointly with him.

Why Use Typologies, and Why Not?

When we observe the "natural" world, what we see, hear, taste, smell, and feel is potentially overwhelming. By itself, "raw experience" does not make sense, but our own cultural upbringing has taught us how to make sense of it through conceptual categories that are embedded in our language. What we experience as an infant is, to quote William James's 1890 *Principles of Psychology* is a "blooming, buzzing confusion" that is slowly put into order as we learn to discriminate objects such as chairs and tables, mother and father, and light and dark, and to associate words with those experienced objects and events.

By the time we are young adults, we have a complete vocabulary and a set of conceptual categories that allow us to discriminate and label most of what we experience. We must not forget, however, that these categories as well as the language that goes with them are learned within a given culture and such learning continues as we move into new cultures such as occupations and organizations. The engineer learns new categories and words, as do the doctor, the lawyer, and the manager.

New concepts become useful if they (1) help to make sense and provide some order out of the observed phenomena, (2) help to define what may be the underlying structure in the phenomena by building a theory of how things work, which, in turn (3) enables us to predict to some degree how other phenomena that may not yet have been observed will look and act. However, in the process of building new categories, we inevitably must become more abstract. As we develop such abstractions, it becomes possible to develop models, typologies, and theories of how things work. The advantage of such typologies and the theories they permit us to postulate is that they attempt to order a great variety of different phenomena.

Culture typologies allow us to "scale" our processing of new information by allowing us to place observations of individual or group behaviors into the norms or patterns that constitute the whole culture model. The disadvantage and danger of typologies is that they are (1) so abstract that they do not reflect adequately the reality of a given set of phenomena being observed, or (2) so simple that they force us to oversimplify relevant (perhaps contrary) details to be consistent with the model to which we adhere (the edges of square pegs are rounded just enough to fit into the roundish hole, but there are important nuances left in the sawdust on the floor). In this sense, typologies can be useful if we are trying to compare many organizations but can be quite useless if we are trying to understand the nuances of one particular organization.

The typologies and models that we use gradually come to be our view of reality, and this simplifies the daily work of making sense of lived experience. Such simplification is useful for reducing anxiety and conserving mental energy. The danger is that we narrow our attention span and become more mindless with respect to what we are observing. Such narrowing can be useful if we are dealing with phenomena of little consequence. Labeling restaurants or banks as being "command-and-control" type organizations is okay if we are just occasional customers. However, if it becomes critical in an economic downturn to decide whether or not to continue to keep our money in a particular bank in our neighborhood, the "type" of bank it is may not give us enough information about its specific financial practices. If we have relied too much on a given typology, we may not have the conceptual tools to analyze our particular bank.

A third issue in using typologies concerns the question of how we arrive at the abstract *label*. A number of the culture models we will review gather data by asking employees how they perceive their organization. The perceptions are then aggregated and combined into a more abstract concept. The concept is often derived from factor-analyzing a broad set of questionnaire responses to determine which items hang together and, therefore, suggest a category that is based on employees' perceptions. Those "factors" are then labeled and described in summary fashion. For example, the label "strategic direction and intent" (Denison, 1990) along with the culture score on that dimension is based on combining employee ratings of their own organizations regarding the following items:

- There is a long-term purpose and direction.
- Our strategy leads other organizations to change the way they compete in the industry.
- There is a clear mission that gives meaning and direction to our work.
- There is a clear strategy for the future.
- Our strategic direction is unclear to me (reverse scoring).

That final score can be a reliable measure of employee perception and a valid indicator of the degree to which a given set of employees believes that their organization has a strong or weak strategy. Still, the question remains whether that score can be a measure of culture as defined in this book, because the *cultural* element of strategy has to do with its *content*, not whether or not there is one. Ciba-Geigy would have been rated as having a very strong strategy, but until the company bought Airwick, it was not aware that culturally it had a strategy that rejected being associated with a consumer-oriented air-freshener company.

Issues in the Use of Surveys to "Measure" Culture

A number of the typologies we will review depend on employee surveys that are scored in the manner described; therefore, we need to ask what are the problems and issues in the use of surveys as culture measures.

Not Knowing What to Ask. If we define culture as covering all of the internal and external dimensions that have been reviewed in this book, we would need a huge survey to cover all of those possible dimensions. What this means for a particular organization is that basically we would not know what questions to put into the survey, and if we used existing surveys we would not know which ones to use. We would not know which dimensions are salient for the organization around the problem or change program we have identified, and we would not know from a survey which are the basic assumptions of our cultural DNA. Some dimensions could be irrelevant and not worth surveying at all. Each survey claims to analyze "the culture" or important "dimensions of the culture," but there would be no a priori way of knowing how to evaluate those claims.

Employees May Not Be Motivated to Be Honest. Employees are always encouraged to be frank and honest in their answers and are usually given the assurance that their answers will be kept completely confidential. The fact that such assurances need to be given in the first place implies that our original assumption is that employees would not be open if their answers were known. Because culture is a living reality, we ought to use a method that allows people to be open. Too many questions in the surveys require evaluations and judgments that cause employees to be careful in how they answer.

Employees May Not Understand the Questions or May Interpret Them Differently. An item like "There is a clear strategy for the future" presumes that the employees have similar definitions of the word "strategy." If we cannot make this assumption, then amalgamating their answers does not make sense. It can therefore be very difficult to infer a "shared" concept from individual responses.

What Is Measured May Be Accurate but Superficial. It is difficult to get at the deeper levels of a culture from paper-and-pencil perceptions. Culture is an intrinsically shared phenomenon that manifests itself only in inter-action; whatever dimensions are measured by the survey are bound to be superficial. As noted previously, it may be critically important to measure how individuals respond within their group context. The company's climate and culture is a function of group behavior as much or more than individual behavior. Just surveying individuals misses the derivative effect of individual responses in subgroup contexts.

The Sample of Employees Surveyed May Not Be Representative of the Key Culture Carriers. Most survey administrators assume that if they have done a careful job of sampling and testing their sample against total organizational demographics, they can validly describe the whole based on the sample. This logic may not work for culture, because the driving forces in a culture can be the executive subculture, and, as Martin (2002) has pointed out, the culture may be fragmented and differentiated around many subcultures that the survey would have no way of identifying statistically. With qualitative knowledge of the organization based on observation and group interviews, we can more quickly identify certain groups and test for survey differences, but we would need to do the qualitative analysis first to identify the sub-groups to be compared.

The Profile of Dimensions Does Not Reveal Their Interaction or Patterning into a Total System. The survey reports are often presented as profiles or as scores on the spokes of a wheel to give an impression of an integrated measure, but the deep interactions of assumptions about dimensions is missing. For example, in the DEC case, the perceptions that the nature of truth could be found only through intense conflict in an egalitarian organization would not have revealed itself in a survey irrespective of its comprehensiveness.

The Impact of Taking the Survey Will Have Unknown Consequences, Some of Which May Be Undesirable or Destructive. Answering questions forces employees to think about categories that may never have occurred to them and to make value judgments in areas that are controversial. Not only are individuals influenced in this way, but if they share value judgments, such as discovering that they are each very cynical about the leadership of the organization, negative group attitudes can be built up that will damage the organization's ability to function. Furthermore, expectations are set in employees that once management has the results, they will take action to improve areas in which employees have voiced complaints. If management does not respond, morale can go down, and the surveys may not provide any explanation as to why.

We have presented these various cautions because the incentive to quickly obtain a quantitative picture of "the culture" is incredibly seductive, and the designers and purveyors of surveys either ignore or minimize the issues we have identified. There are many things that can be measured very well by surveys, but when dealing with a complex concept like *culture*, caution is in order.

When to Use Surveys

Having identified some of the issues with surveys as measures of a particular organization's culture, there are times when surveys can be useful and appropriate, as described next.

Determining Whether Particular Dimensions of Culture Are Systematically Related to Some Element of Performance. To that end, we need to study a large number of organizations and need a way of comparing them on just those dimensions and on their performance. Doing full ethnographic studies is either impractical or too expensive, so we settle for an operational definition of the abstract dimension we want to measure and design a standardized interview, observational checklist, or survey to arrive at a rating or score for each organization. These scores can then be correlated with various other performance measures across many organizations (Cooke & Szumal, 1993; Corlett & Pearson, 2003; Denison, 1990; Denison & Mishra, 1995; Gittell, 2016).

Giving a Particular Organization a Profile of Itself to Stimulate a Deeper Analysis of the Culture of that Organization. The assumption here is that the scores on the dimensions measured are presented as "how the employees perceive this organization" not as an absolute measure of the culture. These perceptions can then become a stimulus for further work on improving organizational performance. To facilitate such improvement, the surveys ask both "how do you perceive your organization in the present" and "how would you like your organization to be in the future." In terms of the preceding example, employees might indicate on the *strategic intent* dimension that they have a low score in the present and would like their organization to be higher on this dimension. When using surveys in this way, it is important to follow up the cultural deciphering with other methods and not to assume that a given profile is "the culture."

Comparing Organizations with Each Other on Selected Dimensions as Preparation for Mergers, Acquisitions, and Joint Ventures. This approach can be useful if we have some idea of the dimensions that are to be compared and if we can assume that the employees will willingly take the survey and answer honestly.

Testing for Subculture Differences. It is often useful to test whether certain subcultures that we suspect to be present can be objectively differentiated and defined in terms of preselected dimensions that a survey can identify. If we suspect that the engineering subculture and the operator subculture have different assumptions along the lines described in Chapter 11, we can design a survey to check this out, provided we can get valid samples and assuming that we are getting honest answers.

Educating Employees about Certain Important Dimensions that Management Wants to Work On. For example, if the future performance of the organization depends on consensus and commitment to a certain strategy, the survey questions reviewed previously can become a vehicle both for testing present perceptions and for launching change programs for building commitment to the strategy.

In each of these cases, the principle applies that we should think carefully whether or not giving the survey would have possible negative consequences, and we should involve the relevant parties in making the decision as to whether or not to go ahead. Having provided this background, we can now look at several typologies that are based on theoretical categories and "measured" with survey data.

Typologies that Focus on Assumptions about Authority and Intimacy

Organizations are ultimately the result of people doing things together for a common purpose. The basic relationship between the individual and the organization can, therefore, be thought of as the most fundamental cultural dimension around which to build a typology, because it will provide critical categories for analyzing assumptions about authority and intimacy. One of the most general theories here is Etzioni's (1975) fundamental distinction between three types of organizations that exist in every society and evolve fundamentally different organizational cultures.

1. Coercive Organizations

The individual is essentially captive for physical or economic reasons and must, therefore, obey whatever rules are imposed by the authorities. Examples include prisons, military academies and units, mental hospitals, religious training organizations, prisoner of war camps, cults, and so on. The cultures that evolve in such organizations usually generate strong countercultures among the participants as defenses against the arbitrary authority, and relationships would be expected to be minus 1 as described in Exhibit 6.4.

2. Utilitarian Organizations

These organizations are based on the model of the human being as a rational economic actor trading off his or her work for pay, or as many employees express it, "a fair day's work for a fair day's pay" and therefore abiding by whatever rules are essential for the overall performance of the organization. Examples include business organizations of all sorts. Relationships are expected to be transactional, Level 1, and role based. As has been found in most such organizations, they also develop countercultural norms so that employees can protect themselves from exploitation by the authorities.

3. Normative Organizations

The individual contributes his or her commitment and accepts legitimate authority because the goals of the organization are basically the same as the individual's goals. Examples include churches, political parties, voluntary organizations, hospitals, and schools. Relationships are expected to be Level 2 and personal but not intimate except around specific tasks.

Authority in the coercive kind of organization is arbitrary and absolute; in the utilitarian system (i.e., the typical business), authority is a negotiated relationship in the sense that the employee is presumed to accept the method by which people in higher ranks have achieved their status. In the normative system, authority is more informal and more subject to personal consent in that the employees or members can exit if they are not satisfied with the treatment they receive.

This typology is important because these types of organizations and the macro cultures in which they are nested differ in the degree to which they expect members to be subordinate, calculative, or normatively engaged. In multicultural organizations real conflict can arise when the authority expects obedience while the employee expects to be valued and engaged. One of the main challenges of globalism is that some of the Western utilitarian and normative management styles that we also believe to be the "correct" style simply don't work in macro cultures that are typically more coercive.

Assumptions about peer relationships and intimacy are also illuminated by this typology. In the coercive system, close peer relationships develop as a defense against authority, leading to unions and other forms of self-protective groups that develop strong countercultures. In the utilitarian system, peer relations evolve around the work group and typically reflect the kind of incentive system that management uses. Because such systems are often built around task performance, close relationships are discouraged on the assumption that they might get in the way of clear task focus. In the normative system, relationships evolve naturally around tasks and core beliefs in support of the organization. In such organizations, more intimate relationships are typically seen as aiding the members in building strong motivation and commitment to the goals of the organization. For this reason, some businesses attempt to be normative organizations by involving ("engaging") employees in the mission of the organization and encouraging more intimate relationships. Professional organizations such as law firms or service organizations that consist of groups of "partners" combine some of the elements of the utilitarian and normative systems (Greiner & Poulfelt, 2005; Jones, 1983; Shrivastava, 1983).

The value of this typology is that it enables us to differentiate the broad category of utilitarian business organizations from coercive total institutions such as prisons and mental hospitals, and from normative organizations such as schools, hospitals, and not-for-profits (Goffman, 1961). The difficulty, however, is that within any given organization, variations of all three authority systems may be operating, which requires us to rely on still other dimensions to capture the uniqueness of a given organization.

To deal with variations of authority within an organization, a number of typologies have been proposed that focus specifically on how authority is used and what level of participation is expected within the organization: (1) autocratic, (2) paternalistic, (3) consultative or democratic, (4) participative and power sharing, (5) delegative, and (6) abdicative (which implies delegating not only tasks and responsibilities but power and controls as well) (Bass, 1981, 1985; Harbison & Myers, 1959; Likert, 1967; Vroom & Yetton, 1973).

These organizational typologies deal much more with aggression, power, and control than with love, intimacy, and peer relationships. In that regard, they are always built on underlying assumptions about human nature and activity. A manager who holds the assumptions of Theory X (that people cannot be trusted) would automatically go toward the autocratic management style and stay there. However, the manager who holds the assumptions of Theory Y (that people are motivated and want to do their job) would select a management style according to the task requirements and vary his or her behavior. Some tasks require autocratic authority, as in carrying out a military mission whereas others should be totally dele-gated because the subordinates have all the information (McGregor, 1960; Schein, 1975).

The arguments that managers enter into about the "correct" level of participation and use of authority usually reflects the different assumptions they are making about the nature of the subordinates they are dealing with. Looking at participation and involvement as a matter of cultural assump-tions makes clear that the debate about whether leaders should be more autocratic or participative is ultimately colored by the assumptions of a particular group in a particular context. The search for the universally cor-rect leadership style is subject to errors of oversimplification, if not entirely doomed to failure, because of cultural variations by country, by industry, by occupation, by the particular history of a given organization, and, most important, by the actual tasks to be performed.

Typologies of Corporate Character and Culture

Typologies trying to capture cultural essences in organizations were first introduced by Harrison (1979) and Handy (1978) with four "types" based on their primary focus. Harrison's four types were

- Power-oriented: organizations dominated by charismatic or autocratic founders
- Achievement-oriented: organizations dominated by task results
- Role-oriented: public bureaucracies
- Support-oriented: nonprofit or religious organizations

Charles Handy drew a parallel between types of organizations and what some of the main Greek gods represented:

- Zeus: the *club* culture
- Athena: the *task* culture
- Apollo: the *role* culture
- Dionysus: the *existential* culture

Both of these typologies are measured with brief questionnaires and are used to help an organization get some insight into its "essence" (Handy, 1978; Harrison & Stokes, 1992).

The concept of corporate "character" was introduced by Wilkins (1989), who saw it as a component of culture consisting of "shared vision," "motivational faith" that things would be fair and that abilities would be used, and "distinctive skills." In his view, building character was possible by emphasizing programs dealing with each of the components, but he did not build a typology around the dimensions. Building on personality dimensions, Corlett and Pearson present a more elaborate model based on the theory of 12 Jungian archetypes—ruler, creator, innocent, sage, explorer, revolutionary, magician, hero, lover, jester, caregiver, and every person (Corlett & Pearson, 2003). They measure, using a self-report questionnaire, how things are done within the organization and then score the results for the 12 archetypes to determine which are the most salient in the organization. By obtaining self-insight, the organization is presumed to be more able to be effective.

Goffee and Jones (1998) saw character as equivalent to culture and created a typology based on two key dimensions: "solidarity" (the tendency to be like-minded) and "sociability" (the tendency to be friendly to each other). These dimensions are measured with a 23-item self-description questionnaire. They closely resemble and are derived from the classical group-dynamics distinction between task variables and building and maintenance variables. Goffee and Jones use these dimensions to identify four types of cultures:

- Fragmented: low on both dimensions
- Mercenary: high on solidarity, low on sociability
- Communal: high on sociability, low on solidarity
- Networked: high on both

Each type has certain virtues and liabilities that are described, but the typology misses a crucial dimension that has been identified by Ancona (1988) and others: the relationship between the group (organization) and its external environments, which is the boundary-management function that must be added to the task and maintenance functions. Without a model of what happens at the boundary, it is not possible to determine which type of culture is effective under different environmental conditions.

Cameron and Quinn (1999, 2006) also developed a four-category typology based on dimensions and the earlier work of Ouchi and Johnson (1978) and Williamson (1975); but in their case, however, the dimensions are more structural—how stable or flexible the organization is and how externally or internally focused it is. These dimensions are seen as "perpetually competing values," which leads to the following typology:

- Clan: internal focus and flexible; collaborative, friendly, family-like
- Hierarchy: internal focus and stable; structured, well coordinated
- Adhocracy: external focus and flexible; innovative, dynamic, entrepreneurial
- Market: external focus and stable; competitive, results oriented

Whereas the Goffee and Jones (1998) typology was built on basic dimensions that derived from group dynamics (task versus maintenance), the Cameron and Quinn (1999, 2006) typology was built on factor-analyzing large numbers of indicators of organizational performance and finding that these reduce to two clusters that correlate closely with what cognitive researchers have found to be "archetypical" dimensions as well.

In this typology, as in the previous one, we don't know the relative importance of these dimensions within the organization being analyzed, we don't know which typology is the more relevant, and we don't know whether a short questionnaire can validly "type" a culture. However, the questionnaire focuses on managerial behavior, so it may be a useful diagnostic for determining the kinds of climate that managers set for their subordinates and correlating that with performance. The Cameron and Quinn (1999, 2006) "competing values framework" is also based on the theoretical idea that the poles of any given dimension are inevitably in conflict with each other and the cultural solution involves reconciling them. This is the same idea as the Hampden-Turner and Trompenaars (2000) model of showing organizations how cultural solutions are always some level of integration of the extremes of the dimension. For example, all cultures have to be both collectivist and individualistic; the way they solve this dilemma gives them their distinctive flavor.

Another culture model that has been noted in reference to the software development world is William Schneider's culture matrix proposed in the 1994 work *The Reengineering Alternative*. It is a "competing values" 2×2 matrix model that proposes that most companies or subgroups (such as an R&D department) array within the four dimensions of "control" (or command and control), "collaboration," "cultivation," and "competence."

The Schneider (1994) model has been endorsed by some in software development because it provides an appropriate language for describing the conditions necessary for Agile, a predominant software development framework. Agile derives in part from historical precedents such as the Toyota Production System and the lean methodologies that were documented by Womack, Jones, and Roos in *The Machine That Changed The World* (1990). Agile also derives from a widely held sentiment of the later 20th century that the common "waterfall" framework of software development was top-down, slow, and inflexible and ultimately led to an insufficient quality-assurance and development pace.

Although there is no explicit association between Agile and any particular culture model, there are some Agile consultants and designers who have adopted the Schneider (1994) model because the two axes are useful for describing the cultural substrate that Agile may need to be able to flourish in an innovative development organization. Michael Sahota explains in detail (www.methodsandtools.com/archive/agileculture.php) how critical culture is to implementing Agile, "doing Agile is not being agile," and by implication, being agile requires the right kind of culture. He has adapted the Schneider model to describe this distinction and to show how Agile differs from Kanban and Lean.

Sahota suggests that R&D leaders need to understand that implementing Agile is not just about the language and the tools. It is about the norms and assumptions that form the foundation for the development endeavor. A command-and-control culture that has adopted a Kanban-based development system may not find it easy to quickly adopt Agile tools because the cultural substrate that Agile is built on is categorically different. Kanban is most closely associated with a control culture. A competence culture may favor a software craftsmanship approach, which can yield very high quality but can also be oppressive, inflexible, and slow in its insistence on superior craftsmanship. Collaboration-and-cultivation cultures are where Agile flourishes. Schneider's (1994) culture model is used in this way to illuminate these cultural substrate distinctions and their importance to different product-development approaches.

Examples of Survey-Based Profiles of Cultures

There are a number of culture models reinforced by survey instruments and many years worth of survey data aggregated across industries, companies, and geographies. One such model, illustrated by Denison (1990), identifies a number of dimensions of culture that are presumed to be relevant to a given organizational outcome such as performance, growth, innovation, or learning. The survey questions are then focused on just the dimensions considered relevant, and if those dimensions cannot conveniently be measured with a survey, the researcher or consultant can supplement with interviews and observations. This approach worries less about creating a typology and more about measuring key dimensions in many organizations and then relating those to performance. For example, Denison's survey measures the following 12 dimensions under four general headings:

- Mission
  - Strategic direction and intent
  - Goals and objectives
  - Vision
- Consistency
  - Core values
  - Agreement
  - Coordination and integration
- Involvement
  - Empowerment
  - Team orientation
  - Capability development

- Adaptability
  - Creating change
  - Customer focus
  - Organizational learning

Scores on each of the 12 dimensions are shown in a circular profile of the group and can be compared to norms based on a large sample of organizations that have been rated as more or less effective. Notice that the categories are quite abstract, so we have to go back to the actual items to discover just what was meant by each dimension.

Human Synergistics International (HSI) offers a similar approach with its "organizational culture inventory" (Cooke & Szumal, 1993). HSI's 12 dimensions, also shown as a "circumplex" profile, are organized around three basic organizational styles:

- Constructive styles
  - Achievement
  - Self-actualizing
  - Humanistic-encouraging
  - Affiliative
- Aggressive-defensive styles
  - Oppositional
  - Power
  - Competitive
  - Perfectionistic
- Passive-defensive styles
  - Avoidance
  - Dependent
  - Conventional
  - Approval

The HSI organizational culture inventory and the related organizational effectiveness inventory offer statistically valid comprehensive analytics with global, historical, and normative data sets to provide companies using these surveys with a great deal of comparative data. Their research shows clearly that organizations that use the constructive style fare better than organizations that are aggressive or passive in their style.

Given the analytical heft (surveys consisting of hundreds of "items"), however, it may not be easy for companies using these instruments to analyze and re-survey without the assistance of third-party experts to help administer and interpret the results. This raises a potential concern with this approach: should insiders be able to decipher their own deep cultural dimensions without complex survey methods or specialized statisticians to illuminate the data. With deeply analytical approaches such as Human Synergistics' "these things take time and effort" caveats certainly apply. Still, all of this analytical gravitas may also help reinforce a commitment to serious change work in which movement toward a more "constructive" culture may be a critical element.

As in all of these analytical approaches, scoping and focusing the instrument is a critical consideration. The HSI assessment focuses on "the shared beliefs and values guiding how members of an organization interact and work." Certainly how workers interact and work is critical, but rather than blanket surveying all aspects of this domain, it may also be important to focus more specifically on issues of authority and intimacy (the forest not just the trees), which run the risk of being lost in these large multiple-item surveys. HSI offers customizations with additional items that can get at idiosyncratic focus areas, and here the only trade-off will be the additional time required to complete what are typically extensive and involved surveys.

The O'Reilly, Chatman, and Caldwell (1991) "organizational culture profile" (OCP) offers another alternative. The OCP distinguishes attributes associated with "preferred work environments." How culture is expressed in preferred work environments can be useful for anticipating new-hire fit and crafting overall company branding. The OCP focuses on seven key dimensions: innovation, stability, people orientation, outcome orientation, easy going, detail orientation, and team orientation. To assess where one fits into these dimensions, 54 value statements are sorted by respondents according to their relative importance. Methodologically, the O'Reilly OCP is different in using "Q Sort factor analysis," which ranks importance of factors in relation to each other and may be, therefore, more likely to identify which dimensions of culture are closest to the essence or the DNA of the culture.

It will be up to consultants or company experts managing the survey project to decide whether a methodology using a 5-point Likert scale or a Q Sort factor-analysis approach is better suited to the project at hand. Because the OCP includes up to 54 items (for "sorting"), it covers a wide range of values, aspirations, beliefs, and so forth that may contribute to culture formation or maintenance. The OCP is also notably flexible in how it is administered, allowing companies to fine-tune the items to best fit the "culture problem" they encounter.

One other culture assessment is worthy of note here; the "culture compass" provided by the Hofstede Centre and ITIM International builds on the Hofstede national culture model reviewed in Chapter 6. This 15-minute individual survey uses 42 pairs of statements which build on the original Hofstede dimensions: "power distance," "individualism," "masculinity," "uncertainty avoidance," "long-term orientation," and "indulgence." The purpose of the survey is to assess individual fit—for a job in a new culture, for an ex-pat assignment, presumably for even a merger that involves combining individuals into new national cultures, and so on. This assessment does not attempt to measure organizational culture per se. While it may appear similar to the other assessments described previously, the intended use of the culture compass is to gauge how well an individual subject might perform within the norms of a work context in a particular cultural milieu (e.g., "How well would I perform in a Chinese company in Shanghai?").

The key point here is that the "culture problem" still needs to be defined at the outset—what is our goal in conducting a culture assessment? It does not make sense to engage in one of these involved assessment projects just to diagnose the culture without having some definition of what the presenting problem is and what we might seek to change.

Automated Culture Analysis with Software-as-a-Service

As of this writing in late 2016, a growing number of software-as-a-service (SaaS) companies have been formed and richly funded to provide surveys and analytics for customers wanting to get a better understanding of their climate, culture, and employee engagement. Of hundreds of companies providing software and services to help automate and apply big data analytics to human resources variables, we have found about 20 that focus on providing software and cloud solutions for surveying corporate culture, climate, and employee engagement. Although we will not attempt to touch on all of these companies, there are a few that provide some context and indication of how this trend may affect the analysis of organizational culture.

TinyPulse. The first company worthy of note is TinyPulse, www.tinypulse .com. With about $10 million in venture funding from two venture rounds and five investors, TinyPulse is poised to grow its business of providing rapid and frequent "engagement" and "performance" feedback for HR and senior management. It has developed a platform and an app for short, targeted surveys pushed to employees' devices and desktops. One of the central promises of TinyPulse is that the short app-delivered confidential and anonymous surveys are so quick and easy that response rates are nearly 100 percent and data reporting is nearly real-time. In TinyPulse's words, this pulse survey approach is "time-saving, effective, transparent." Regardless of what we think of the quality of the data, the ease of collection and compelling visual presentation in beautiful dashboards clearly appeal to a segment of the market for employee engagement measurement. To be able to simply ask employees the same short list of questions and report on a dashboard chart the degree of improvement or deterioration on a daily basis is an attractive proposition, one that provides near real-time pulse readings on how team members are feeling. For many managers, the relative trend up or down in the metrics may be quite meaningful, whether or not these snapshots have any validity with respect to underlying cultural drivers.

Glint. Glint (www.glintinc.com) is another SaaS vendor that also bases its employee engagement system on frequent "pulse" surveys. As of mid 2016 Glint has raised nearly $16 million from top-tier Silicon Valley investors. While its product focus appears to be on well-presented employee engagement metrics measured frequently, it is worth noting that Glint describes its product suite as an "organizational development platform for the digital age." Glint is promising "visibility insight action," the implication being that frequent measurement of simple engagement questions will provide the understanding that senior leaders need to make changes to incentive systems, feedback and communication, work styles and spaces, and other artifacts and espoused values that contribute to climate and culture. It is too early to know whether new "OD platforms" such as this provide sufficient insight into the deepest levels of culture that persist through many iterations of climate improvements.

CultureIQ. Delving further in to SaaS analysis of culture, we find CultureIQ (www.cultureiq.com) whose system promises to enable companies to manage their culture to drive employee engagement and success. This system reduces culture to "10 measurable qualities of high-performance cultures— collaboration, innovation, agility, communication, support, wellness, work environment, responsibility, performance focus, mission and value alignment." The CultureIQ system offers a simple survey instrument built around these 10 dimensions. In addition, it offers analytics and dashboards for deriving insights—a "cultureIQ" score, 0–100, where we can assume that a score in the 80s–90s is most "successful," graphical displays of results, and customized presentations to stakeholders.

CultureIQ also offers consulting services to help clients interpret the data and "strengthen their culture." In this sense, CultureIQ offers a straightforward model of what a good culture is and helps companies become stronger along these deterministic dimensions of "good" culture. The CultureIQ system also emphasizes applying big data analytics to uncover unknowns about their climate and culture. A big data approach to measuring and "changing" culture clearly appeals to a market hungry for immediate and tangible answers. For now, we will refrain from questioning whether *strength* of successful dimensions of culture is an appropriate way to think about the problem. The promise of CultureIQ is simple and expedient results, which may be just what some leaders are looking for when they wake up one day with that sudden "insight" that they may have a problem with their culture.

RoundPegg. RoundPegg offers another "culture and engagement platform" (http://roundpegg.com). This company has raised about $6 million in five rounds from five investors. The RoundPegg platform "makes it dead simple for leaders to solve business problems and achieve strategic goals by measuring and managing their single biggest business driver, company culture." A seven-minute culture survey asks respondents to make binary choices between "most important" and "least important" aspects of work life—for example, "creating order" or "paying attention to detail." RoundPegg calls this seven-minute survey the "CultureDNA assessment" to see how employees' shared values align with corporate mission, to hire employees that fit best with company culture, to "empower managers with better insight into what each member of their team values most," and to measure engagement.

The claim is that companies can use their culture data to understand how to motivate employees. This interesting description of the RoundPegg platform implies that the simple seven-minute survey is neither anonymous nor confidential; otherwise it would not illuminate how to alter individual incentives based on what each team member values the most. For now, we will leave RoundPegg with the question of whether we can accept the notion of characterizing a company's cultural DNA based in any way on the responses to a seven-minute survey of an employee who may not even have been at the company for seven days.

CultureAmp. CultureAmp (www.cultureamp.com) describes its business as "people analytics for your company." Founded in Melbourne, Australia, CultureAmp has a strong presence on the west coast of the United States, with a respectable list of customers (mostly web services and e-commerce companies). It is not immediately clear what is different about CultureAmp relative to many other products in this space. CultureAmp does appear to be one of the pioneers in this category, but that does not suggest that their survey approach is different or superior. Like others, they closely link engagement and culture. The culture diagnosis process starts with an engagement survey and offers options for "pulse" surveys (frequently repeated) as well. They will probably continue to add variants of surveys to complement their "life cycle" and "performance" diagnostic instruments.

The company is composed of at least as many software engineers as industrial psychologists or organizational culture experts. This seems common among this category of rapid-engagement culture-diagnostics competitors. CultureAmp describes its staff as "people geeks." The question for CultureAmp "people geeks" and for the others in the segment is whether their mission is about understanding customer companies, their people and their culture, or whether it is about software for rapid surveying and analytics on data about employees. The "datafication" of people is happening, everything is becoming instrumented. The question remains whether all this recently collected and accessed big data about people is actionable and transformational, or whether a number of hi-res snapshots miss the forest for the trees.

It is anybody's guess whether these SaaS providers of culture and engagement surveys will survive, flourish, and redefine the cultural quantitative-diagnostics landscape. Given that many of them are venture backed, we should expect that a likely outcome for many of these SaaS specialists will be that they are absorbed into larger full-service providers of "people operations" platforms (e.g., Workday, Salesforce, Oracle, etc.). Or perhaps these engagement survey SaaS platforms can complement the existing consultative survey providers such as HSI and Denison (or perhaps Gallup, NBRI, or SurveyMonkey).

At any rate, these SaaS start-ups create new approaches that challenge our assumptions about surveys and may cause enough disruption in the market to bring about real change. SaaS customers work directly with the platforms; expert consultants administering research and interpreting results are not needed in this approach. Global channels of expert consultants certainly raise entry barriers that protect the established culture survey players, but it may be that SaaS providers are gambling on the premise that many clients prefer a more expedient and direct approach that does not rely on expert intermediaries, longer committed engagements, and added expense.

Therefore, we may see the dynamics of culture *diagnostics* change. This will not, however, alter the realities of what culture is and how it changes. If there is one point that the SaaS providers like to trumpet that must be challenged, it is the suggestion that culture can be shifted or altered as easily as the SaaS surveys are administered. This pace-of-change argument may be applied accurately to elements of *climate* that bear directly on engagement and performance. Culture is deeper and does not change at the pace of rapid surveys. Culture-change programs are intense, involved, social, and iterative. Rapid diagnosis, even if quite accurate, is only a small piece of the culture change process.

Still, all of the buzz about rapid, "pulse" survey approaches does amplify that it is now mainstream for leaders to accept the centrality of culture for their business health. Do modern leaders expect that these rapid approaches will paint an adequate if not complete picture of their companies' culture? Engagement is symptomatic; culture is causal. Can rapid approaches get to root causes? Previous chapters have built the argument that culture derives from history, that it takes time to fully uncover and decipher cultural DNA. Even though the rapid-survey approaches may quickly tap espoused values, will they capture the subtleties in artifacts and tacit assumptions? Reflecting on the SaaS survey approaches, we can see a distinction between the industrial-organizational psychology methodological bias centered on quantitative analysis of a sample of individuals' surveys and the social and ethnographic methodologies centered on observation, individual and group interviews, data collection over time, group interactions, and group interpretations.

Consider this navigational analogy: Rapid survey approaches may provide silhouettes of landforms as seen from a few miles out. And the in-depth surveyors (e.g., HSI, Denison, etc.), may provide a great deal of contour and detail of the observed landforms (shorelines, beaches, cliffs, etc.). Yet recalling Sahlins and the Captain Cook example, understanding deep layers of cultural subtlety requires stepping off of the metaphorical observation vessel and, stepping in to immersive dialogue with members of the subject group—about past, present, and future—to figure out *what they think* is right, *what they think* is wrong, and *what they believe* is really going on.

Summary and Conclusions

The value of typologies is that they simplify thinking and provide useful categories for sorting out the complexities we must deal with when we confront organizational realities. The weakness of culture typologies is that they oversimplify these complexities and may provide us categories that are incorrect in terms of their relevance to what we are trying to understand. They can limit our perspective by prematurely focusing us on just a few dimensions, they can limit our ability to find complex and derivative patterns among a number of dimensions, and they may not reveal what a given group feels *most intensely* about.

Typologies also introduce a bias toward what Martin (2002) calls the "integration perspective" in culture studies—an approach that emphasizes the dimensions on which there is a high degree of consensus. Martin reminds us that many organizations are "differentiated" or even "fragmented" to the extent that there is little consensus on any cultural dimensions. An integrated culture might be one in which the whole organization shares a single set of assumptions; a differentiated culture is an organization in which powerful subcultures disagree on certain crucial issues, such as labor and management; and a fragmented culture is an organization such as a financial conglomerate that has a great many subcultures and no single overarching set of shared assumptions. Clearly the effort to classify a given organization into a single typological category (e.g., "clan" or "networked") presumes not only integration around two dimensions but the assumption that those dimensions can be measured well enough to determine the degree of consensus.

Some typologies attempt to reduce all organizations to a few types, while others rely more on profiling organizations in terms of a number of dimensions that are separately measured by means of employee surveys. We have reviewed the pros and cons of using such surveys to "measure" cultures. The main issue is whether individual responses on a survey can get at the deeper levels of shared tacit assumptions that may reveal themselves only in actual group interaction. What surveys measure may be valid, but it may not get at cultural essence or culture DNA.

The main conclusion for the change leader is to stay focused on the change problem and really think through whether the measurement approach will be helpful or whether some qualitative work must precede any culture assessment as well as whether culture itself is better understood qualitatively.

Suggestions for the Reader

1. Think of several organizations with which you are familiar either as a customer, an employee, or a manager. Take two or three of the typologies discussed in this chapter and see whether you can clearly slot each of your organizations into one of them.

2. If you have trouble fitting some organizations into the types, try to figure out which dimensions don't work and use them to create new types for yourself.

3. Ask yourself whether or not you believe that quantifying culture dimensions is useful, and under what conditions.

15

THE DIALOGIC QUALITATIVE CULTURE ASSESSMENT PROCESS

The dialogic qualitative approach to assessment is based on three crucial premises:

1. The purpose of the assessment is to help the change leader make an assessment that will help move the change process forward.

2. It is crucial that the change leader engage in an assessment process that will reveal the elements of the culture that bear on the change problem.

3. It is *not* important for the outside consultant to understand the client's culture, but the consultant must be very clear about the change implications of the assessment process itself.

Defining change targets does not tell the change leader what might be involved in the implementation of the change process itself. Will the cultural elements of the culture we have, the culture we have built, and the culture that is present today, *help* or *hinder* "the new way of working" that the change goals define? With the targets clearly in mind, the assessment process has to answer this fundamental question.

The change process does not begin at cultural ground zero; the organization has built a culture whose basic assumptions, its DNA, are the source of its success. The organization has probably also built up cultural elements that are now perceived to be a source of the problems that the change process is supposed to "fix."

Because of the inevitable differentiation into various subcultures, it is likely that there are conflicts and tensions within the different units of the organization that must be diagnosed and understood for the change process to work effectively. But, paradoxically, it is not important for the outside "expert diagnostician" to gain this understanding, while it is essential for the change leader to gain it.

In the diagnostic quantitative model the assumption is made that the outsider can "measure" the dimensions of the culture and "explain" the culture to the insiders and the change leader. In the dialogic qualitative model, the role of the outside expert is to help the insiders, especially the change leader, to figure out which elements of the existing culture will aid or hinder the change process.

In the measurement model the intervention energy goes into making sure that the numbers are "scientifically" valid and accurate; in the qualitative model the intervention energy goes into helping the client to gain insight into how the culture that he or she lives in will affect the change process.

In the measurement model the ethics of "science" prevail in that the data should be as accurate as possible around issues of sampling and using the best statistical methods. In the qualitative model the ethics of "intervention" prevail in asking whether the assessment process itself could be harmful to the client system.

In the measurement model the outside helper is in the role of an *expert* on culture diagnosis by measuring the system. In the qualitative model the outsider is in the role of a "humble process consultant" who may know a lot about culture dynamics in general but whose expertise is in facilitating a process that enables the client (the change leader) to diagnose his or her own culture (Schein, 2016).

There is no formula for this dialogic qualitative process because it depends on the nature of the problem, the macro-cultural context, and the kind of relationship that is built up between client and helper. The best way to explain this approach, therefore, is through a few illustrative cases.

Case 4: MA-COM—Revising a Change Agenda as a Result of Cultural Insight

Culture assessment done for one purpose can reveal cultural elements that were not anticipated yet explain much of the observed behavior of the organization and its leaders. In this case, once the deeper and unanticipated elements of the culture had been identified, the change agenda was revised to arrive at a better solution.

A newly appointed CEO of MA-COM, a high-tech company that consisted of 10 or more divisions, asked me to help him figure out how the organization could develop a "common culture." He felt that its history of decentralized autonomous divisions was now dysfunctional and that the company should work toward a common set of values and assumptions.

The CEO, the director of human resources, and I were the planning group who were to decide how to approach the problem. We reached the conclusion that all of the division directors, all of the heads of corporate staff units, and various other individuals who were considered to be relevant to the discussion would be invited to an all-day meeting where we would identify the elements of a common *corporate* culture for the future. Thirty people attended the meeting.

We began with the CEO as "change leader" stating his goals and why he had asked the group to come together. He introduced me as the person who would "stage-manage" the day while making it clear that we were working on his agenda. I then gave a 30-minute lecture on how to think about culture based on the three-level model and launched into the self-assessment by asking some of the less senior people in the group to share what it was like to enter this company. As people brought out various artifacts and norms, I wrote them down on flip-charts and hung up the filled pages around the room. It appeared clear that there were powerful divisional subcultures, but it was also clear that there were many common artifacts across the group.

My role, in addition to writing things down, was to ask for clarification or elaboration when people threw in abstractions like, "it was a teamwork organization." I would then ask for an example of what the person meant. As we worked into our second and third hours, some central value conflicts began to emerge. The various divisional units really favored the traditional assumption that high degrees of decentralization and divisional autonomy were the right way to run the overall business. At the same time, they longed for strong centralized leadership and a set of core values that they could rally around as a total company.

My role at this point shifted to helping the group to confront this conflict and to try to understand both its roots and its consequences. We broke at lunchtime and instructed randomly selected subgroups of seven to eight members to continue the analysis of these values and assumptions for a couple of hours after lunch. We then met at around three o'clock for a final two-hour analysis and wrap-up session.

To start off the final session, I asked each group to give a brief report of the assumptions that it felt aided and those it felt hindered the achievement of a common corporate culture. In these presentations, the same divisional versus corporate conflict kept emerging, so when the reports were done, I encouraged the group to dig into this a little more. What was this conflict really about, and why could they not resolve it? I had noticed that some mention had been made of "strong founders," so I asked the group to talk further about how the divisions had been created. This discussion led to a major insight.

It turned out that almost every division had been acquired with its founder still in place; the corporate headquarters policy of granting autonomy to divisions had encouraged those founders to stay on as CEOs even though they had given up ownership. Most of the managers in the room had grown up under those strong leaders and had enjoyed that period of their history very much. Each division had created its own culture under the strong leadership of the founders.

Now, however, all the founders had retired, left, or died, and the divisions were led by general managers who did not have the same charisma the founders had. What the group longed for now was the sense of unity and security they each had had in their respective divisions under their founders. They now realized that they did not, in fact, want a strong unified *corporate* culture and leadership because the different businesses needed autonomy to operate effectively. They realized that their desire for a stronger corporate culture was misplaced. What they really wanted was the same autonomy they had always enjoyed, but with stronger leadership at the divisional level.

These insights, based on historical reconstruction of how the corporate culture had been formed, led to a very different set of proposals for the future. The group, with the blessing of corporate leadership, agreed that they needed only a few common corporate policies in such areas as public relations, human resources, and research and development. They did not need common values or assumptions, though if such developed naturally over time that would be fine. However, they wanted stronger leadership at the divisional level and a development program that would maximize their chances to obtain such leadership. Finally, they wanted to strongly reaffirm the value of divisional autonomy to enable them to do the best possible job in each of their various businesses.

Lessons Learned

This case illustrates the following important points about deciphering culture and managing cultural assumptions:

- The process started with a CEO who was worried about "the lack of a common corporate culture" and wanted "to create one." I was willing to examine this issue and suggested a planning group that would "own" the problem. The planning group then worked with me to design a one-day qualitative intervention to assess the existing culture. We agreed that a one-day intervention would be a start and that whatever else was needed would be decided after the day. I think of this as a "qualitative intervention."

- A senior management group with the help of an outside facilitator would be able to decipher key assumptions that pertain to a particular business problem—in this case, whether or not to push for a more centralized common set of values and assumptions.

- The qualitative analysis of artifacts and values by the members of the organization revealed several DNA-level basic assumptions that were centrally related to the business problem, as judged by the participants. Other elements of the culture that were also clearly revealed in the self-analysis were judged to be not relevant. Inasmuch as every culture includes assumptions about almost everything, it is important to have an assessment technique that permits individuals to set priorities and to discover what aspects of a culture are relevant.

- The resolution of the business problem did not require any *culture* change. In fact, the group reaffirmed one of its most central cultural assumptions. In this context, the group did, however, define some new priorities for future action: to develop common policies and practices in certain business areas and to develop stronger divisional leaders. Often what is needed is a change in *business practices* within the context of the given culture, not necessarily a *change* in culture but an *evolution* of that existing culture.

Case 5: U.S. Army Corps of Engineers Reassessing Their Mission

This case example illustrates the culture-deciphering process in a different type of organization. As part of a long-range strategy-planning process, I was asked in 1986 to conduct an analysis of the culture of the U.S. Army Corps of Engineers because of concerns that their mission was changing and they were uncertain what the future sources of funding would be. In attendance were the 25 or so senior managers, both military and civilian, with the specific purpose of analyzing their culture (1) to remain adaptive in a rapidly changing environment, (2) to conserve those elements of the culture that were a source of strength and pride, and (3) to manage the evolution of the organization realistically. The managers knew that the Corps's fundamental mission had changed over the past several decades and that the survival of the organization hinged on obtaining an accurate self-assessment of its strengths and weaknesses.

We followed a 10-step assessment procedure that I sometimes use with a small group that wants quickly to discover the key elements of their culture.

Step 1: Obtain Top Leadership Commitment

Deciphering cultural assumptions and evaluating their relevance to some organizational change program must be viewed as a major intervention in the organization's life and, therefore, must be undertaken only with the full understanding and consent of the formal leaders of the organization. This means probing why the leaders in an organization want to do this assessment and fully describing the process and its potential consequences to obtain their full commitment to the group meetings that will be involved. In this case it was the leaders who came to me with the approval of their government superiors.

Step 2: Select Groups for Self-Assessment

The next step is for the facilitator to work with the formal leaders to determine how best to select some groups representative of the corporate culture. The criteria for selection usually depend on the concrete nature of the problem to be solved. Groups can either be homogeneous with respect to a given department or rank level or made deliberately heterogeneous by selecting diagonal slices from the organization. The group can be as small as 3 and as large as 30. In this case the leaders and I selected the group that would have the most experience with this issue.

Step 3: Select an Appropriate Setting for the Group Self-Assessment

The group meeting should stimulate perceptions, thoughts, and feelings that are ordinarily implicit. The room in which the meeting is to be held must therefore be comfortable, allow people to sit in a circular format, and permit the hanging of many sheets of flip-chart paper on which cultural elements would be written. In addition there should be available a set of breakout rooms in which subgroups can meet, especially if the basic group is larger than 15 or so participants.

Step 4: Explain the Purpose of the Group Meeting (15 Minutes)

The meeting should start with a statement of its purpose by someone from the organization who is perceived to be in a leadership or authority role, so that openness of response is encouraged. The organizational-change problem should be clearly stated and written down, allowing for questions and discussion. The purpose of this step is both to be clear as to why this meeting is being held and to begin to get the group involved in the process.

The insider then introduces the process consultant as the "facilitator who will help us to conduct an assessment of how our organization's culture will help or constrain us in solving the problem or resolving the issue we have identified." The process consultant can be an outsider, a member of the organization who is part of a staff group devoted to providing internal consulting services, or even a leader from another department if he or she is familiar with how culture works and is familiar with this group process.

Step 5: Understand How to Think about Culture (15 Minutes)

It is essential for the group to understand that although culture manifests itself at the level of artifacts and espoused values, the goal is to try to decipher the shared basic assumptions that lie at a lower level of consciousness. The consultant should, therefore, present the three-level model of artifacts, espoused values, and tacit assumptions shown in Chapter 3 and ensure that everyone understands that culture is a learned set of assumptions based on a group's shared history. It is important for the group to understand that what they are about to assess is a product of their own history and that the culture's stability rests on the organization's past success.

Step 6: Elicit Descriptions of the Artifacts (60 Minutes)

The process consultant then tells the group that they are going to start by describing the culture through its artifacts. A useful way to begin is to find out who has joined the group most recently and ask that person what it felt like to enter the organization and what he or she noticed most upon entering it. Everything mentioned is written down on a flip-chart; as the pages are filled, they are torn off and hung on the wall so that everything remains visible.

If group members are active in supplying information, the facilitator can stay relatively quiet, but if the group needs priming, the facilitator should suggest categories such as dress codes, desired modes of behavior in addressing the boss, the physical layout of the workplace, how time and space are used, what kinds of emotions someone would notice, how people are rewarded and punished, how someone gets ahead in the organization, how decisions are made, how conflicts and disagreements are handled, how work and family life are balanced, and so forth.

Step 7: Identify Espoused Values (15–30 Minutes)

The question that elicits artifacts is "What is going on here?" By contrast, the question that elicits espoused values is "Why are you doing what you are doing?" It is often the case that values already have been mentioned during the discussion of artifacts, so these should be written down on different pages. To elicit further values, I pick an area of artifacts that is clearly of interest to the group and ask people to articulate the reasons why they do what they do.

As values or beliefs are stated, I check for consensus; if there appears to be consensus, I write down the values or beliefs on the new chart pad. If members disagree, I explore why by asking whether this is a matter of different subgroups having different values or there is genuine lack of consensus, in which case the item goes on the list with a question mark to remind us to revisit it. I encourage the group to look at all the artifacts they have identified and to figure out as best they can which values seem to be implied. If I see some obvious values that they have not named, I will suggest them as possibilities—but in a spirit of joint inquiry, not as an expert conducting a content analysis of their data. After we have a list of values to look at, we are ready to push on to underlying assumptions.

Step 8: Identify Shared Underlying Assumptions (15–30 Minutes)

The key to getting at the underlying assumptions is to check whether the espoused values that have been identified really explain all of the artifacts or whether things that have been described as going on have clearly not been explained or are in actual conflict with some of the values articulated. An easy way to do this is to ask the group whether the structure and the processes they use are consistent with the espoused values.

As assumptions surface, the facilitator should test for consensus and then write them down on a separate list. This list becomes important as the visible articulation of the cultural essences that have been identified. This phase of the exercise is finished when the group and the facilitator feel that they have identified most of the critical assumption areas that pertain to the problem they are trying to solve, and participants are now clear on what an assumption is.

Step 9: Identify Cultural Aids and Hindrances (30–60 Minutes)

At this point it is important to review the change goal. What are we trying to do, what will be involved in getting there, and how will our present culture aid or hinder us in getting there.

Step 10: Make Decisions on Next Steps (30 Minutes)

The purpose of this step is to reach some kind of consensus as to what the important shared assumptions are and their implications for what the organization wants to do next. This led to the development of the following themes, stated as either key values or assumptions, depending on how the group itself experienced that element:

- Our mission is to solve problems of river control, dams, bridges, and so forth pragmatically, not aesthetically, but our responsiveness to our environment leads to aesthetic concerns within the context of any given project.
- We always respond to crisis and are organized to do so.
- We are conservative and protect our turf but value some adventurism.
- We are decentralized and expect decisions to be made in the field but control the field tightly through the role of the district engineer.
- We are numbers driven and always operate in terms of cost-benefit analyses, partly because quality is hard to measure.
- We minimize risk because we must not fail; hence, things are overdesigned, and we use only safe, well-established technologies.
- We exercise professional integrity and say no when we should.
- We try to minimize public criticism.
- We are responsive to externalities but attempt to maintain our independence and professional integrity.
- We are often an instrument of foreign policy through our non–U.S. projects.

The group identified as its major problem that the traditional mission of flood control had been largely accomplished, and with changing patterns in Congress, it was not easy to tell what kinds of projects would continue to justify the budget. Financial pressures were seen to cause more projects to be cost-shared with local authorities, requiring degrees of collaboration that the Corps was not sure it could handle. The culture discussion provided useful perspectives on what was ahead but did not provide clues as to the specific strategy to pursue in the future.

Lessons Learned

This case, like the others, illustrates that we can get a group to decipher major elements of its culture in relation to a change goal, and that this can be a useful exercise in clarifying what is strategically possible. It is also evident that a culture assessment need not lead to culture *change* even though that might have been an initial goal.

The process of identifying underlying assumptions through a stepwise process of identifying artifacts and espoused values and then comparing them with each other to look for discrepancies as the locus of the tacit assumptions is effective and can be done within a half day, if necessary.

What makes this process work is a clear initial agreement between the client and the facilitator on the goals, the change problem, and the willingness of the client to own the process and outcomes. Without a clear change goal, the process wanders aimlessly and is often seen as boring and pointless by the group.

Case 6: Apple Assessing Its Culture as Part of a Long-Range Planning Process

Apple Computer decided in 1991 to conduct a cultural analysis as part of a long-range planning exercise focused on human resource issues. How big would the company be in five years, what kind of people would it need, and where should it locate itself geographically under different size scenarios?

A 10-person working group, consisting of several line managers and several members of the human resource function, was assigned the task of figuring out how Apple's culture would influence growth and what impact it might have on the kinds of people who would be attracted to it in the future. The vice president for human resources knew of my work on culture and asked me to be a consultant to this working group. He functioned as its chairman.

The original plan was to sort out various planning tasks and delegate these to other committees for more detailed work because the presentation to the company meeting was six months away. One of these other groups was charged with analyzing the impact of Apple's culture on future growth. My role was to help organize the study, teach the group how best to study culture, and consult with the culture subcommittee down the line.

The first meeting of the group was scheduled for a full day and involved the planning of several different kinds of activities, of which the culture study was just one. When it came to deciding how to study the Apple culture, I had 20 minutes in which to describe the model of artifacts, espoused values, and basic underlying assumptions. I also described in general terms how I had used the model with other organizations to help them decipher their culture through various versions of the foregoing 10-step process. The group was intrigued and decided to try the process immediately. We launched directly into uncovering artifacts and espoused values, to compare them and to come up with a provisional set of tacit assumptions backed by various kinds of data that the group generated. These were written down in draft form on flip-charts, and I was asked to organize them into a more ordered set of what we ended up calling Apple's "governing assumptions."

1. We are not in the business for the business alone but for some higher purpose—to change society and the world, create something lasting, solve important problems, and have fun.

One of Apple's major products was designed to help children learn. Another major product was designed to make computing easier and more fun. Apple engaged in many rituals designed to be fun—for example, after-hours parties, playfulness at work, and magic shows at executive-training events. The group felt that only what is fun and what is unique gets the big rewards.

It was alleged that many people at Apple would object if the company went after the broad business market and if it sold products to selected groups who would misuse the product (e.g., the U.S. Department of Defense).

2. Task accomplishment is more important than the process used or the relationships formed.

The group listed several versions of this assumption:

- When you fail at Apple, you are alone and abandoned; you become a "boat person."
- Seniority, loyalty, and past experience don't count relative to present task achievements.
- When you trip, no one picks you up.

- Out of sight, out of mind; you are only as good as your latest hit; relationships formed at work do not last.
- People are so intent on their mission that they don't have time for you or to form relationships.
- Bonding occurs only around tasks and is temporary.
- Groups are security blankets.
- Apple is a club or a community, not a family.

3. *The individual has the right and obligation to be a total person.*

This showed up as the following assumptions:

- Individuals are powerful, can be self-sufficient, and can create their own destiny.
- A group of individuals motivated by a shared dream can do great things.
- People have an inherent desire to be their best and will go for it.
- Apple neither expects company loyalty from individuals nor does it expect to guarantee employment security to individuals.
- Individuals have the right to be fully themselves at work, to express their own personality and uniqueness, to be different.
- There is no dress code and no restriction on how personal space is decorated.
- Children or pets can be brought to work.
- Individuals have the right to have fun, to play, to be whimsical.
- Individuals have the right to be materialistic, to make lots of money, and to drive fancy cars no matter what their formal status.

4. *Only the present counts.*

- Apple has no sense of history or concern for the future.
- Seize the moment; the early bird gets the worm.
- Apple is not a lifetime employer.
- Longer-range plans and tasks are discussed but not done.
- People do not build long-range, cross-functional relationships.

- Nomadic existence inside Apple is normal; people don't have offices, only "campsites" and "tents."
- The physical environment is constantly rearranged.
- It is easier to fix things than to plan for perfection; flexibility is our greatest skill.
- People are forgotten quickly if they leave a project or the company.
- We learn by doing.

These governing assumptions and the supporting data were passed on to the subcommittee dealing with the Apple culture, where they were tested and refined with further interviews. Interestingly enough, after several more months of work, no substantial changes had been made to the list, suggesting that a group can get at the essentials of its culture very rapidly.

Lessons Learned

This case illustrates the following important points:

- If a motivated insider group is provided with a process for deciphering its culture, members can rather quickly come up with some of their most central basic assumptions. I revisited Apple several years after this event and was shown the same set of assumptions as still being the essence of the culture, though they were stated in a somewhat different order and with some additional comments about areas that needed to change. I have no current data on the Apple culture, but its range of products and the way its stores are run suggests that the earlier description from 1991 is still largely valid.
- With Apple's far more prominent place in today's world of consumer electronics and mobile computing, it is tempting to think of the assumptions here as still reflecting the Apple we know today. It is possible that much of this applies, but it is also highly likely that with four promoted CEOs since this work was done, Apple has evolved its culture significantly. We always have to think of culture as something mutable, organic, and evolutionary, especially with growth and age as I described in Chapter 11.
- Stating these governing assumptions allowed the company managers to assess where their strategy might run into cultural constraints. In

particular, they realized that if they were to grow rapidly and enter the enterprise computing market, they would have to deal with members of their organization who grew up under the assumption that business should involve more than just making money. They also realized that they lived too much in the present and would have to develop longer-range planning and implementation skills.

• Apple reaffirmed its assumptions about task primacy and individual responsibility by starting to articulate explicitly a philosophy of no mutual obligation between the company and its employees. When layoffs became necessary, the company simply announced them without apology and carried them out. Apple was one of the first companies to articulate that employment security would gradually have to give way to employability security, by which they meant that an individual would learn enough during some years at Apple to be attractive to another employer if he or she were laid off. There should be no loyalty in either direction, in that employees should also feel free to leave if a better opportunity came along. Where, then, would commitment and loyalty reside? In the project. The project appeared to be the critical organizational unit around which everything else revolved.

Case 7: SAAB COMBITECH—Building Collaboration in Research Units

The head of the SAAB company research division, Per Risberg, had noted that his six research units that reported to different product divisions of the company had many common technology problems and processes but had built such strong subcultures over the years that they did not realize to what extent collaboration would help all of them. He recruited me to help him develop a three-day workshop that would teach them about culture and enable them to discover where they could helpfully collaborate with each other. Prior to the workshop he sent them each a copy of my culture book and asked them to write me a letter in which they were to compare their own subculture with DEC and Ciba-Geigy, the two detailed cases presented in the book.

On the first day of the workshop, I introduced the culture model, gave them more examples, and briefly reviewed their self-analyses. We then had each group volunteer two of its members to become "ethnographers" who would go into one other group to learn what its culture was like. I provided some dimensions dealing with authority and intimacy and gave them several hours to visit, observe, and inquire about the group's artifacts, espoused values, and tacit assumptions. On the second day, these observations were reported in a plenary session so that each group heard how it was perceived by two "anthropologists." Through this process, we all became highly aware of both the communality of assumptions and the diversity of assumptions across the groups. Groups were encouraged to ask each other questions and explore further each other's cultures.

The third day was devoted to a systematic exploration of the ways in which the research units were interdependent and how they could help each other by sharing more of their technology and know-how. One would argue that this process changed the *corporate* culture toward the assumption that collaboration was more productive than independence, and that at the same time, it evolved each of the subcultures by creating linkages that enabled each of them to do their job better.

Lessons Learned

I learned from this experience that working with the insider leads to better change designs than trying to develop and impose a change design on the system. Risberg knew his people and knew that if he found a way to expose them to each other, they would find that experience valuable and would change their behavior. I might have thought that this was desirable in the abstract, but I would not have been able to figure out the elegant design that we created together.

The dialogic qualitative approach is more intense but overall much faster. In three intensive days we were able to accomplish what might have taken months of measurement and analysis of the subgroups. The change targets made the changes because they became willing clients who felt that the activity of being "forced" into acting as amateur ethnographers helped them.

Case 8: Using A Priori Criteria for Culture Evaluation

A different kind of approach is illustrated in a German publishing company that offered a prize in 2003 to six companies selected from a nominated pool of 63 for the following:

> individual models of excellence in developing and living a corporate culture . . . . An international working commission composed of experts from academia and the business world developed ten critical dimensions of corporate culture in intense discussion . . . . Then a team of researchers from Bertelsman Stiftung and the consulting firm of Booz Allen Hamilton evaluated these companies against the ten dimensions and their related criteria."
>
> (Sackman, 2006, p. 43)

The dimensions chosen were:

1. Common goal orientation

2. Corporate social responsibility

3. Commonly held beliefs, attitudes, and values

4. Independent and transparent corporate governance

5. Participative leadership

6. Entrepreneurial behavior

7. Continuity in leadership

8. Ability to adapt and integrate

9. Customer orientation

10. Shareholder value orientation

The research team then examined the economic performance and publicly available information of each company for the past 10 years to winnow the list down to 10 finalists, who were then evaluated against the 10 criteria. The evaluations were done through company visits and interviews of all levels from board chairs to members of the works council. For each of the 10 factors, detailed checklists were developed to enable the evaluation teams to score each company relatively objectively.

The detailed findings were then reviewed with the original commission leading to the selection of six companies as outstanding examples of the evolution and use of corporate culture in achieving their excellent performance: the BMW Group, Deutsche Lufthansa, Grundfos, Henkel, Hilti, and Novo Nordisk. Sackman (2006) concluded, "the corporate culture that distinguished each of them today [in 2006] has, on the one hand, contributed to their success and, on the other hand, placed them in a strong position as they face challenges to come" (p. 45).

What makes this research valuable is the detailed description of the six companies so that the reader can get past the abstractions that the 10 dimensions represent and see how things actually worked in each company. Note that the 10 criteria involve both issues of survival in the external environment and issues of internal integration. A similar example is the detailed analysis of a corporate culture-change program conducted in HSBC in Hong Kong (O'Donovan, 2006).

What of DEC, Ciba-Geigy, and Singapore? Did Their Cultures Evolve and Change?

The three main cases in this book had different cultural histories. DEC was so enamored of its commitment to innovation and its mix of freedom and strong paternalism that it consciously refused changes that were necessary for economic survival. In some sense DEC lacked the "money gene" in its cultural DNA. But the culture survived in that most DEC alumni still argue that the way DEC was run was what they would advocate for running any company.

Ciba-Geigy was in an evolutionary process stimulated by changing technologies and economic pressures leading first to a restructuring that involved dropping major chemical products and then to a reorientation toward pharmaceuticals that led to merging with Sandoz to become Novartis. Its central assumptions about long-range strategy became more focused around a narrower product set, something DEC could not do, but its values around treating people well remained throughout the downsizing.

Singapore's Economic Development Board has continued to do what it did so well in the beginning and has now become part of a successful modern city-state. A great deal of effort has gone into stimulating entrepreneurship, the one area that had been identified by me and others as being a weak link in their economic development chain.

Summary and Conclusions

The assessment process described and illustrated in this chapter leads to a number of conclusions:

Culture can be assessed by means of various individual and group interview processes; group interviews are preferable because culture is a set of shared beliefs, values, and assumptions, which reveal themselves better in a group setting. Such group-based assessments can be usefully made by insiders with the help of a facilitator in as little as a half-day.

Insiders are capable of understanding and making explicit the shared tacit assumptions that make up the culture, but they need outsider help in this process. The helper or consultant should therefore operate primarily from a process-consulting model and should avoid, as much as possible, becoming an expert on the content of any given group's culture (Schein, 1999a, 2009a, 2016).

The facilitator may never fully understand the culture, but that may not matter as long as the group can move forward on its change agenda. In any case, the contextual meaning of cultural assumptions can be fully understood only by members of the culture; hence, creating a process to facilitate their understanding is more important than for the researcher, consultant, or facilitator to obtain that understanding. If it is important for the outsider or researcher to be able to describe the culture in more detailed terms, additional observations, participant observations, and more group assessments would have to be made until a more complete picture emerges.

A culture assessment is of little value unless it is tied to some organizational problem or issue. In other words, assessing a culture for its own sake is too vast an undertaking, one that can be viewed as boring and useless. However, when the organization has a purpose, a new strategy, a problem to be solved, or a change agenda, determining how the culture affects the issue is not only useful but in most cases necessary. The issue should be related to the organization's effectiveness and should be stated in as concrete a way as possible. We cannot say that the culture itself is an issue or problem. The culture affects how the organization performs, and the initial focus should always be on where the performance needs to be improved.

For a culture assessment to be valuable, it must get to the assumptions level. If the client system does not get to assumptions, it cannot explain the discrepancies that almost always surface between the espoused values and the observed behaviors. The assessment process should identify cultural assumptions and then assess them in terms of whether they are a strength or a constraint on what the organization is trying to do. In most organizational change efforts, it is much easier to draw on the strengths of the culture than to overcome the constraints by changing the culture. Not all parts of a culture are relevant to any given issue the organization may be facing; hence, attempting to study an entire culture in all of its facets is not only impractical but also usually inappropriate. However, in any cultural assessment process, we should be sensitive to the presence of subcultures and be prepared to do separate assessments of them to determine their relevance to what the organization is trying to do.

If changes in the culture are discovered to be necessary, those changes will rarely involve the entire culture; it will almost always be a matter of changing one or two assumptions. Only rarely does the basic paradigm have to change, but if it does, the organization faces a multiyear major change process.

Quantitative assessments such as described in the previous chapter can supplement these qualitative processes but are not essential, as the above cases have tried to show.

Suggestion for the Reader

The best way to test this qualitative model is to bring together a small group (three to five) of people from your own company, club, or other group and take an hour to discuss: (1) what does it feel like to enter this group, (2) what are the values we live by in this group, and (3) what are the deep assumptions that drive us. If you can think of changes you would like to make in how this group operates, ask yourself how what you identified previously would help you or hinder you.

16

A MODEL OF CHANGE MANAGEMENT
AND THE CHANGE LEADER

If you are a leader or a manager and want to create, evolve, or change your culture because you believe that it is some aspect of culture that matters to the functioning of your organization, you need to understand what we have covered so far in this book, but it may not seem very practical to you. What you want and need in addition is a model of the change process itself and some guidelines for how to get started. In this chapter we will define you as the "change leader" and provide you a model for managing change.

We will look first at a general model of how organizational change works, because you can't change culture if you don't understand the general change process in human systems. Before you get to culture change you have to answer first what is the problem, what is worrying you? If you conclude that you do need to change something, you have to get very precise and concrete about what you want to change and why. Paradoxically, you will have to answer these questions without using the word *culture* because culture is just an abstraction that refers to lots of concrete things such as structure, process, beliefs, values, and behavior.

If you think of culture as being for the group or organization what personality or character is to the individual, you will realize that just assessing a personality without having some reason to do so can be an endless and pointless exercise. The same is true for general culture assessment. So when someone who is in a change leadership position approaches me with the question, "Can you help us diagnose our culture?" I find myself first engaging in defining the change problem.

The Change Leader Needs Help in Defining the Change Problem or Goal

The best way to explain how to do this is to provide a hypothetical conversation based on a number of such conversations that I have had.

Client: "Hello, in my company we are getting very interested in your concept of culture and wondered whether you would help us define the main elements of our culture."

EHS: "I am curious to know why you want to do that?"

Client: "Well, we are worried about some recent employee surveys showing that we may be losing employee involvement and thought we should examine our culture to see what might be happening."

(To know what elements of culture might be relevant to this, I need to know more about what the client means by "losing employee involvement" rather than pursuing what she means by "culture.")

EHS: "OK, can you tell me a little more about what is going on that makes you think you are losing employee involvement?"

Client: "Well, we are experiencing unusually high turnover among our younger employees."

EHS: "In all categories, or are you worried about certain ones?"

(The general principle is to push down the abstraction ladder to some specific issue or problem that is worrying the client.)

Client: "It is especially our young recently hired creative engineering group that is losing people within a year or two of coming in, so we need to find out what is going on in our culture that is making that happen; I know there are some good surveys out there that might give us a clue as to where our culture is missing out and what we have to do to build a new culture in the engineering department."

(We now know that it might be a problem of the engineering "subculture," but it is still not clear just what the client wants except some vague diagnosis.)

EHS: "So the problem is you would like to reduce turnover of the recently hired engineers; have I understood that?"

Client: "Yes, exactly, that is why I want a culture survey."

EHS: "So what we need is an assessment process that will help us understand why young engineers are leaving and how the existing culture in your company may be involved in that."

Client: "Isn't that exactly what I asked you about; I want to do a culture survey."

(I now finally have some leverage to get into the complicated issue of what we mean by the word *culture*, and can push ahead to what to do next.)

EHS: "Before we do a survey, which might be a shot in the dark, it might be useful to get together some groups of young engineers and ask them what their perception of the culture of the organization is. If they come up with some relevant dimensions we might know what kind of survey and remedy we might need. We might also want to talk to some of the managers and ask them what their view of the problem is and how they think it relates to culture dimensions."

Client: "Would it not be more efficient to just go ahead with a survey?"

(If the client seemed to have some understanding of culture and had proposed a specific set of dimensions to test, maybe across several engineering departments that had different levels of turnover, I might agree that a survey would be a good next step and help him or her design one or lead him or her to an organization that does surveys around those dimensions, but we still don't know what kind of survey might help.)

EHS: "Not really, because there are many surveys out there dealing with different dimensions and different culture models; they may have nothing to do with the particular problem that is worrying you, so I think it best to start with some group interviews; then we can decide whether to do a survey and what kind of survey."

The principle is not to engage in "culture change" before we know what problem or issue is motivating the change, and then to help the client to understand the change process that would be involved in making "culture changes."

General Change Theory

All planned change starts with some recognition of a problem, a recognition that something is not going as expected. My elaboration of Kurt Lewin's (1947) original change theory is a good starting point for analyzing the whole change process through its various stages. As Lewin noted, human systems are always in a "quasi-stationary equilibrium," by which he meant that there are always many forces acting toward change, many other forces acting toward maintaining the present, and that the system is always seeking some kind of equilibrium.

Human systems are "open," in the sense of being perpetually involved with their physical and social environment and, therefore, perpetually being influenced and, in turn, trying to influence that environment. We need to understand what then triggers "managed" change, the desire for someone to deliberately change something that is currently in a quasi-stationary equilibrium? What are the conditions needed for such deliberate managed change to be successful, to accomplish the goals of the change project? Are these conditions different if the change involves cultural DNA, the basic assumptions by which the group or organization has been working? How does such deliberate, managed change begin, and what stages does such a change process involve?

Why Change? Where Is the Pain?

A desire for change, for doing something differently, for learning something new, *always begins with some kind of pain or dissatisfaction*. This can take many forms—an unexpected negative result of some program, a drop in sales, people leaving unexpectedly, a loss of morale. Failure to achieve something that was wanted or expected could be equally painful, especially if it created disappointment or disillusionment. The desire to change something can even result from a reminder that something intended had not yet been done. In all cases the common factor is some kind "pain."

Formal leaders may not be hurting or dissatisfied, but they will not start a change program unless they see someone whom they care about in pain or dissatisfied. That could be a customer, a client, a subordinate, a peer, or someone above her or him. Many of the most significant change programs in health care have begun with leaders observing that *patients* are having a difficult time with the medical system, resulting in the launching of programs to improve patient satisfaction or *the quality of the patient experience*. A hospital administrator may observe that some doctors are unnecessarily rude to nurses or even patients, and decide that this is not only hurtful to the nurses but lowers their morale, which in turn influences patient care.

We can think of the process of seeing or experiencing something that causes the pain as "disconfirmation," which starts the change process by creating some motivation to change. This launches what we can think of as a series of stages of the change process as shown in Exhibit 16.1.

Exhibit 16.1   The Stages and Cycle of Learning/Change

Stage 1 Creating the Motivation to Change (Unfreezing)

- Disconfirmation
- Creation of survival anxiety or guilt
- Learning anxiety produces resistance to change
- Creation of psychological safety to overcome learning anxiety

Stage 2 Learning New Concepts, New Meanings for Old Concepts, and New Standards for Judgment

- Imitation of and identification with role models
- Scanning for solutions and trial-and-error learning

Stage 3 Internalizing New Concepts, Meanings, and Standards

- Incorporation into self-concept and identity
- Incorporation into ongoing relationships

The Stages and Steps of Change Management

Stage 1: Creating Motivation and Readiness for Change

If any part of the core cognitive or emotional structure is to change in more than minor incremental ways, the system must first experience enough disequilibrium to force a coping process that goes beyond just reinforcing the assumptions that are already in place. Lewin (1947) called the creation of such disequilibrium *unfreezing*, or creating a motivation to change. To understand this we have to define four very different processes, each of which must be present to a certain degree for the system to develop motivation to change and launch into the change process.

Disconfirmation. Disconfirmation is any information that shows someone in the organization that some of its goals are not being met or that some of its processes are not accomplishing what they are supposed to. Someone is hurting somewhere. Disconfirming information can be economic, political, social, or personal—as when a charismatic leader chides a group for not living up to its own ideals and thereby induces guilt. Scandals or embarrassing leaks of information are often the most powerful kind of disconfirmation.

However, the information is usually only symptomatic. It does not automatically tell the organization what the underlying problem might be; it only creates disequilibrium in pointing out that something is wrong somewhere.

Change leaders then have to use the disconfirming data that already exists or even be the source of it by defining the problem themselves, sometimes creating a crisis to create change motivation.

Survival Anxiety and Learning Anxiety (Coutu, 2002). Disconfirmation does not, by itself, automatically produce a motivation to change, because members of the organization can deny the validity of the information or rationalize that it is irrelevant. For example, if employee turnover suddenly increases, leaders or organization members can say, "It is only the bad people who are leaving, the ones we don't want anyway." Or if sales are down, it is possible to say, "This is only a reflection of a minor recession."

For disconfirming information to create *survival anxiety* or *guilt*, it has to imply that some important goal is not being met or some important value is being compromised. Even when survival anxiety is felt, denial and repression can arise because of the realization that new ways of perceiving, thinking, feeling, and behaving may be very hard to learn, thus creating what I have called *learning anxiety*, a feeling that "I cannot learn new behaviors or adopt new attitudes without losing my position, my feeling of self-esteem, or my group membership."

For example, the Alpha Power Company had to become environmentally responsible, which meant that the electrical workers had to change their self-image from being employees who heroically kept power and heat on to being responsible stewards of the environment, preventing and cleaning up spills produced by their trucks or transformers. The new rules required them to report incidents that might be embarrassing to their group, and even to report on each other if they observed environmentally irresponsible behavior in fellow workers. At the same time, they were in a panic because they did not know how to diagnose environmentally dangerous conditions—how to determine, for example, whether a spill required a simple mop-up or was full of dangerous chemicals such as PCBs, or whether a basement was merely dusty or was filled with asbestos dust.

Sometimes disconfirming data have existed for a long time, but because of insufficient survival anxiety and a great deal of learning anxiety, the organization has collectively avoided change by denying the data's relevance, validity, or even its existence. It is our capacity both as individuals and as organizations to deny or even repress disconfirming data that make whistle-blowing or scandals such powerful change motivators. The Alpha Power Company launched its major change program only after it was revealed that an explosion had blown dangerous chemicals into the environment, chemicals that the organization had claimed were not in the transformers.

The failure to pay attention to disconfirming data occurs at two levels: (1) leaders who are in a position to act, deny, or repress the data for personal psychological reasons, or (2) the information is available in various parts of the organization but is suppressed in various ways. For example, in the analysis of major accidents, it is routinely found that some employees had observed various hazards and did not report them, were not listened to, or were actually encouraged to suppress their observations (Gerstein, 2008; Perin, 2005). The organization may deny information, because to accept it would compromise its ability to achieve other values or goals or would damage the self-esteem or face of the organization itself. When these face-maintaining forces are strong, the survival anxiety is not experienced in the first place. Hence, a scandal is often needed for disconfirming data to be acknowledged so that a change program can be launched.

Learning Anxiety Produces Resistance to Change. If the disconfirming data "get through" the organization's denial and defensiveness, it will recognize the need to change, the need to give up some old habits and ways of thinking, and the need to learn some new habits and ways of thinking. However, the launching of a change program produces learning anxiety. It is the interaction of these two anxieties that creates the complex dynamics of change.

To illustrate this in different terms, let's look at what happens with tennis. The process starts with disconfirmation; you are not beating some of the people you are used to beating, or your aspirations for a better score or a better-looking game are not met, so you feel the need to improve your game. But, as you contemplate the actual process of unlearning your old stroke and developing a new stroke, you realize that you may not be able to do it, or you may be temporarily incompetent during the learning process. These feelings exemplify "learning anxiety."

Such feelings can arise when the change proposed requires new learning, i.e., becoming computer competent, changing your supervisory style, transforming competitive relationships into teamwork and collaboration, changing from a high-quality, high-cost strategy into becoming the low-cost producer, moving from engineering domination and product orientation to a marketing and customer orientation, learning to work in nonhierarchical diffuse networks, and so on. In the health care industry there are many change programs that require doctors to give up some of the autonomy that they have always assumed was intrinsic to their role, or to learn new behavior patterns vis-à-vis patients, nurses, and technicians.

It is important to understand that the resistance to change based on learning anxiety can result for one or more valid reasons:

- **Fear of loss of power or position:** With new learning, we may have less power or status than we had before.

- **Fear of temporary incompetence:** During the learning process, we will feel incompetent because we have given up the old way and have not yet mastered the new way. The best examples come from the efforts to learn to use computers.

- **Fear of punishment for incompetence:** If it takes a long time to learn the new way of thinking and doing things, we fear that we will be punished for lack of productivity. In the computer arena, there are some striking cases in which employees never learned the new system sufficiently to take advantage of its potential because they felt they had to remain productive and thus spent insufficient time on the new learning.

- **Fear of loss of personal identity:** We may not want to be the kind of person that the new way of working would require us to be. For example, some electrical workers in Alpha Power resigned or retired because they could not stand the self-image of being environmental stewards.

- **Fear of loss of group membership:** The shared assumptions that make up a culture also identify who is in and who is out of the group. If by developing new ways of thinking or new behavior we will become a deviant in our group, we may be rejected or even ostracized. This fear is perhaps the most difficult to overcome, because it requires the whole group to change its ways of thinking and its norms of inclusion and exclusion.

One or more of these forces lead to what we end up calling "resistance to change." It is usually glibly attributed to "human nature," but as I have tried to indicate, it is actually a rational response to many situations that require people to change. As long as learning anxiety remains high, an individual will be motivated to resist the validity of the disconfirming data or will invent various excuses for why he or she cannot really engage in a learning process right now. These responses often come in the following stages (Coghlan, 1996):

1. **Denial:** convincing ourselves that the disconfirming data are not valid, are temporary, don't really count, or someone is just crying "wolf"

2. **Scapegoating, passing the buck, dodging:** convincing ourselves that the cause is in some other department, that the data do not apply to us, that others need to change first

3. **Maneuvering, bargaining:** wanting special compensation for the effort to make the change; wanting to be convinced that it is in our own interest and will benefit us

Given all of these bases of resistance to change, how then does the change leader create the conditions for change—that is, how is new learning to begin? Two crucial principles come into play.

Principle 1: Survival Anxiety or Guilt Must Be Greater than Learning Anxiety

From the change leader's point of view, it might seem obvious that the way to motivate learning is simply to increase the survival anxiety or guilt. The problem with that approach is that greater threat or guilt may simply increase defensiveness to avoid the threat or pain of the learning process. With more forces operating in the whole system, the overall tension in the system increases, leading to more unpredictable and undesirable resistance to change. That realization leads to a key insight about change embodied in Principle 2.

Principle 2: Learning Anxiety Must Be Reduced Rather than Increasing Survival Anxiety

The change leader must reduce learning anxiety by increasing the learner's sense of psychological safety and reducing external barriers to change. Figuring out how to do this and having the consulting and helping skills to turn the change target into a client now becomes the most difficult phase of the change process. The involvement of the change target in the change process now becomes critical.

Creating Psychological Safety. The person or group that becomes the target of change, that must unlearn something and learn something new, must come to feel that it is possible and in its own interest. Paradoxically, the person who is the change *target* must become a *client*, must begin to see that change is possible and is beneficial, and that the change leader can become a helper in the new learning process. Creating such psychological safety for organizational members who are undergoing a change process involves eight activities that must be carried on almost simultaneously. They are listed in chronological order, but the change leader must be prepared to implement all of them:

1. **Provide a compelling positive vision:** The targets of change must come to believe that they and the organization will be better off if they learn the new way of thinking and working. Such a vision must be articulated and widely held by senior management, who must spell out in clear behavioral terms what "the new way of working" will be. It must also be recognized that this new way of working is nonnegotiable.

2. **Provide formal training:** If the new way of working requires new knowledge and skill, members must be provided with the necessary formal and informal training. For example, if the new way of working requires teamwork, then formal training on team building and maintenance must be provided. If the new skills are complex, it may require a period of coaching until the new behavior is well embedded (Nelson, Batalden, Godfrey, and Lazar, 2011).

3. **Involve the learner:** If the formal training is to take hold, the learners must have a sense that they can manage their own informal learning process. Each learner will learn in a slightly different way, so it is essential to involve learners in designing their own optimal learning process. The goals of learning may be nonnegotiable, but the method of learning and the new way of working can often be highly individualized.

4. **Train relevant "family" groups and teams:** Because cultural assumptions are embedded in groups, informal training and practice must be provided to whole groups so that new norms and new assumptions can be jointly built. Learners should not feel like deviants if they decide to engage in the new learning.

5. **Provide resources:** These include time, practice fields, coaches, and feedback. Learners cannot learn something fundamentally new if they don't have the time, the space, the coaching, and valid feedback on how they are doing. Practice fields are particularly important so that learners can make mistakes without disrupting the organization (Kellogg, 2011).

6. **Provide positive role models:** The new way of thinking and behaving may be so different from what learners are used to that they may need to be able to see what it looks like before they can imagine themselves doing it. They must be able to see the new behavior and attitudes in others with whom they can identify, especially others at higher levels in the organization.

7. **Provide support groups in which learning problems can be aired and discussed:** Learners need to be able to talk about their learning frustrations and difficulties with others who are experiencing similar difficulties so that they can support each other and jointly learn new ways of dealing with those difficulties.

8. **Remove barriers and build new supporting systems and structures:** Organizational structures, reward systems, and control systems must be made consistent with the new way of thinking and working. For example, if the goal of the change program is to learn how to be more of a team player, the individualized competitive sales target system must be removed and the reward system must become group oriented; the discipline system must begin to punish instead of rewarding individually

competitive, aggressive, or selfish behavior; and the organizational structures must make it possible to work as a team.

In any complex system if you change one part, it will have repercussions in other parts of the system, which must be anticipated and dealt with. For example, a program to have nurses visit patients the night before a critical operation or treatment program was abandoned because the record-keeping system could not or would not provide the necessary patient information to make the visits possible. Most change programs fail because they do not create the eight conditions outlined here. When we consider the difficulty of achieving all eight conditions and the energy and resources that have to be expended to achieve them, it is small wonder that changes are often short-lived or never get going at all. However, when an organization sets out to really transform itself by creating psychological safety, real and significant cultural changes can be achieved.

Stage 2: The Actual Change and Learning Process

In analyzing the actual change and learning process, we have to discuss both what actually changes and by which mechanism the change occurs. I discuss the learning mechanisms first and then show how they are related to what actually changes.

Imitation and Identification versus Scanning and Trial-and-Error Learning

There are basically two mechanisms by which we learn new behavior, beliefs, and values:

1. Imitating a role model and psychologically identifying with that person
2. Scanning our environment and using trial and error as we keep inventing our own solutions until something works

In practice we use both methods of learning in the sense that the things we want to try out are often based on imitation of a role model. The reason for distinguishing the two methods in models of planned change is that the change leader has a choice of whether or not to make "the new way of working" visible by providing role models, or deliberately withholding such role models to force the learner to scan and find his or her own things to try out.

Imitation and identification work best when it is clear what the new way of working is to be and when the new beliefs and values to be adopted are themselves clear. For example, the leader can "walk the talk" in the sense of making himself or herself a role model of the new behavior that is expected. As part of a training program, the leader can provide role models through case materials, films, role-playing, or simulations. Learners who have acquired the new concepts can be brought in to encourage others to get to know how they did it. This mechanism is also the most efficient, but it comes with the risk that what the learner learns does not integrate well into his or her personality or is not acceptable to the groups he or she belongs to. This means that the new learning may not be internalized, and the learner will revert to prior behavior after the coercive pressure to perform the new behavior is no longer there.

If we are talking about new beliefs and values, they can sometimes be acquired immediately through identifying with a charismatic change leader or others whom he or she brings into the change process. When this does not work, the change leader must rely more on hoping that the new behavior, which may initially have been coerced, is successful in improving the situation and that the learner will then adopt the beliefs and values that justify the new behavior.

If the change leader wants us to learn things that really fit into our personality, he or she must encourage us to scan our environment and develop our own solutions. As an example of *scanning*, when Amoco changed the role of "engineer" from embedded resource to freelance consultant, the company could have developed a training program for how to be a consultant, built around engineers who had made the shift successfully. However, senior management felt that such a shift was so personal that they decided merely to create the structure and the incentives, but to let individual engineers figure out for themselves how they wanted to manage the new kinds of relationships. In some cases, this meant that some people left the organization. But those engineers who learned from their own experience how to be consultants genuinely evolved to a new kind of career that they integrated into their total identities. This process did not rule out imitation, but it gave the choice of whom to imitate to the learners.

The explicit use of *imitation and identification* was illustrated in the Alpha Power program to create a "culture of environmental responsibility." Both the goals and the methods of how to be environmentally responsible were clear and nonnegotiable. Employees therefore had to be trained in how to identify hazards and spills as well as how to clean things up, which meant giving them the time and resources to learn how to do it along with role models and coaching for all the situations that might come up. There were clear principles and rules to be followed—for example, "even a few drops of oil on the pavement have to be cleaned up," and "if you see a hazardous condition, you must report it immediately."

The general principle here is that the change leader must be clear about the ultimate goals (i.e., the new way of working that is to be achieved), but that does not necessarily imply that everyone will reach that goal in the same way. Involvement of the learner does not imply that the learner has a choice about the ultimate goals, but it does imply that he or she can be given a choice of the means to get there when that seems appropriate.

Change Beliefs and Values First or Behavior First? Some change theorists argue that one must change beliefs and values first and the desired behavior will then automatically follow; others argue that one must change behavior first, and then beliefs and values will follow to justify the behavior. The first theory is simpler but harder to implement, because when it comes to culture it is not easy to convince people that the present cultural beliefs and values need to change, given that those same beliefs and values have been the source of the organization's success. The first theory also falls short when the connection between beliefs and behavior is not clearly specified. Many organizations espouse teamwork and employees agree that it is important, but what they consider to be teamwork *behavior* is not aligned with the beliefs that the change agent sold.

Changing behavior first avoids this problem because it begins with having to define clearly what is actually expected of employees in the future if the change program is successful. If you want teamwork, what would team behavior look like and what kind of training and supporting structures would be needed to support such behavior? The more clearly the desired behavior is specified, the easier it becomes to identify the sources of learning anxiety and the kind of psychological safety that would have to be provided. It is for this reason that clearly specifying future behavior has to be an integral part of initially deciding what the problem is and what changes are desired. "Let's create a teamwork culture" is, from this point of view, a useless goal unless the specific desired behavior is defined concretely.

Behavior change can be "coerced" by threatening job loss or other punishment if the change targets do not agree at least to go through the motions. This works if the behavior is something simple, but becomes irrelevant if the new behavior requires learning new skills or requires coordinated activity. Of course, the training can also be coerced. For example, I know of many efforts to introduce information technology into workflows by training the employees in the new process, declaring victory when the training is finished, only to discover that the hoped-for productivity does not increase and the employees grumble about the unwanted side effects of the new system.

This situation is occurring right now in the introduction of electronic patient records systems, which require doctors to learn how to enter all patient information into computers to create "a more safe and efficient safety culture in medicine." In some hospitals the doctors were involved, were given adequate training, and now find that the new system not only works well but is clearly "the way of the future." In some other hospitals the doctors were "coerced" to use the system, found it cumbersome and time consuming, claimed that it interfered with maintaining good eye contact with patients, and therefore were sure that "we will go back to the old system."

In other words, behavior change leads to culture change only if the new behavior is perceived to make things better and therefore becomes internalized and stable. Employees who are coerced and who are not involved in the change process are not likely to experience the results as "better" and will therefore only continue to go through the motions. We need next to understand how new beliefs and values come about.

New Beliefs and Values through Cognitive Redefinition. The new learning can happen through either scanning, identification, or both, but in any case the essence of the new learning that can be legitimately described as cultural (i.e., new beliefs and values) involves some "cognitive redefinition" of some of the core concepts in the learner's assumption set. For example, when companies that assume that they are lifetime employers who would never lay off anyone are faced with the economic necessity of reducing payroll costs, they cognitively redefine layoffs as "transitions" or "early retirements," make the transition packages generous, provide long periods of time during which the employees can seek alternative employment, offer extensive counseling, provide outplacement services, and so on, all to preserve the assumption that "we treat our people fairly and well." This process is more than rationalization. It is a genuine cognitive redefinition on the part of the senior management of the organization and is viewed ultimately as "restructuring." A publicly espoused value of lifetime employment is subordinated to other values such as company survival and beneficial treatment of the people who are fired.

As I have argued previously, most change processes should emphasize the need for specific behavior change. Such change is important in laying the groundwork for cognitive redefinition, but behavior change alone will not last unless it is accompanied by cognitive redefinition. For example, Alpha's environmental program began with the enforcement of rules, but eventually it became internalized when employees saw the benefits of their own behavior change and therefore were able to cognitively redefine their job role and their identity. Some engineers at Amoco were able to redefine their self-image quickly, become comfortable with the new job structure, and went on to tout the value of engineering as an independent consulting service. Some of the doctors who were forced to use the electronic patient records system saw its benefits, shifted their concepts of its value, and noticed that eye contact was not critical as long as they demonstrated in other ways that they were really listening.

Learning New Concepts and New Meanings for Old Concepts. New concepts are often promulgated first in the vision of the change leader—"a new independent engineer" in Amoco, "an environmentally responsible organization" in Alpha Power, and a "a world-class clean, non-corrupt city-state" in the case of Singapore. Bushe & Marshak (2015) call such visionary concepts "generative metaphors" in that a metaphor such as "sustainability" or "saving the planet" is a clear positive goal without specifying just how the goal would be accomplished. In the many changes that are occurring in the culture of medicine, it is "patient involvement," a "better patient experience," and an emphasis on "population health" (instead of curing disease) that have become such generative metaphors.

Beyond these broad new concepts, if someone has been trained to think in a certain way and has been a member of a group that has also thought that way, how can that person imagine changing to a new way of thinking? If you were an engineer in Amoco, you would have been a member of a division working as an expert technical resource with a clear career line and a single boss. In the new structure of a centralized engineering group "selling its services for set fees," you were now asked to think of yourself as a member of a consulting organization that sells its services to customers who could purchase those services elsewhere if they did not like your deal. For you to make such a transformation would require you to develop several new concepts—"freelance consultant," "selling services for a fee," and "competing with outsiders who could underbid you." In addition, you would have to learn a new meaning for the concept of what it meant to be an "engineer" and what it meant to be an "employee of Amoco." You would have to learn a new reward system—that you would now be paid and promoted based on your ability to bring in work. You would have to learn to see yourself as much as a salesperson as an engineer. You would have to define your career in different terms and learn to work for many different bosses. This kind of change is not necessarily benign and certainly not easy!

Developing New Standards of Evaluation. Along with new concepts come new standards of evaluation. Production targets, quality standards, and safety requirements require new behavior on which the change targets will now be evaluated. When these new targets and criteria are not carefully thought through in terms of what the "new way of working would look like" to achieve them, we often get organizational pathology in the form of employees claiming to accomplish the targets when, in fact, they were not meeting them. In the Alpha change program, monitors had to be installed all over the system for a while to enforce the standard of cleaning up *all spills*.

In the 2014 scandal in the Veteran's Administration, it was discovered that the targets set in Washington of seeing a certain number of patients within a set time limit were not being met, but, worse, were claimed by many offices to have been met, which left many veterans without care for long periods of time. Such events again highlight the importance of defining the problem clearly and thinking through what the change program would involve to have the new way of working to be implemented successfully. The cheating on emission standards that was revealed in Volkswagen in 2016 was similarly a case of senior management setting targets without considering whether or not the system could meet them.

For the individual change target, all of this means that you will now be evaluated differently. Whereas in the former Amoco structure the engineers were evaluated largely on the quality of their work, now they had to estimate more accurately just how many days a given job would take, what quality level could be achieved in that time, and what it would cost if they tried for the higher-quality standard they were used to. This might require a whole new set of skills involving making estimates and creating accurate budgets.

What was hardest for the Alpha employees to learn were the new standards of what it meant to be environmentally responsible; they thought they already were, but never considered that cleaning up a few drops of oil was now considered essential. If they encountered a potential hazard, as responsible engineers they always checked the data carefully before reporting it. The idea that "the possibility of something dangerous" had to be reported *immediately*, even before the lab could check whether or not the danger was real was hard for Alpha engineers to accept. A more extreme version of a change in standards was what the Singaporean citizens had to learn, given the newly required standards of cleanliness and non-corruption that had to be accepted to reach the larger economic goals.

In the case of DEC, the engineers had certain standards for what was a good computer based on what their sophisticated customers valued. When the market shifted to "dumb users" who just wanted a turnkey product, the DEC engineers explicitly rejected that as a new standard to work to. When they finally decided to build some simple desktop products, they used their own standards for evaluating what a customer expected; they over-designed them and built in far too many bells and whistles, which made the computers too expensive and too hard to use. The DNA of the DEC culture never changed.

Setting new standards is perhaps clearest in change programs to "improve safety." Most organizations claim that they are concerned about safety and carefully measure themselves on the OSHA statistics, but one hospital got serious about patient safety only when the CEO announced with great feeling that "he was not about to go to yet one more family to tell them that a family member had died because of a hospital mistake." In high-hazard industries change programs that are directed to improving safety really take hold only when the CEO becomes personally involved and provides a role model through his or her own behavior and defines the standards to be met.

Stage 3: Refreezing, Internalizing, and Learning Agility

The final step in any given change process is refreezing, by which Lewin (1947) meant that the new learning will not stabilize until it is reinforced by actual results. The Alpha employees discovered that not only could they deal with environmental hazards but that it was satisfying and worthwhile to do so; hence, they internalized the attitude that a clean and safe environment was in everyone's interest even if it meant slowing jobs down when a hazard was encountered. If the change leaders have correctly diagnosed the behavior that is needed to fix the problems that launched the change program, the new behavior will produce better results and will be confirmed.

If it turns out that the new behavior does not produce better results, this information will be perceived as disconfirming information and will launch a new change process. Human systems are, therefore, potentially in perpetual flux; the more dynamic the environment becomes, the more that may require an almost perpetual change and learning process.

Cautions in Regard to "Culture" Change

When an organization encounters disconfirming information and launches a change program, it is not clear at the outset whether culture change will be involved and how the culture will aid or hinder the change program. To clarify these issues, a culture assessment process of the kind described in the preceding two chapters becomes appropriate. However, it is generally better to be very clear about the change goals before launching the culture assessment.

1. **The change goal must be defined concretely in behavioral terms not as "culture change."** For example, in the Alpha Power case, the court said that the company had to become more environmentally responsible and more open in its reporting. The change goal was to get employees (1) to become more aware of environmental hazards, (2) to report them immediately to the appropriate agencies, (3) to learn how to clean up the hazardous conditions, and (4) to learn how to prevent spills and other hazards from occurring in the first place.

In what way the "culture" needed to be changed was not known when the change program was launched. Only as specific goals were identified could the change leaders determine whether or not cultural elements would aid or hinder the change. In fact, it turned out that large portions of the culture could be used positively to change some specific elements in the culture that did have to be changed. The fact that Alpha was quite autocratic and very training oriented enabled it to train the entire workforce immediately in how to identify hazards and what to do about them. The bulk of the existing culture was used to change some peripheral cultural elements.

One of the biggest mistakes that leaders make when they undertake change initiatives is to be vague about their change goals and to assume that "culture change" would be needed. When someone asks me to help him or her with a "culture-change program," my most important initial question is "What do you mean? Can you explain your goals without using the word *culture?*"

2. **Old cultural elements can be destroyed by eliminating the people who "carry" those elements, but new cultural elements can be learned only if the new behavior leads to success and satisfaction over a period of time.** Once a culture exists, once an organization has had some period of success and stability, the culture cannot be changed directly unless the group itself is dismantled. A leader can impose new ways of doing things, can articulate new goals and means, and can change reward and control

systems, but none of those changes will produce culture change unless the new way of doing things actually works better and provides the members a new set of shared experiences that eventually become perceived to be a change in the culture.

3. **Changes in the basic assumptions of the culture always require a period of unlearning that is psychologically painful.** Many kinds of changes that leaders impose on their organizations require only new learning and therefore will not be resisted. These are usually new behaviors that make it easier to do what we want to do anyway. However, once we are adults and once our organizations have developed routines and processes that we have become used to, we may find that new proposed ways of doing things such as learning a new software program to make our work on the computer more efficient may look easy to the change leaders but may be hard for the employees to learn. We may feel comfortable with our present software and may feel that to learn a new system is not worth the effort. The change leader therefore needs a model of change that includes "unlearning" as a legitimate stage and that can deal with transformations, not just seeming enhancements.

4. **As task complexity and systemic interdependency increases, change becomes perpetual.** We talk in terms of stages, but with technological complexity and cultural diversity the change process is becoming more or less perpetual in most organizations. Even as some new behaviors are "refrozen," they elicit new reactions from the environment, which creates a new cycle of disconfirmation, survival anxiety, and motivation for further change. New beliefs, values, and behavior have to be thought of as "adaptive moves" rather than "solutions" to problems. Though the change process can be analyzed in terms of stages, it is increasingly becoming in many organizations a perpetual way of life (Schein, 2016).

Summary and Conclusions

This chapter describes a general change model that acknowledges from the outset the difficulty of launching any transformative change because of the anxiety associated with new learning. The change process starts with disconfirmation, which produces two anxieties: (1) *survival anxiety or guilt*, the feeling that we must change, and (2) *learning anxiety*, the realization that we might have to unlearn something and learn new things that might challenge our competencies, our role or power position, our identity elements, and possibly our group membership. Learning anxiety causes denial and resistance to change. The only way to overcome such resistance is to reduce the learning anxiety by making the learner feel "psychologically safe."

The conditions for creating psychological safety were described. If new learning occurs, it usually reflects "cognitive redefinition," which consists of learning new concepts, learning new meanings for old concepts, and adopting new standards of evaluation. Such new learning occurs either through identification with role models or through trial-and-error learning based on scanning the environment.

The change goals should initially be focused on the concrete problems to be fixed; only when those goals are clearly defined in terms of desired future behavior is it appropriate to initiate a culture assessment to determine how the culture will aid or hinder the change process.

Suggestions for Readers

1. Apply these stages to some change that you have personally experienced, some habit that you tried to break, or some new skill you tried to learn.

2. Determine which stage and which process was most difficult.

3. Now think about an organizational change you want to make and apply the same thinking.

17

THE CHANGE LEADER AS LEARNER

The various predictions about globalism, knowledge-based organizations, the information age, the bio-tech age, the loosening of organizational boundaries, networks, and so on all have one theme in common: we basically do not know what the world of tomorrow will really be like, except that it will be different, more complex, more fast-paced, and more culturally diverse (Drucker Foundation, 1999; Global Business Network, 2002; Michael, 1985, 1991; Schwartz, 2003).

This means that organizations, their leaders, and all the rest of us will have to become perpetual learners (Kahane, 2010; Michael, 1985, 1991; Scharmer, 2007; Senge, Smith, Kruschwitz, Laur, & Schley, 2008). When we pose the issue of perpetual learning in the context of cultural analysis, we confront a paradox. Culture is a stabilizer, a conservative force, and a way of making things meaningful and predictable. Many management consultants and theorists have asserted that "strong" cultures are desirable as a basis for effective and lasting performance. But strong cultures are, by definition, stable and hard to change.

If the world is becoming more turbulent, requiring more flexibility and learning, does this not imply that strong cultures will increasingly become a liability? Does this not mean that the process of culture creation is itself potentially dysfunctional because it stabilizes things, whereas flexibility might be more appropriate? Or is it possible to imagine a culture that, by its very nature, is learning oriented, adaptive, and flexible? Can we stabilize perpetual learning and change? What would a culture look like that favored perpetual learning and flexibility? What would a leader look like who promoted such a culture?

To translate that question into leadership terms, what is the direction in which the leaders of today should be pushing cultural evolution to prepare for the surprises of tomorrow? What sort of characteristics and skills must a leader have to perceive the needs of tomorrow and to implement the changes needed to survive?

What Might a Learning Culture Look Like?

The ideas spelled out in this chapter originally resulted from many conversations with the late Donald Michael (1985, 1991) and with my colleagues Tom Malone (2004), Peter Senge (1990; et al., 2008), and Otto Scharmer (2007) about the nature of organizations and work in the future. They have been tested in many workshops where I have heard first-hand from leaders in both the private and nonprofit sectors how rapidly the world is evolving into new uncharted territory. As I have experienced Silicon Valley in the last five years, these ideas have been reinforced and enhanced.

1. *Proactivity.* A learning culture must assume that the appropriate way for humans to behave in relationship to their environment is to be proactive problem solvers and learners. If the culture is built on fatalistic assumptions of passive acceptance, learning will become more and more difficult as the rate of change in the environment increases.

Learning-oriented leadership must portray confidence that active problem solving leads to learning, thereby setting an appropriate example for other members of the organization. It will be more important to be committed to the learning process than to any particular solution to a problem. In the face of greater complexity, the leader's dependence on others to generate solutions will increase, and we have overwhelming evidence that new solutions are more likely to be adopted if the members of the organization have been involved in the learning process (Schein, 2009a, 2009b, 2016).

2. *Commitment to "Learning to Learn."* The learning culture must have in its DNA a "learning gene," in the sense that members must hold the shared assumption that learning is a good thing worth investing in and that learning to learn is itself a skill to be mastered. "Learning" must include both learning about changes in the external environment and learning about internal relationships and how well the organization is adapted to the external changes. For example, one way of understanding the failure of

DEC is to note that the company was committed to continued technological innovation, but there was very little reflection or commitment to learning how to deal with the destructive intergroup competition that success, growth, and age had spawned.

The key to learning is to get feedback and to take the time to reflect, analyze, and assimilate the implications of what the feedback has communicated. Feedback is useful only if the learner has asked for it, so one of the key traits of the learning leader must be willingness to ask for help and accept it (Schein, 2009a, 2016). A further key to learning is the ability to generate new responses, to try new ways of doing things, to accept errors and failure as learning opportunities. This takes time, energy, and resources. A learning culture must therefore value reflection and experimentation and must give its members the time and resources to do it.

3. *Positive Assumptions about Human Nature.* Learning leaders must have faith in people and must believe that ultimately human nature is basically good and, in any case, malleable. The learning leader must believe that humans can and will learn if they are provided the resources and the necessary psychological safety. Learning implies some desire for survival and improvement. If leaders start with assumptions that people are basically lazy and passive or that people have no concern for organizations or causes above and beyond themselves, they will inevitably create organizations that will become self-fulfilling prophecies. Such leaders will train their employees to be lazy, self-protective, and self-seeking, and then they will cite those characteristics as proof of their original assumption about human nature. The resulting control-oriented organizations may survive and even thrive in certain kinds of stable environments, but they are certain to fail as environments become more turbulent and as technological and global trends cause problem solving to become increasingly more complex.

Knowledge and skill are becoming more widely distributed, forcing leaders—whether they like it or not—to be more dependent on other people in their organizations. Under such circumstances, a cynical attitude toward human nature is bound to create, at best, bureaucratic rigidity, and, at the worst extreme, counter-organizational subgroups.

4. Belief that the Environment Can Be Managed. A learning culture must contain in its DNA a gene that reflects the shared assumption that the environment is to some degree manageable. The learning leader who assumes that organizations must symbiotically accept their niche will have more difficulty in learning as the environment becomes more turbulent. Adaptation to a slowly changing environment is also a viable learning process, but I am assuming that the way in which the world is changing will make that less and less possible. In other words, the more turbulent the environment, the more important it will be for leadership to argue for and show that some level of management of the environment is desirable and possible.

A powerful argument along these lines is made by O'Reilly & Tushman (2016) in their concept of *lead and disrupt*, which shows that companies that have survived for a long time have managed both to retain their core businesses and simultaneously build new and adaptive businesses within themselves.

5. Commitment to Truth through Inquiry and Dialogue. A learning culture must contain the shared assumption that solutions to problems derive from a deep commitment to inquiry and a pragmatic search for "truth" through a dialogic process that permits different cultures to begin to understand each other. The inquiry process itself must be flexible and reflect the nature of the environmental changes encountered. What must be avoided in the learning culture is the automatic assumption that wisdom and truth reside in any one source or method. This point is especially important in that in the macro-cultural world even what is considered "scientific" varies considerably; we cannot take some of the physical science models of science as being the only way to truth.

As the problems we encounter change, so too will our learning method have to change. For some purposes, we will have to rely heavily on "normal science"; for other purposes, we will have to find truth in dialogues among experienced practitioners, because scientific proof will be impossible to obtain. For still other purposes, we will collectively have to experiment and live with errors until a better solution is found. Knowledge and skill can be found in many forms, and what I am calling a clinical research process—in which helpers and clients work things out together—will become more and more important, because no one will be "expert" enough to provide an answer. In the learning organization, everyone will have to learn how to learn (Scharmer, 2007; Senge, 1990).

The toughest problem for learning leaders is to come to terms with their own lack of expertise and wisdom. Once we are in a leadership position, our own needs and the expectations of others dictate that we should know the answer and be in control of the situation. Yet if we provide answers, we are creating a culture that will inevitably take a moralistic position in regard to reality and truth. The only way to build a learning culture that continues to learn is for leaders themselves to realize that there is much that they do not know, and to realize that they must teach others to accept that there is much that they do not know (Schein, 2009a). The learning task then becomes a shared responsibility and requires leaders at all levels to build more personal, open, and trusting relationships with their subordinates (Schein, 2016).

I am often asked how to make someone more sensitive to culture. My short answer is "Travel more." It is through giving ourselves more varied experiences in more different kinds of cultures that we learn about cultural variation and develop cultural humility. The learning leader should make it a point to spend a lot of time outside his or her organization and travel to as many other cultures as is practical and build personal relationships with members of those cultures.

6. *Positive Orientation toward the Future.* The optimal time orientation for learning appears to be somewhere between the far future and the near future. We must think far enough ahead to be able to assess the systemic consequences of different courses of action, but we must also think in terms of the near future to assess whether or not our solutions are working. If the environment is becoming more turbulent, the assumption that the best orientation is to live in the past or to live in the present clearly seems dysfunctional.

7. *Commitment to Full and Open Task-Relevant Communication.* The learning culture must be built on the assumption that communication and information are central to organizational well-being and must therefore contain a multichannel communication system that allows everyone to connect to everyone else. This does not mean that all channels will be used or that any given channel will be used for all things. What it does mean is that anyone must be able to communicate with anyone else, and everyone must assume that telling the truth as best they can is positive and desirable. This principle of "openness" does not mean that we suspend all the cultural rules pertaining to face and adopt a definition of openness as equivalent to the proverbial "letting it all hang out." There is ample evidence that interpersonal openness can create severe problems across hierarchical boundaries and in multicultural settings.

But we must use our own cultural insight to know when to move from a Level 1 transactional relationship to a more personal Level 2 relationship within the bounds of our task or joint goals that permits us to be as open as possible about task-relevant information. Full task-relevant information can be achieved only if the members of the group have learned to trust each other, and trust is basically built when the parties tell each other the truth as far as the rules of the social order will allow. One of the major challenges for learning leadership is how to establish trust in a network where people may not have face-to-face contact.

To achieve any of this, one of the most important skills of the learning leader is the ability to be personal when it is appropriate and necessary.

8. Commitment to Cultural Diversity. The more turbulent the environment, the more likely it is that the organization with the more diverse cultural resources will be better able to cope with unpredicted events. Therefore, the learning leader should stimulate diversity and promulgate the assumption that diversity is desirable at the individual and subgroup levels. Such diversity will inevitably create subcultures, and those subcultures will eventually be a necessary resource for learning and innovation.

For diversity to be a resource, however, the subcultures or the individuals in a multicultural task group must be connected and must value each other enough to learn something of each other's culture and language. A central task for the learning leader is to ensure good cross-cultural communication and understanding. Some ideas of how this can be accomplished were presented in Chapter 7. Creating diversity does not mean letting diverse parts of the system run on their own without coordination. Laissez-faire leadership does not work, because it is in the nature of subgroups and sub-cultures to protect their own interests. To optimize diversity, therefore, requires some higher-order coordination mechanisms and mutual cultural understanding.

9. *Commitment to Systemic Thinking.* As the world becomes more complex and interdependent, the ability to think systemically, to analyze fields of forces and understand their joint causal effects on each other, and to abandon simple linear causal logic in favor of complex mental models will become more critical to learning. The learning leader must believe that the world is intrinsically complex, nonlinear, interconnected, and "over-determined" in the sense that most things are multiply caused. The ability to think in this complex manner has come to be a critical interpersonal competence in the analysis of safety in high-hazard industries and in health care and is well captured in the concept of "group sense making" (Weick & Sutcliffe, 2001).

10. *Belief in the Value of Internal Cultural Analysis.* In a learning culture, leaders and members must believe that analyzing and reflecting on their own culture is a necessary part of the learning process. Internal cultural analysis reveals important mechanisms by which groups and organizations function in completing their tasks. Without internal cultural analysis, it is difficult to understand how groups are created, how they become organizations, and how they evolve throughout their existence. But most important, without internal cultural analysis, how can we hope to understand other cultures? Having said this, I still believe that such internal analysis is really useful only in the context of a learning and change agenda.

Why These Dimensions?

Many other dimensions could be analyzed as being relevant to learning. I have chosen to ignore those where the conclusion as to what would aid learning seemed unclear. For example, with respect to the dimension of individualism versus groupism, the best prescription for learning is to accept the notion that every system has both elements in it, and the learning culture will be the one that optimizes individual competition and collaborative teamwork, depending on the task to be accomplished. A similar argument can be made around the dimension of task orientation versus relationship orientation. An optimal learning system would balance these as required by the task rather than opting for either extreme.

With respect to degree of hierarchy, autocracy, paternalism, and participation, it is again a matter of the task, the kind of learning required, and the particular circumstances. In the Alpha Power example, we saw that knowledge of environmental hazards and how to deal with them was initially learned in a very autocratic, top-down training program; as experience in the field accumulated, the learning process shifted to local innovation, which was then circulated to the rest of the organization. Innovative solutions to environmental, health, and safety issues were captured in videotapes and circulated throughout the organization. Monthly award lunches were held, at which successful teams met with senior management and each other to share "how they did it" and to communicate solutions to other teams.

In the end, we have to recognize that even the concept of learning is heavily colored by cultural assumptions and that learning can mean very different things in different cultures and subcultures. The dimensions I listed previously reflect only my own cultural understanding and should therefore be taken only as a first approximation of what a learning culture should emphasize.

The role of learning-oriented leadership in a turbulent world, then, is to promote these kinds of assumptions. Leaders themselves must first hold such assumptions, become learners themselves, and then be able to recognize and systematically reward behavior based on those assumptions in their immediate subordinates. Only if the subordinates exhibit the same behavior is there any hope of the various levels below them adopting such behavior themselves.

Learning-Oriented Leadership

Having described the generic characteristics of a learning culture and the implications in general for the learning leader, it remains to examine briefly whether learning-oriented leadership varies as a function of the different stages of organizational evolution.

Learning Leadership in Culture Creation

In a rapidly changing world, the learning leader or founder must not only have vision but must be able both to impose it and to evolve it further as external circumstances change. Just as the new members of an organization arrive with prior organizational and cultural experiences, a common set of assumptions can be forged only by clear and consistent messages as the group encounters and survives its own crises. The culture-creation leader therefore needs persistence and patience, yet as a learner must be flexible and ready to change.

As groups and organizations develop, certain key emotional issues arise: those having to do with dependence on the leader, with peer relationships, and with how to work effectively. At each of these stages of group development, leadership is needed to help the group identify the issues and deal with them. During these stages, leaders often have to absorb and contain the anxiety that is unleashed when things do not work as they should (Hirschhorn, 1988; Schein, 1983, Frost, 2003). The leader may not have the answer, but he or she must provide temporary stability and emotional reassurance while the answer is being worked out. This anxiety-containing function is especially relevant during periods of learning, when old habits and ways must be given up before new ones are learned. If the world is becoming more changeable, such anxiety may be perpetual, requiring the learning leader to play a perpetually supportive role.

The difficult learning agenda for founders or leaders is discovering how to be simultaneously clear and strong in articulating their vision and yet open to change as that very vision becomes maladaptive in a turbulent environment.

Learning Leadership in Organizational Midlife

Once the organization develops a substantial history of its own, its culture becomes more of a cause than an effect. The culture now influences the strategy, the structure, the procedures, and the ways in which the group members will relate to each other. Culture becomes a powerful influence on members' perceiving, thinking, and feeling, and these predispositions, along with situational factors, will influence the members' behavior. Because it serves an important anxiety-reducing function, culture will be clung to even if it becomes dysfunctional in relation to environmental opportunities and constraints.

Midlife organizations show two basically different patterns, however. Some, under the influence of one or more generations of leaders, develop a highly integrated culture even though they have become large and diversified; others allow growth and diversification in cultural assumptions as well and, therefore, can be described as culturally diverse with respect to their business, functional, geographical, and even hierarchical subunits. How leaders manage culture at this stage of organizational evolution depends on which pattern they perceive and which pattern they decide is best for the future.

Leaders at this stage need, above all, the insight and skill to help the organization evolve into whatever will make it most effective in the future. In some instances, this may mean increasing cultural diversity, allowing some of the uniformity that may have been built up in the growth stage to erode; in other instances, it may mean pulling together a culturally diverse set of organizational units and attempting to impose new common assumptions on them. In either case, the leader needs (1) to be able to analyze the culture in sufficient detail to know which cultural assumptions will aid and which ones will hinder the fulfillment of the organizational mission and (2) to have the intervention skills to make desired changes happen.

Most of the prescriptive analyses of how to bring organizations through this period emphasize that the leader must have certain insights, clear vision, and the skills to articulate, communicate, and implement the vision, but they say nothing about how a given organization can find and install such a leader. In U.S. organizations in particular, the outside board members probably play a critical role in this process, but if the organization has had a strong founding culture, its board may be composed exclusively of people who share the founder's vision. Consequently, real changes in direction may not become possible until the organization faces serious survival difficulties and begins to search for a person with different assumptions to lead it.

Leadership in Mature and Declining Organizations

In the mature organization, if it has developed a strong unifying culture, that culture now defines even what is thought of as "leadership," what is heroic or sinful behavior, how authority and power are allocated and managed, and what the rules of intimacy are. Thus, what leadership has created now either blindly perpetuates itself or creates new definitions of leadership, which may not even include the kinds of entrepreneurial assumptions that started the organization in the first place. The first problem of the mature and possibly declining organization is to create a succession process to find and empower a potential leader who may have enough insight and power to overcome some of the constraining cultural assumptions.

Leaders capable of such managed culture change can come from inside the organization, if they have acquired objectivity and insight into elements of the culture. However, the formally designated senior managers of a given organization may not be willing or able to provide such culture-change leadership. If a leader is imposed from the outside, he or she must have the skill to diagnose accurately what the culture of the organization is, which elements are well adapted, which elements are problematic for future adaptation, and how to change whatever needs changing.

Leadership conceived of in this way is, first of all, the capacity to surmount your own organizational culture, to be able to perceive and think about ways of doing things that are different from what the current assumptions imply. Learning leaders therefore must become somewhat marginal and must be somewhat embedded in the organization's external environment to fulfill this role adequately. At the same time, learning leaders must be well connected to those parts of the organization that are themselves well connected to the environment—the sales organization, purchasing, marketing, public relations, legal, finance, and R&D. Learning leaders must be able to listen to disconfirming information coming from these sources and to assess its implications for the future of the organization. Only when they truly understand what is happening and what will be required in the way of organizational change can they begin to take action in starting a new cultural learning process in connection to whatever organizational survival problems they encounter.

Much has been said of the need for "vision" in leaders, but too little has been said of their need to listen, to absorb, to search the environment for trends, to seek and accept help, and to build the organization's capacity to learn (Schein, 2009a). Especially at the strategic level, the ability to see and acknowledge the full complexity of problems becomes critical. The ability to acknowledge complexity may also imply the willingness and emotional strength to admit uncertainty and to embrace experimentation and possible errors as the only way to learn (Michael, 1985). In our obsession with leadership vision, we may have made it difficult for the learning leader to admit that his or her vision is not clear and that the whole organization together will have to learn. And, as I have repeatedly argued, vision helps only when the organization has already been disconfirmed, and members feel anxious and in need of a solution. Much of what the learning leaders must do occurs before vision even becomes relevant.

A Final Thought: Discover the Culture within My Own Personality

I have discovered that I learn the most about culture when something surprises and puzzles me. I often did not know that I would react in a certain way to what happened or what was said. What I have learned that is most useful to me is to use that moment to look into myself—why did I react the way I did, why is this other person's behavior a puzzle, what does it say about me? So I am joining the millions of philosophers who have said "know thyself." My twist on that is "know the cultures that are inside you."

References

Adizes, I. 1990. *Corporate life cycles*. Englewood Cliff, NJ: Prentice-Hall.

Aldrich, H.E., & Ruef, M. 2006. *Organizations evolving* (2nd ed.). London, UK: Sage.

Allan, J., Fairtlough, G., & Heinzen, B. 2002. *The power of the tale*. London, UK: Wiley.

Allen, T.J. 1977. *Managing the flow of technology*. Cambridge, MA: MIT Press.

Amalberti, R. 2013. *Navigating safety*. New York, NY: Springer.

Ancona, D.G. 1988. Groups in organizations. In C. Hendrick (Ed.), *Annual review of personality and social psychology: Group and intergroup processes*. Beverly Hills, CA: Sage.

Ang, S., & Van Dyne, L. (Eds.). 2008. *Handbook of cultural intelligence*. Armonk, NY: M.E. Sharpe.

Argyris, C. 1964. *Integrating the individual and the organization*. New York, NY: Wiley.

Argyris, C., & Schon, D.A. 1974. *Theory in practice: Increasing professional effectiveness*. San Francisco, CA: Jossey-Bass.

Argyris, C., & Schon, D.A. 1978. *Organizational learning*. Reading, MA: Addison-Wesley.

Argyris, C., & Schon, D.A. 1996. *Organizational learning II*. Reading, MA: Addison-Wesley.

Argyris, C., Putnam, R., & Smith, D.M. 1985. *Action science*. San Francisco, CA: Jossey-Bass.

Ashkanasy, N.M., Wilderom, C.P.M., & Peterson, M.F. (Eds.). 2000. *Handbook of organizational culture and climate*. Thousand Oaks, CA: Sage.

Bailyn, L. 1992. Changing the conditions of work: Implications for career development. In D.H. Montross and C.J. Shinkman (Eds.), *Career development in the 1990s: Theory and practice* (pp. 373–386). Springfield, IL: Charles C. Thomas.

Bailyn, L. 1993. *Breaking the mold*. New York, NY: Free Press.

Baker, M.N. 2016. Organizational use of self: A new symbol of leadership. *Leader to Leader*, 81, 47–52. doi: 10.1002/ltl.20245.

Bales, R.F. 1958. Task roles and social roles in problem solving groups. In N. Maccoby et al. (Eds.), *Reading in social psychology* (3d ed.). New York, NY: Holt, Rinehart, & Winston.

Barley, S.R. 1984. *Technology as an occasion for structuration: Observations on CT scanners and the social order of radiology departments*. Cambridge, MA: Sloan School of Management, MIT.

Barley, S.R., & Kunda, G. 2001. Bringing work back in. *Organization Science, 12*, 76–95.

Bartunek, J.M., & Louis, M.R. 1996. *Insider/Outsider research*. Thousand Oaks, CA: Sage.

Bass, B.M. 1981. *Stogdill's handbook of leadership* (rev. ed.). New York, NY: Free Press.

Bass, B.M. 1985. *Leadership and performance beyond expectations*. New York, NY: Free Press.

Beckhard, R., & Harris, R.T. 1987. *Organizational transitions: Managing complex change*. Reading, MA: Addison-Wesley.

Bennis, W., & Nanus, B. 1985. *Leaders*. New York, NY: Harper & Row.

Bennis, W.G., & Shepard, H.A. 1956. A theory of group development. *Human Relations, 9*, 415–43

Berg, P.O., & Kreiner, C. 1990. Corporate architecture: Turning physical settings into symbolic resources. In P. Gagliardi (Ed.), *Symbols and artifacts* (pp. 41–67). New York, NY: Walter de Gruyter.

Bion, W.R. 1959. *Experiences in groups*. London, UK: Tavistock.

Blake, R.R., & Mouton, J.S. 1964. *The managerial grid*. Houston, TX: Gulf.

Blake, R.R., & Mouton, J.S. 1969. *Building a dynamic organization through grid organization development*. Reading, MA: Addison-Wesley.

Blake, R.R., Mouton, J.S., & McCanse, A.A. 1989. *Change by design*. Reading, MA: Addison-Wesley.

Bradford, L.P., Gibb, J.R., & Benne, K.D. (Eds.). 1964. *T-group theory and laboratory method*. New York, NY: Wiley.

Busco, C., Riccaboni, A., & Scapens, R.W. 2002. When culture matters: Processes of organizational learning and transformation. *Reflections: The SoL Journal, 4*, 43- 54.

Bushe, G.R. 2009. *Clear leadership* (Rev. ed.). Mountain View, CA: Davis-Black.

Bushe, G.R., & Marshak, R.J. 2015. *Dialogic organization development*. Oakland, CA: Berrett/Koehler.

Cameron, K.S., & Quinn, R.E. 1999. *Diagnosing and changing organizational culture*. Reading, MA: Addison-Wesley.

Cameron, K.S., & Quinn, R.E. 2006. *Diagnosing and changing organizational culture*. San Francisco, CA: Jossey-Bass.

Chandler, A.D., Jr. 1962. *Strategy and structure*. Cambridge, MA: MIT Press.

Chapman, B., & Sisodia, R. 2015. *Everybody matters*. New York, NY: Penguin.

Christensen, C.M. 1997. *The innovator's dilemma: When new technologies cause great firms to fail*. Boston, MA: Harvard Business School Press.

Coghlan, D. 1996. Mapping the progress of change through organizational levels. *Research in Organizational Change and Development, 9*, 123–150.

Coghlan, D., & Brannick, T. 2005. *Doing action research in your own organization.* Thousand Oaks, CA: Sage.

Conger, J.A. 1989. *The charismatic leader.* San Francisco, CA: Jossey-Bass.

Conger, J.A. 1992. *Learning to lead.* San Francisco, CA: Jossey-Bass.

Cook, S.N., & Yanow, D. 1993. Culture and organizational learning. *Journal of Management Inquiry, 2*(4), 373–390.

Cooke, R.A., & Szumal, J.L. 1993. Measuring normative beliefs and shared behavioral expectations in organizations: The reliability and validity of the Organizational Culture Inventory. *Psychological Reports, 72,* 1299–1330.

Corlett, J.G., & Pearson, C.S. 2003. *Mapping the organizational psyche.* Gainesville, FL: Center for Application of Psychological Type.

Coutu, D.L. 2002. The anxiety of learning (interview of Edgar Schein). *Harvard Business Review,* March.

Dalton, M. 1959. *Men who manage.* New York, NY: Wiley.

Darling, M.J., & Parry, C.S. 2001. After-action reviews: Linking reflection and planning in a learning practice. *Reflections, 3*(2), 64–72.

Deal, J. J. & Levenson, A. 2016. *What Millennials Want From Work.* New York: McGraw Hill Education.

Deal, T.E., & Kennedy, A.A. 1982. *Corporate cultures.* Reading, MA: Addison-Wesley.

Deal, T.E., & Kennedy, A.A. 1999. *The new corporate cultures.* New York, NY: Perseus.

Denison, D.R. 1990. *Corporate culture and organizational effectiveness.* New York, NY: Wiley.

Denison, D.R., & Mishra, A.K. 1995. Toward a theory of organizational culture and effectiveness. *Organizational Science, 6*(2), 204–223.

Donaldson, G., & Lorsch, J.W. 1983. *Decision making at the top.* New York, NY: Basic Books.

Douglas, M. 1986. *How institutions think.* Syracuse, NY: Syracuse University Press.

Drucker Foundation, Hesselbein, F., Goldsmith, M., & Somerville, I. (Eds.). 1999. *Leading beyond the walls.* San Francisco, CA: Jossey-Bass.

Dubinskas, F.A. 1988. *Making time: Ethnographies of high-technology organizations.* Philadelphia, PA: Temple University Press.

Dyer, W.G., Jr. 1986. *Culture change in family firms.* San Francisco, CA: Jossey-Bass.

Dyer, W.G., Jr. 1989. Integrating professional management into a family-owned business. *Family Business Review, 2*(3), 221–236.

Earley, P.C., & Ang, S. 2003. *Cultural intelligence: Individual interactions across cultures.* Stanford, CA: Stanford University Press.

Edmondson, A.C. 2012. *Teaming: How organizations learn, innovate, and compete in the knowledge economy.* San Francisco, CA: Jossey-Bass.

Edmondson, A.C., Bohmer, R.M., & Pisano, G.P. 2001. Disrupted routines: Team learning and new technology implementation in hospitals. *Administrative Science Quarterly, 46,* 685–716.

Ehrhart, M.G., Schneider, B., & Macey, W.H. 2014. *Organizational climate and culture: An introduction to theory, research and practice*. United Kingdom: Routlege.

England, G. 1975. *The manager and his values*. Cambridge, MA: Ballinger.

Etzioni, A. 1975. *A comparative analysis of complex organizations*. New York, NY: Free Press.

Festinger, L.A. 1957. *Theory of cognitive dissonance*. New York, NY: Harper & Row.

Friedman, R. 2014. *The best places to work: The art and science of creating an extraordinary workplace*. New York, NY: Penguin.

Frost, P.J. 2003. *Toxic emotions at work*. Boston, MA: Harvard Business School Press.

Gagliardi, P. (Ed.). 1990. *Symbols and artifacts: Views of the corporate landscape*. New York, NY: Walter de Gruyter.

Geertz, C. 1973. *The interpretation of cultures*. New York, NY: Basic Books.

Gersick, C. J.C. 1991. Revolutionary change theories: A multilevel exploration of the punctuated equilibrium paradigm. *Academy of Management Review, 16*, 10–36.

Gerstein, M.S. 2008. *Flirting with disaster*. New York, NY: Union Square.

Gerstein, M.S. 1987. *The technology connection: Strategy and change in the information age*. Reading, MA: Addison-Wesley.

Gerstner, L.V. 2002. *Who says elephants can't dance*. New York, NY: Harper Collins.

Gibbon, A., & Hadekel, P. 1990. *Steinberg: The breakup of a family empire*. Toronto: MacMillan of Canada.

Gibson, C.B., & Dibble, R. 2008. Culture inside and out: Developing a collaboration's capacity to externally adapt. In S. Ang & L. Van Dyne (Eds.), *Handbook of cultural intelligence*. Armonk, NY: M.E. Sharpe.

Gittell, J.H. 2016. *Transforming relationships for higher performance*. Stanford, CA: Stanford University Press.

Gladwell, M. 2008. *Outliers*. New York, NY: Little Brown.

Global Business Network. 2002. *What's next? Exploring the new terrain for business*. Cambridge, MA: Perseus Books.

Goffee, R., & Jones, G. 1998. *The character of a corporation*. New York, NY: Harper Business.

Goffman, E. 1959. *The presentation of self in everyday life*. New York, NY: Doubleday.

Goffman, E. 1961. *Asylums*. New York, NY: Doubleday Anchor.

Goffman, E. 1967. *Interaction ritual*. Hawthorne, NY: Aldine.

Goldman, A. 2008. Company on the couch: Unveiling toxic behavior in dysfunctional organizations. *Journal of Management Inquiry, 17*(3), 226–238.

Greiner, L.E. 1972. Evolution and revolution as organizations grow. *Harvard Business Review, 76*(3), 37–46.

Greiner, L.E., & Poulfelt, L. (Eds.). 2005. *Management consulting today and tomorrow*. New York, NY: Routledge.

Grenier, R., & Metes, G. 1992. *Enterprise networking: Working together apart.* Maynard, MA: Digital Press.

Hall, E.T. 1959. *The silent language.* New York, NY: Doubleday.

Hall, E.T. 1966. *The hidden dimension.* New York, NY: Doubleday.

Hampden-Turner, C.M., & Trompenaars, A. 1993. *The seven cultures of capitalism.* New York, NY: Doubleday Currency.

Hampden-Turner, C.M., & Trompenaars, A. 2000. *Building cross-cultural competence.* New York, NY: Wiley.

Handy, C. 1978. *The gods of management.* London, UK: Pan Books.

Harbison, F., & Myers, C.A. 1959. *Management in the industrial world.* New York, NY: McGraw-Hill.

Harrison, R. 1979. Understanding your organization's character. *Harvard Business Review, 57*(5), 119–128.

Harrison, R., & Stokes, H. 1992. *Diagnosing organizational culture.* San Francisco, CA: Pfeiffer.

Hassard, J. 1999. Images of time in work and organization. In S.R. Clegg & C. Hardy (Eds.), *Studying organization* (pp. 327–344). Thousand Oaks, CA: Sage.

Hatch, M.J. 1990. The symbolics of office design. In P. Gagliardi (Ed.), *Symbols and artifacts.* New York, NY: Walter de Gruyter.

Hatch, M.J., & Schultz, M. (Eds.). 2004. *Organizational identity: A reader.* Oxford, UK: Oxford University Press.

Hatch, M.J., & Schultz, M. 2008. *Taking brand initiative: How companies can align strategy, culture, and identity through corporate branding.* San Francisco, CA: Jossey-Bass.

Hirschhorn, L. 1988. *The workplace within: Psychodynamics of organizational life.* Cambridge, MA: MIT Press.

Hofstede, G. 1991. *Cultures and organizations.* London, UK: McGraw-Hill.

Hofstede, G. 2001. *Culture's consequences* (2nd ed.). Beverly Hills, CA: Sage. (Original work published 1980.)

Hofstede, G., Hofstede, G.J., & Minkov, M. 2010. *Cultures and organizations: Software of the mind.* New York, NY: McGraw-Hill.

Holland, J.L. 1985. *Making vocational choices* (2nd ed.). Englewood Cliffs, NJ: Prentice-Hall.

Homans, G. 1950. *The human group.* New York, NY: Harcourt Brace Jovanovich.

House, R.J., et al. (Eds.). 2004. *Culture, leadership, and organizations: The GLOBE study of 62 societies.* Thousand Oaks, CA: Sage.

Hughes, E.C. 1958. *Men and their work.* Glencoe, IL: Free Press.

Isaacs, W. 1999. *Dialogue and the art of thinking together.* New York, NY: Doubleday.

James, W. 1890. *The principles of psychology.* New York: Henry Holt & Company.

Johansen, R., Sibbet, D., Benson, S., Martin, A., Mittman, R., & Saffo, P. 1991. *Leading business teams.* Reading, MA: Addison Wesley.

Jones, G.R. 1983. Transaction costs, property rights, and organizational culture: An exchange perspective. *Administrative Science Quarterly, 28,* 454–467.

Jones, M.O., Moore, M.D., & Snyder, R.C. (Eds.). 1988. *Inside organizations*. Newbury Park, CA: Sage.

Kahane, A. 2010. *Power and love*. San Francisco, CA: Berrett-Koehler.

Kantor, D. 2012. *Reading the room: Group dynamics for coaches and leaders*. San Francisco, CA: Jossey-Bass.

Kaplan, R., & Norton, D.P. 1992. The balanced scorecard: Measures that drive performance. *Harvard Business Review* (January–February), 71–79.

Keegan, R., & Lahey, L.L. 2016. *An everyday culture*. Cambridge, MA: Harvard Business School Press.

Kellogg, K.C. 2011. Challenging operations. Chicago, IL: Univ. of Chicago Press.

Kets de Vries, M.F.R., & Miller, D. 1984. *The neurotic organization: Diagnosing and changing counterproductive styles of management*. San Francisco, CA: Jossey-Bass.

Kets de Vries, M.F.R., & Miller, D. 1987. *Unstable at the top: Inside the troubled organization*. New York, NY: New American Library.

Kilmann, R.H., & Saxton, M.J. 1983. *The Kilmann-Saxton culture gap survey*. Pittsburgh, PA: Organizational Design Consultants.

Kleiner, A. 2003. *Who really matters?* New York, NY: Doubleday Currency.

Kluckhohn, F.R., & Strodtbeck, F.L. 1961. *Variations in value orientations*. New York, NY: Harper & Row.

Kotter, J.P., & Heskett, J.L. 1992. *Culture and performance*. New York, NY: The Free Press.

Kunda, G. 1992. *Engineering culture*. Philadelphia, PA: Temple University Press.

Kunda, G. 2006. *Engineering culture* (rev. ed.). Philadelphia, PA: Temple University Press.

Leavitt, H.J. 1986. *Corporate pathfinders*. Homewood, IL: Dow Jones-Irwin.

Lewin, K. 1947. Group decision and social change. In T.N. Newcomb & E.L. Hartley (Eds.), *Readings in social psychology* (pp. 459–473). New York, NY: Holt, Rinehart and & Winston.

Likert, R. 1967. *The human organization*. New York, NY: McGraw-Hill.

Louis, M.R. 1980. Surprise and sense making. *Administrative Science Quarterly, 25*, 226–251.

Malone, T.W. 2004. *The future of work*. Boston, MA: Harvard Business School Press.

Malone, T.W., Yates, J., & Benjamin, R. (1987). Electronic markets and electronic hierarchies. *Communications of the ACM, 30*, 484–497.

Marshak, R.J. 2006. *Covert processes at work*. San Francisco, CA: Berrett-Koehler.

Martin, J. 2002. *Organizational culture: Mapping the terrain*. Newbury Park, CA: Sage.

Martin, J., & Powers, M.E. 1983. Truth or corporate propaganda: The value of a good war story. In L.R. Pondy, P.J. Frost, G. Morgan, & T.C. Dandridge (Eds.), *Organizational symbolism*, 93–107. Greenwich, CT: JAI Press.

Maslow, A. 1954. *Motivation and personality*. New York, NY: Harper & Row.

McGregor, D.M. 1960. *The human side of enterprise*. New York, NY: McGraw-Hill.

Merton, R.K. 1957. *Social theory and social structure* (rev. ed.). New York, NY: Free Press.

Michael, D.N. 1985. *On learning to plan—and planning to learn.* San Francisco, CA: Jossey-Bass.

Michael, D.N. 1991. Leadership's shadow: The dilemma of denial. *Futures,* Jan./Feb., 69–79.

Mirvis, P., Ayas, K., & Roth, G. 2003. *To the desert and back.* San Francisco, CA: Jossey-Bass.

Nelson, E.C., Batalden, P.B., Godfrey, M.M., & Lazar, J.S. (Eds.) 2011. *Value by design.* San Francisco, CA: Jossey Bass, Wiley.

Neuhauser, P.C. 1993. *Corporate legends and lore.* New York, NY: McGraw-Hill.

O'Donovan, G. 2006. *The corporate culture handbook.* Dublin, Ireland: Liffey Press.

O'Reilly, C.A., III, & Chatman, J.A. 1996. Culture as social control: Corporations, cults and commitment. In B.M. Staw, & L.L. Cummings (Eds.), *Research in organizational behavior 18* (pp. 157–200). Greenwich, CT: JAI.

O'Reilly, C.A., III, Chatman, J.A., & Caldwell, D.F. 1991. People and organizational culture. *Academy of Management Journal, 34,* 487–516.

O'Reilly, C.A., III, & Tushman, M.L. 2016. *Lead and disrupt: How to solve the innovator's dilemma.* Stanford, CA: Stanford University Press.

Oshry, B. 2007. *Seeing systems.* San Francisco, CA: Berrett-Koehler.

Ouchi, W.G. 1981. *Theory Z.* Reading, MA: Addison-Wesley.

Ouchi, W.G., & Johnson, J. 1978. Types of organizational control and their relationship to emotional well-being. *Administrative Science Quarterly, 23,* 293–317.

Packard, D. 1995. *The HP way.* New York, NY: Harper Collins.

Pascale, R.T., & Athos, A.G. 1981. *The art of Japanese management.* New York, NY: Simon & Schuster.

Perin, C. 1991. The moral fabric of the office. In S. Bacharach, S.R. Barley, & P.S. Tolbert (Eds.), *Research in the sociology of organizations* (special volume on the professions). Greenwich, CT: JAI Press.

Perin, C. 2005. *Shouldering risks.* Princeton, NJ: Princeton University Press.

Peters, T.J., & Waterman, R.H., Jr. 1982. *In search of excellence.* New York, NY: Harper & Row.

Peterson, B. 2004. *Cultural intelligence.* Boston, MA: Intercultural Press.

Pettigrew, A.M. 1979. On studying organizational cultures. *Administrative Science Quarterly, 24,* 570–581.

Plum, E. 2008. *CI: Cultural intelligence.* London, UK: Middlesex University Press.

Pondy, L.R., Frost, P.J., Morgan, G., & Dandridge, T. (Eds.). 1983. *Organizational symbolism.* Greenwich, CT: JAI Press.

Porras, J., & Collins, J. 1994. *Built to last.* New York, NY: HarperBusiness.

Redding, S.G., & Martyn-Johns, T.A. 1979. Paradigm differences and their relation to management, with reference to Southeast Asia. In G.W. England, A.R. Neghandi, & B. Wilpert (Eds.), *Organizational functioning in a cross-cultural perspective*. Kent, OH: Comparative Administration Research Unit, Kent State University.

Ritti, R.R., & Funkhouser, G.R. 1987. *The ropes to skip and the ropes to know* (3rd ed.). Columbus, OH: Grid.

Roethlisberger, F.J., & Dickson, W.J. 1939. *Management and the worker* Cambridge, MA: Harvard University Press.

Sackman, S.A. 2006. *Success factor: Corporate culture*. Guetersloh, Germany: Bertelsman Stiftung.

Sahlins, M. 1985. *Islands of history*. Chicago, IL: University of Chicago Press.

Sahlins, M., & Service, E.R. (Eds.). 1960. *Evolution and culture*. Ann Arbor, MI: University of Michigan Press.

Salk, J. 1997. Partners and other strangers. *International Studies of Management and Organization, 26*(4), 48–72.

Savage, C.M. 1990. *Fifth generation management: Integrating enterprises through human networking*. Maynard, MA: Digital Press.

Scharmer, C.O. 2007. *Theory U*. Cambridge, MA: Society for Organizational Learning.

Schein, E.H. 1961a. *Coercive persuasion*. New York, NY: Norton.

Schein, E.H. 1961b. Management development as a process of influence. *Industrial Management Review (MIT), 2*, 59–77.

Schein, E.H. 1968. Organizational socialization and the profession of management. *Industrial Management Review, 9*, 1–15.

Schein, E.H. 1969. *Process consultation: Its role in organization development*. Reading, MA: Addison-Wesley.

Schein, E.H. 1971. The individual, the organization, and the career: A conceptual scheme. *Journal of Applied Behavioral Science, 7*, 401–426.

Schein, E.H. 1975. In defense of theory Y. *Organizational Dynamics*, Summer, 17–30.

Schein, E.H. 1978. *Career dynamics: Matching individual and organizational needs*. Reading, MA: Addison-Wesley.

Schein, E.H. 1980. *Organizational psychology* (3rd ed.). Englewood Cliffs, NJ: Prentice-Hall. (Original work published 1965; 2nd ed. published 1970.)

Schein, E.H. 1983. The role of the founder in creating organizational culture. *Organizational Dynamics*, Summer, 13–28.

Schein, E.H. 1987a. *The clinical perspective in fieldwork*. Newbury Park, CA: Sage.

Schein, E.H. 1987b. Individuals and careers. In J.W. Lorsch (Ed.), *Handbook of organizational behavior* (pp. 155–171). Englewood Cliffs, NJ: Prentice-Hall.

Schein, E.H. 1988. *Process consultation. Vol. 1: Its role in organization development* (2nd ed.). Reading, MA: Addison-Wesley.

Schein, E.H. 1992. The role of the CEO in the management of change. In T.A. Kochan, & M. Useem (Eds.), *Transforming organizations* (pp. 80–96). New York, NY: Oxford University Press.

Schein, E.H. 1993a. On dialogue, culture, and organizational learning. *Organizational Dynamics*, Autumn, *22*, 40–51.

Schein, E.H. 1993b. *Career anchors (rev. ed.)*. San Diego, CA: Pfeiffer & Co. (Jossey-Bass).

Schein, E.H. 1993c. How can organizations learn faster? The challenge of entering the green room. *Sloan Management Review, 34*, 85–92.

Schein, E.H. 1996a. Three cultures of management: The key to organizational learning. *Sloan Management Review, 38*(1), 9–20.

Schein, E.H. 1996b. *Strategic pragmatism: The culture of Singapore's Economic Development Board*. Cambridge, MA: MIT Press.

Schein, E.H. 1999a. *Process consultation revisited*. Englewood Cliffs, NJ: Prentice- Hall (Addison-Wesley).

Schein, E.H. 1999b. *The corporate culture survival guide*. San Francisco, CA: Jossey-Bass.

Schein, E.H. 2001. Clinical inquiry/research. In P. Reason & H. Bradbury (Eds.), *Handbook of action research* (pp. 228–237). Thousand Oaks, CA: Sage Press.

Schein, E.H. 2003. *DEC is dead; Long live DEC*. San Francisco, CA: Berrett/ Kohler.

Schein, E.H. 2008. Clinical inquiry/research. In P. Reason & H. Bradbury (Eds.), *Action research* (2nd ed., pp. 266–279). Thousand Oaks, CA: Sage.

Schein, E.H. 2009a. *Helping*. San Francisco, CA: Berrett/Koehler.

Schein, E.H. 2009b. *The corporate culture survival guide* (2nd ed.). San Francisco, CA: Jossey-Bass.

Schein, E.H. 2013. *Humble inquiry: The gentle are of asking instead of telling*. San Francisco: Berrett-Koehler.

Schein, E.H. 2016. *Humble consulting: How to provide real help faster*. San Francsico: Berrett-Koehler.

Schein, E.H., & Bennis, W.G. 1965. *Personal and organizational change through group methods*. New York, NY: Wiley.

Schein, E.H., & Van Maanen, J. 2013. *Career anchor: The changing nature of work and careers* (4th ed.). San Francisco: Wiley.

Schmidt, E., & Rosenberg, J. 2014. *How Google works*. New York, NY: Grand Central.

Schneider, B. (Ed.). 1990. *Organizational climate and culture*. San Francisco, CA: Jossey-Bass.

Schneider, W. 1994. *The reengineering alternative: A plan for making your current culture work*. New York, NY: McGraw Hill (Irwin Professional).

Schultz, M. 1995. *On studying organizational cultures*. New York, NY: De Gruyter.

Schwartz, P. 2003. *Inevitable surprises*. New York, NY: Gotham Books.

Senge, P.M. 1990. *The fifth discipline*. New York, NY: Doubleday Currency.

Senge, P., Smith, B., Kruschwitz, N., Laur, J., & Schley, S. 2008. *The necessary revolution*. Cambridge, MA: Society for Organizational Learning.

Shrivastava, P. 1983. A typology of organizational learning systems. *Journal of Management Studies, 20*, 7–28.

Silberbauer, E.R. 1968. *Understanding and motivating the Bantu worker*. Johannesburg, South Africa: Personnel Management Advisory Services.

Sithi-Amnuai, P. 1968. The Asian mind. *Asia*, Spring, 78–91.

Smircich, L. 1983. Concepts of culture and organizational analysis. *Administrative Science Quarterly, 28*, 339–358.

Snook, S.A. 2000. *Friendly fire.* Princeton, NJ: Princeton University Press.

Steele, F.I. 1973. *Physical settings and organization development.* Reading, MA: Addison-Wesley.

Steele, F.I. 1981. *The sense of place.* Boston, MA: CBI Publishing.

Steele, F.I. (1986). *Making and managing high-quality workplaces.* New York, NY: Teachers College Press.

Tagiuri, R., & Litwin, G.H. (Eds.). 1968. *Organizational climate: Exploration of a concept.* Boston, MA: Division of Research, Harvard Graduate School of Business.

Thomas, D.C., & Inkson, K. 2003. *Cultural intelligence.* San Francisco, CA: Berrett/Kohler.

Tichy, N.M., & Devanna, M.A. 1987. *The transformational leader.* New York, NY: Wiley.

Trice, H.M., Beyer, J.M. 1984. Studying organizational cultures through rites and ceremonials. *Academy of Management Review, 9,* 653–669.

Trice, H.M., & Beyer, J.M. 1985. Using six organizational rites to change culture. In R.H. Kilmann, M.J. Saxton, & R. Serpa, *Gaining control of the corporate culture* (pp. 370–399). San Francisco, CA: Jossey-Bass.

Trice, H.M., & Beyer, J.M. 1993. *The cultures of work organizations.* Englewood Cliffs, NJ: Prentice-Hall.

Tuchman, B.W. 1965. Developmental sequence in small groups. *Psychological Bulletin, 63,* 384-399.

Tushman, M.L., & Anderson, P. 1986. Technological discontinuities and organizational environments. *Administrative Science Quarterly, 31,* 439–465.

Tyrrell, M.W.D. 2000. Hunting and gathering in the early Silicon age. In N.M. Ashkanasy, C.P.M. Wilderom, & M.F. Peterson (Eds.), *Handbook of organizational culture and climate* (pp. 85–99). Thousand Oaks, CA: Sage.

Van Maanen, J. 1973. Observations on the making of policemen. *Human Organization, 4,* 407–418.

Van Maanen, J. 1976. Breaking in: Socialization at work. In R. Dubin (Ed.), *Handbook of work organization and society,* 67–130. Skokie, IL: Rand McNally.

Van Maanen, J. 1979. The self, the situation, and the rules of interpersonal relations. In W. Bennis, J. Van Maanen, E.J. Schein, & F.I. Steele, *Essays in interpersonal dynamics* (pp. 43–101). Homewood, IL: Dorsey Press.

Van Maanen, J. 1988. *Tales of the field: On writing ethnography.* Chicago: University of Chicago Press.

Van Maanen, J., & Schein, E.H. 1979. Toward a theory of organizational socialization. In B.M. Staw, & L.L. Cummings (Eds.), *Research in organizational behavior* (vol. 1), 209–264. Greenwich, CT: JAI Press.

Van Maanen, J., & Barley, S.R. 1984. Occupational communities: Culture and control in organizations. In B.M. Staw, & L.L. Cummings (Eds.), *Research in organizational behavior* (vol. 6), 265–287. Greenwich, CT: JAI Press.

Van Maanen, J., & Kunda, G. 1989. Real feelings: Emotional expression and organizational culture. In B. Staw (Ed.), *Research in organizational behavior* (vol. 11), 43–103. Greenwich, CT: JAI Press.

Vroom, V.H., & Yetton, P.W. 1973. *Leadership and decision making.* Pittsburgh, PA: University of Pittsburgh Press.

Watson, T.J., Jr., & Petre, P. 1990. *Father, son & Co.: My life at IBM and beyond.* New York, NY: Bantam Books.

Weick, K. 1995. *Sensemaking in organizations.* Thousand Oaks, CA: Sage.

Weick, K., & Sutcliffe, K.M. 2001. *Managing the unexpected.* San Francisco, CA: Jossey-Bass.

Wilderom, C.P.M., Glunk, U., & Maslowski, R. 2000. Organizational culture as a predictor of organizational performance. In N.M. Ashkanasy, C.P.M. Wilderom, & M.F. Peterson (Eds.), *Handbook of organizational culture and climate* (pp. 193–209). Thousand Oaks, CA: Sage.

Wilkins, A.L. 1983. Organizational stories as symbols which control the organization. In L.R. Pondy, P.J. Frost, G. Morgan, & T. Dandridge (Eds.), *Organizational symbolism*, 81–92. Greenwich, CT: JAI Press.

Wilkins, A.L. 1989. *Developing corporate character.* San Francisco, CA: Jossey-Bass.

Williamson, O. 1975. *Markets and hierarchies, analysis and anti-trust implications: A study in the economics of internal organization.* New York, NY: Free Press.

Womack, J.T., Jones, D.T., & Roos, D. 1990. *The machine that changed the world.* New York, NY: Free Press.

Zuboff, S. 1984. *In the age of the smart machine.* New York, NY: Basic Books.

Index

A

Accountability
  changes, nature of, 209–210
  characteristics of, 227
  examples of, 159
Acculturation process, 12
Acknowledgment, 101
Acquisitions, 248–249
Activity interaction, 95–96
Adaptation
  external, 150
  learning and, 346
  mutual, 117
  in problem solving, 7–8
  summary, 178
  to technology, 213
After Action Reviews, 111
Agile, 284
Agilent, 145
Airwick, 155–156, 274
Alcoa, 184
Alpha Power Company, 184,
    332, 334
  change anxiety at, 324–325
  change program at, 335–337
  hazard knowledge of, 350
  product diversity of, 217
  rites/rituals of, 200
"Ambidextrous organizations," 49–50

Amelio, Gilbert, 143
Amoco
  evaluation at, 336
  learning at, 331, 334–335
  rewards/punishment at,
    175–176
Analysis
  artifact level, 1719
  automated, 288–293
  belief in, 349
  internal, risk of, 264–266
  professional obligations in,
    266–267
  risks in, 263–264
Anticipatory socialization, 12
Anxiety, 324–328
Apple
  CEO succession at, 238
  cultural change at, 244
  founding of, 142–143
  inspiration by, *xvi*
  jargon of, 9
  long-range planning process,
    307–311
Army Core of Engineers, 302–307
Artifacts
  Ciba-Geigy, 45–50
  DEC, 32–35
  definition of, 17